Fireworks Don't Last

By Dr. Lee Roberson

Pastor Emeritus Highland Park Baptist Church;
Founder and Chancellor Tennessee Temple University,
Chattanooga, Tennessee

University Publishers
P.O. Box 3571
Chattanooga, Tennessee 37404

Fireworks Don't Last

DR. LEE ROBERSON

University Publishers

Copyright 1982
Second Edition 1986
All Rights Reserved

ISBN 0-931117-07-0

Camp Joy

*Where Boys
And Girls
Begin To Live*

Camp Joy is close to my heart - it bears the name of our baby who is with the Lord.

Camp Joy is built on the principle: The greatest need of boys and girls is Jesus Christ, the Saviour.

Since 1946, the camp has been in operation - more than 80,000 children have attended (FREE of any charge). Many thousands have made professions of faith in Christ. Hundreds of letters have come from children and parents, thanking us for the blessing of Camp Joy.

From the beginning, we decided that the camp would operate on the "by faith" concept. The children attend free. We pray for our needs and present our works to friends who believe in giving young people a little special help. We are grateful to the thousands who have made contributions - large and small.

Send your gifts to Camp Joy, 1901 Union Avenue, Chattanooga, Tennessee 37404. May God bless you.

Sincerely,

Lee Roberson, Pastor Emeritus
Highland Park Baptist Church
Chancellor, Tennessee Temple
University
Chattanooga, Tennessee

FREE...

TO BOYS AND GIRLS
AGES 9 thru 14

OVER 80,000 BOYS
AND GIRLS HAVE
ATTENDED CAMP JOY
SINCE 1946

OVER 16,000 HAVE
MADE PROFESSIONS
OF FAITH IN CHRIST

CAMP JOY
NEEDS OUR PRAYERS
AND FINANCIAL
SUPPORT. ASK GOD
WHAT HE WOULD
HAVE YOU TO DO.

**THREE VIEWS OF THE
HIGHLAND PARK BAPTIST CHURCH
CHATTANOOGA, TENNESSEE**

THE UNION GOSPEL MISSION
16 E. MAIN STREET
CHATTANOOGA, TENNESSEE

THE UNION GOSPEL MISSION, A DOWNTOWN MINISTRY OF THE HIGHLAND PARK BAPTIST CHURCH, WAS ORGANIZED IN 1950. SINCE THEN THE MISSION HAS REACH OVER 850,000 MEN. OVER 30,000 OF THESE HAVE MADE PROFESSIONS OF FAITH IN CHRIST.

ANOTHER VIEW OF THE NEW CHURCH AUDITORIUM.

CHARLES F. WEIGLE MUSIC CENTER

TENNESSEE TEMPLE UNIVERSITY

McGILRAY MEMORIAL GYMNASIUM

ORCHARD KNOB BUILDING

ADMINISTRATION
BUILDING

TENNESSEE TEMPLE ELEMENTARY
SCHOOL CLASSROOM BUILDING

CHARLES F. WEIGLE
MUSIC CENTER

NEW 553 BED DORMATORY FOR LADIES AT T.T.U.

Table of Contents

1. The Day of the Bulldozer 1
2. How to Prepare For the Coming Crash 13
3. The Episode of the Fifth Rib 27
4. The Hourglass Sermon..........................39
5. Fireworks Don't Last 51
6. One Tiny Conjunction..........................63
7. How to Change Your Life in Thirty Minutes......75
8. The World's Greatest Ordination Service........89
9. God and A Worm 99
10. Please, Please, No Flowers, No Telegrams, No Cards, No Sunshine Baskets, No Family Visitation Hour 111
11. The Verse That Jumped From the Page..........125
12. The Wrap-Up On The Second Coming.............137
13. Life Is A Lollipop 153
14. This Bus Stops At Calvary....................167
15. Cure for Excusitis 173
16. America — Where Are Thy Gods That Thou Hast Made? 187

Tabernacle Revival Sermons (after page 198)

Chapter 1
The Day of the Bulldozer

Buy the truth, and sell it not; also wisdom, and instruction, and understanding.
The father of the righteous shall greatly rejoice: and he that begetteth a wise child shall have joy of him.
Thy father and thy mother shall be glad, and she that bare thee shall rejoice.
My son, give me thine heart, and let thine eyes observe my ways. — Prov. 23:23-26.

* * * * * * *

Howbeit Jesus suffered him not, but saith unto him, Go home to thy friends, and tell them how great things the Lord hath done for thee, and hath had compassion on thee. — Mark 5:19.

Sometime ago, while making a call in a certain section of a city, I saw a number of my friends, people I knew at least by acquaintance, sitting on the front porch of a large two-story home. I spoke to them and went on my way.

A couple days later I came back to the same section of town to make some more calls. To my surprise, the big two-story house was completely gone. Every stick of lumber was removed from the yard. The ground was touched by the scraper. The dirt was showing and looked strangely clean.

Parked over to one side of the lot was a big bulldozer which had been used in doing the job.

THE DAY OF THE BULLDOZER

When I saw that scene, I thought of the home. I thought of the day of the bulldozer and the things now happening. As the bulldozer cleared away the house and everything on the lot, so does the bulldozer of sin work in our lives and homes. For that reason, I want to emphasize this truth tonight.

We need to beware of the bulldozer of sin - low standards, strong drink, immorality, loose, vulgar speech.

There is the bulldozer of disobedience to God.

There is the bulldozer of indifference, not caring what happens.

There is the bulldozer of the rejection of Jesus Christ.

This is a message of the home, the Christian home. I trust we can press some things on your mind.

I. THE VALUE OF A HOME

A man died in 1852 in a foreign land, in Africa, and was buried there. Not too much was said about him. However, about thirty years after his death, in 1882 or 1883, this man's body was brought back to the United States, to Washington, D.C., and carried down Pennsylvania Avenue. The stands were put up for the President, the Vice-President, the Cabinet, the senators, the House of Representatives. Thousands assembled at the sides of the streets as they carried the body of the man down Pennsylvania Avenue.

The interesting thing is this: they were recognizing this man and the work he had done thirty years after his death, after his burial in Africa, his writing of words which became a song. The man was John Howard Payne. The song - "Home Sweet Home." One phrase says, "Be it ever so humble, there's no place like home."

It was as simple as A-B-C; yet, somehow, this song about home touched people's hearts.

For most of us, speaking about home stirs some memories. For some of us who are older, it makes us think of days gone by. If you are away from home, it makes you think of your home, what it means to you, how sacred it is. This is the

THE DAY OF THE BULLDOZER

value of a home.

Where is the strength of a home? <u>First, the strength of a home and nation depends upon the Christian home.</u> This we know. Our nation is weak because of home failure. It will become strong if homes become strong. The nation will stand if homes will stand for God. But if they fail to stand, the whole thing fails.

<u>Second, the work of the Saviour begins in the home.</u> Mother and Dad can give their convictions to the little ones, as they teach them, as they stand for these convictions themselves, as they seek to win souls to the blessed Saviour. The work of our Saviour begins in the home.

<u>Third, the salvation of the soul should begin in the home.</u> Parents should be Christians, and mothers and dads should transmit the message of the Lord Jesus Christ to their children. They should tell them of the sweetest story ever told - the story of Jesus and His love.

When a little boy or girl comes forward, do not look at that one and say, "He is so young." I watch when you sit in the back. You ease up in your seat to see if you can see the child. He is a very tiny thing, maybe six or seven years old. By his side will be his mother or father, or both. The child has come for a profession of faith in Jesus Christ. And some of you think, *I wonder if this is right. I wonder if this could be true.*

Then I take the child up for baptism. Father may be standing on this side and Mother over here. They are both rejoicing in the salvation of their child. You may think, *Can it be? Have they done right?*

My dear parent, let me say this to you: Have a great concern for your children and seek to bring them early to the Saviour. Do not be disturbed by anything that others may think. If they are young in years, still give them the message in the same way. Don't change one bit. Be sincere. Give the Word of God to the little ones. If you have transmitted the message of the Lord Jesus Christ and they accept Him, or

THE DAY OF THE BULLDOZER

say they are doing so, God Himself will straighten it out later if there is some mistake.

Some of you, with concern, have come to me regarding this. I'm not worried about that one bit. If you have done your best, if you are seeking to get your children to the Lord, do not worry. The value is found only in having Jesus in the center of that home.

II. THE DESTRUCTION OF THE HOME

The bulldozer of sin is ever working. The Devil wants to destroy your home and mine. He wants to control the home.

What do people do? <u>Some people lock the door on Christ.</u> They shut Him outside. He is knocking but they refuse to open the door. They lock outside the greatest Friend they could ever have - the Lord Jesus Christ. They lock outside the One who could stabilize the home and make it to stand in spite of all obstacles, difficulties and adversaries. They lock away the sinner's Friend. They lock away the One who can help them when all others fail. They lock Jesus outside.

Second, <u>some people close their minds and hearts to the Word of God.</u> Here is the Book, the Bible; yet the home is never taught the Word of God. You have locked it outside. The Devil rejoices because this brings the home to powerlessness and weakness.

Locking the Bible outside will destroy the home as sure as you live. If the home is going to stand, there must be a recognition of the Word and the teaching of the Book.

Third, <u>some people lose the way to the house of God.</u> Weeds grow up alongside the pathway to the church. They turn away. Satan is back of this. The Bible tells us, "Not forsaking the assembling of ourselves together, as the manner of some is . . . . "

The New Testament church epitomizes the good things of God. The church has a message for every sinner. It has help for every child of God. The church furnishes direction for the wandering. It strengthens the weak. You are your

THE DAY OF THE BULLDOZER

strongest when you keep in close touch with the house of God and with preaching. You hurt yourself when you lose your way to God's house.

Fourth, some people let Satan rule the home. The Devil comes in. You had better recognize his work, for he will try to destroy your home. Mothers and fathers, he will try to destroy your influence and impact upon your children. You must watch this all the time.

Frederick the Great was listening to a minister. This fellow was exalting man, talking about how great he is. Frederick the Great became incensed by what he was saying. Turning to a friend next to him, he muttered, "That man does not know the devil in the human heart."

This is true. Satan is working all of the time. He will get into your heart and try to tear it down. He will try to tear down your home and keep it from being what God wants it to be.

It is bad when you speak as the Devil wants you to speak - with profanity, with vulgar speech. No matter what they are doing on television and radio, you be clean for God!

I tune in once in a while television or radio to hear certain things that I think will interest me. I turn it off when I hear vulgarity and profanity spewing out. Our homes can be destroyed if we come to speak as Satan directs.

Fifth, homes behave as Satan prescribes. The Devil has encouraged strong drink until millions are now alcoholics. They are away from God, away from decent society because of their drinking. The Devil is encouraging this. He encourages that purity and the standards of life be cast aside. People want to live as Satan wants them to live, turning from the pure life as the Bible prescribes and behaving as Satan prescribes.

Sixth, some people fail to care for the home. They do not have a real concern for the home that God has given them.

Dr. M. R. DeHaan, a preacher who is now in Glory, was visiting in Oregon in a home of thirteen children. Eight of

THE DAY OF THE BULLDOZER

them were Korean orphans, while five belonged to the family. Mr. and Mrs. Harry Holton and the children gathered together with the Word of God. Dr. DeHaan said, "I have never seen anything so impressive as the eight children from Korea, the five of this family, and Mother and Father - all gathered together around the Word of God and in prayer. I could see how much they cared, how much they loved the children, how much they sought to help them, and what they were doing for them."

Then Dr. DeHaan said, "A strange thing is that many children are spiritual orphans. Mother and Dad seeem not to care. They do not read the Bible with and pray for their children. Neither do they seek to guide or help them in any way."

Do you have a family altar? Is there a time every day when you get the Bible and read the Word of God with your family? If you care for your home and have a concern for the family, you will take time for the Bible and prayer each day. You take time for other things - the newspaper, the magazines, recreation and other things. Why not take time for the Word of God and prayer?

Put your Bible out on the table where you have breakfast and other meals, and keep it there. AND USE IT!!

Read the Word of God. Pray for the family. Do you care that much?

Dr. DeHaan said, "I saw how much they cared. I saw what God was doing for a little couple who had taken in eight orphans from Korea and how they were being brought up in the nurture and admonition of the Lord."

It is important that we get hold of this. Many are burdened by Satan's tricks and suggestions. Instead of following what God says in His Word, they turn away from the things of God.

A lady was having some trouble. She was worrying about her life and concerned about a number of things. As she slept one night, she had a dream. In the dream she was troubled with all kinds of burdens. Little imps were standing along the way - Satan's emissaries - and were casting more and more on her all the time.

In the dream, she met Jesus and said to Him, "Jesus, help me get rid of all these things, this load that I have on my back. Get rid of every bit of it."

The Lord replied in this dream, "I will take care of you, but I did not put on you the burdens. You get rid of them. I will supply the grace day by day that you need, but these things Satan has put on you."

Some of you tonight need to pray, "O God, I have been allowing the Devil to get hold of my life, to control my home. I have allowed him to bring into my home things that are wrong. I need to get rid of these things. God, give me guidance day by day, hour by hour. Help me do what You want me to do." Do not go around all burdened down.

This is the second thing: the destruction of the home. This is hitting all around the country today. This is the reason for the divorce rate rising with such a rapid rate. So many happenings constantly come to mind. People are weeping over their broken homes. They call me on the phone. Most of the time these people have turned away from God and have listened to the Devil's suggestions. They are not doing what God wants them to do.

III. THE SAVING OF THE HOME

First, we discussed the value of the home; second, the destruction of the home; now, third, the saving of the home. So many things are written on this subject in this day and time. *Reader's Digest* had an article entitled, "What Makes a Successful Family?" I cut it out for future reference.

It tells the story of a man, Reuben Hill, who wrote a book that sold for $11.25. The article in *Reader's Digest* gives the summary of Dr. Hill's conclusion about what makes a successful family. This is exactly as it was written in the article. Six different points he had written down:

THE DAY OF THE BULLDOZER

1. Do not be in a rush to marry.
2. Have fewer children.
3. Be prepared to cope with the unexpected.
4. Discuss decisions freely.
5. Choose the decision-maker wisely. The husband and wife should make the decision in the case of the older child.
6. Rely on your relatives.

Boy, that is a smart man! And people paid $11.25 for that! Not one mention of Jesus Christ. Not a single reference to the Son of God or to the Bible. This is the sadness of it all. This is the trend of the day in which we live. There was not one mention of the spiritual needs of men, not one mention of the Word of God and prayer, not a thing said about seeking the face of God and living for Him.

We come to the question of the saving of the home. What will save a home?

First of all, faith in God. There must be a faith in Christ for salvation. Look to Him; come to Him. Put away your pride and confess, "To save my home, I must know Christ as my Saviour."

There must be faith in God to guide you day by day, to guide you in life's every situation.

There must be faith in God to supply your every need. Rest upon this. Watch that you do not get ahead of God. Do not let self get in and push God out. Exercise faith in God for the needs of your heart and life.

There must be faith in God to save your home. When self rises and begins to say "thus and so," you say, *Wait a minute! I am going to exercise faith in God and depend on Him for my every need.*

While driving through a city where I used to pastor, I saw a fine man standing on the corner waiting for a bus. In his hand was a satchel. He was going home from work. I knew him, so I pulled over and picked him up. We began to talk. He said, "Brother Roberson, I have been working here at

THE DAY OF THE BULLDOZER

this one job for twenty years. I have a good job, but I've an aspiration. I have wanted to be a judge in a certain court. Now that place is vacated. I am as happy as I can be. This is a realization of all my dreams, all that I have ever wanted. Now I am going to have it."

I thought to myself, *That is a strange thing. A church member, a professing Christian, but he has his whole life wrapped up in the job that he feels he will get next week.*

When we got to his home and I had stopped to let him out of the car, he turned around, briefcase in hand, tapped me on the shoulder and said, "It's been good talking to you. I am sure looking forward to my future days and what it is going to mean to my family."

I have never seen him again. Why? He did not get the job. It was given to someone else. When he failed to get the job, his mind cracked. The last time I heard about him, he was at an institution for those who were mentally deranged.

Wait a minute! This man lacked faith in God. He was looking to man, trusting in man for help instead of trusting in God.

Second, there must be positive action. It takes more than negative words and a negative attitude.

I know a man who constantly fought sin. He was vigorous in his act against evil. He fought sin in his home. He fought sin in his ministry. He hated the sin of strong drink and would everywhere voice his opposition. All he did was to fight sin. His wife left him. His business folded up. He failed completely.

What was wrong? This man was living a negative life. He was fighting sin but he was not doing all God wanted him to do.

I believe in fighting sin. We should fight it, but there must also be the positive side.

Be faithful in church attendance. That is positive. Be faithful in having the family altar. That is positive. Be faithful in soul winning. That is positive. That is active, that is doing

THE DAY OF THE BULLDOZER

something. Be faithful in your giving. That is positive. That is active, and it brings results. Positive action is a necessity for us all.

Third, there must be tearful concern. What will save the home? First, faith in God. Secondly, positive action - doing things in a positive, definite way. Number three, a tearful concern for others.

In our city there is a church organization dedicated to the improvement of family relationships. For fifteen dollars you will get three lessons which discuss the following things:

(1) Finding more effective ways of relating to your children and spouse;
(2) Learning to hear what members of your family are really saying to you;
(3) Aiding you in developing ways to work through a particular family problem.

This may be well and good, except that everything fails unless Jesus Christ is in the forefront. If you neglect and ignore the Son of God, your family fails and your individual life fails. You must have the Lord God with you. You must rest upon Him and on His promises.

What does it mean? It means the tearful concern for others. A concern for your children who may be lost in sin. A concern for your relatives and friends who are unsaved. A concern for a dear one close to you in your home. You need to continually pray for that person and seek his salvation.

This is a concern for that individual. Are you doing it? Do you have that concern? Are you showing that for your home, or do you simply pass it by nonchalantly? Do you say, "It will be all right. They will come out on the right side after a while. Everything will turn out just right"? There must always be that concern on your part, a tearful concern for others. Help others be what God wants them to be.

What an interesting story is given about a boy named Joseph. The lad went to Sunday school. The teacher was not

THE DAY OF THE BULLDOZER

very kind. Because of that, the boy turned away from Sunday school.

This crippled lad went on to school, finished up his elementary and high school work. He went to college and then to the university. He got a Ph.D. degree.

After he got a Ph.D degree, a man came, put his arm around him and said, "I need you. You are my kind. I want you to help me, to work with me, to be my propaganda minister." So he, Joseph Goebbels, became the propaganda minister for Adolf Hitler, this crippled man with a Ph. D. degree who had been ignored by his Sunday school class. Instead of being a follower of the lowly Nazarene, he became the follower of the Nazis, a regime which resulted in millions coming to their tragic death.

Let's sum up everything we have said tonight. If the home is going to stand, if it is to amount to anything, there must be a Saviour, Jesus Christ, the Son of God. We must emphasize Christ and build everything around Him - His kindness, His love, His compassion, His peace. Build your home around the Saviour.

There must be a Book, a guide Book for your home, and that is the Bible. There is a strange thing about this Book. I have never met any situation yet that it has not had the answer.

The matter of what women should wear is in the Word of God. It tells how long should be the dress. You want to ask me about it? I will give it to you. It is there. How long should the hair be? That, too, is given in the Bible. It is all in the Word of God. Not one single thing is missing in the Word of God for your home, your children, for you. The Word of God prescribes every bit of it.

There must be the church. I speak of the church of the Lord Jesus Christ, the New Testament church, such as this one. It is a church that stands for Christ, stands for salvation through faith in Him, and stands for the second coming of our Saviour. Surround your life and build it in the things of

THE DAY OF THE BULLDOZER

the church and your home will stand.

There must be faith, a Book, and a church. I am trying to simplify it. Let this get hold of you. Let your home be blessed of God. Let it be a happy place. Put out self. Get out all the things that antagonize and irritate. Settle all upon the things of God. Pray, "O God, guide me. Show me what You want me to be."

The first thing is to come to Jesus Christ and be saved. Mother, Father and children, the first need is to come to the Saviour. Do not wait for anybody else. If you want Christ, He is ready to save you. He said, "Behold, I stand at the door, and knock..."

Holman Hunt painted a picture, "The Light of the World," a picture of Jesus on the outside knocking on the door. There is no knob on the outside; it is on the inside. It is your life. He will not enter against your will. You must open the door and invite Him into your heart.

Someone has said, "The free will is an awful gift." Yes, with the free will you can reject. The people of Jerusalem turned away. Jesus said, ".... ye would not!"

By your free will tonight choose Jesus Christ. Will you say, "I want Him as my Saviour. I take Him now. I want to follow Him "?

Choose Christ today.

Chapter 2
How to Prepare For the Coming Crash

Watch therefore, for ye know neither the day nor the hour wherein the Son of man cometh.
— Matt. 25:13

The world is in sore trouble today, but it has been in trouble since the Garden of Eden. Since sin came into the world, this world has been in serious trouble. When man fell to Satan's temptation, then death passed upon the whole earth. Sin brings temptation, sorrow, heartache, bloodshed, and death.

Today, my friend, there seems to be a special anxiety about this world of ours, about this nation of ours. You have noticed this on the part of many. The world conditions, the decisions of Washington, D.C., and its lack of decisions, are causing some trouble, some questions. Strange answers are being given to some of the questions in this day and time.

I want to touch on this in this message. I trust that I can cause you to think a little as we talk about "How to Prepare for the Coming Crash."

The editor of the *Wall Street Journal* had this to say in condemnation of the ministers of this day:

> "Who is it in our society that makes significant and prophetic statements about the events of our time? Astronauts, artists, novelists, newscasters, politicians, and so on.
> But, the preachers are missing. They are not saying it."

It goes on to say a word of condemnation about ministers who do not call attention to things as they are in this world of ours.

HOW TO PREPARE FOR THE COMING CRASH

Then the writer comes down to another statement.

"The Presidency, the economy, the dollar, education, national security, minorities, government secrecy, blue collar workers, students, the church, foreign aids, arms control, love, marriage - everything seems to have come apart lately.

Nothing seems to work out right. Families are failing, familiar ways are being lost. No satisfactory new ways are being found."

Now here is another person's view which I picked from letters coming to me. This is also out of Washington, D.C.:

"I've never really worried about our nation's revival or survival until just recently. I would like to tell you that I am troubled now. I'm hoping that something can be done to relieve the situation."

He also said this:

"America is no longer the world's first military power. We are now second to Russia. The communists are widening their lead every week."

Most writers are speaking about saving America. Can America be saved? Of course, they are referring to all that is happening now in Washington, D.C. In the Presidency, in the Vice-Presidency and in almost every place in the nation at this moment, certain things are happening.

Some people take a rather dim view toward it all. I do not join with the people in this. I think perhaps this is weakening what we are doing. I'm referring to a little portion of this in a communication sent to me. The man is condemning the nation and saying that something needs to be done about a lot of things. He points out so many things of the past. He said Franklin D. Roosevelt lived with three women at the same time. He said he could prove it. All this was written in articles. Now, this is strange - digging back in the past.

Then he said that John Kennedy did so and so when he was nominated for the Presidency. (I shall not go into the evil part.) Then he said 141 tapes were discovered in the White House made by President Kennedy.

He goes on to say that Bobby Kennedy bugged everybody,

HOW TO PREPARE FOR THE COMING CRASH

including his friend, Martin Luther King, and he says much about that. I tore out a brief portion of that just to let you know how people are thinking. This one is also thinking that something needs to be done, referring to all of the situations in the world today.

Recently someone sent to me a book, *How To Prepare for the Coming Crash,* written by Robert Preston. It sold about 200,000 copies, which is a pretty good sale for a book anytime. There are 121 pages.

Mr. Preston says the following:

> "We will soon witness the greatest crash and depression the nation has ever known."

In his book he tells us how to prepare for this crash in a physical and material way, what we should do. He tells us that a great financial crash is just ahead.

> ". . . billions will be out of work. Millions will starve. Riots, killings and plunderings will sweep the nation."

He bases this coming crash on the fact that we have used our money in the wrong way. In the book by Mr. Preston, there is no mention of the Bible, no quoting the Scripture at all. He is dealing with this thing from another side altogether. But he bases the coming crash on the fact of the wrong use of money in our nation.

> "Our present prosperity, like a ballon, can get so big and then it must burst. A depression is coming."

He speaks in the book of how to store food and prepare for the depression days. Of course that is entirely on the physical side. He is not basing his predictions on the Word of God.

I do not doubt that there may be some kind of financial depression or some kind of revolution in our nation. I do not doubt that it would come because of that which is happening today.

This is a time of tragic upsets. This is a time when people are a bit uncertain about how to feel and what to say. They are troubled about the nation, about the leadership, about the conditions overseas. They are troubled about many

HOW TO PREPARE FOR THE COMING CRASH

facts - about Russia and our alliances with Russia in various ways. They are troubled about the happenings in the Near East.

I doubt not that something will happen some day to shake this nation. It may happen in our time, in these years before the coming of our Lord. Why? We have too much luxurious living, too many cars, too many clothes, too many vacations, too much money and we have very little Christianity, very little responsibility, too little decency, not much concern for others. We have too little respect for the Word of God, for God's day, for God's house.

Satan's power is rampant. This we see and feel in every place - on the radio, on the television, in the newspapers, in the magazines, in all of society. Sin is on the increase throughout the world, sin of the worst kind, the overt kinds that people can see and know and talk about.

Man is helpless to solve his problems. We can see it around us very clearly.

My concern is for the souls of men, for people being saved. The next event in God's program is the coming of Christ. He is coming again.

I cannot prophesy about a coming economic crash, or a depression. I do not know about it. But, my friend, with positive assurance, I can prophesy and preach this: Christ is coming again! "I will come again. . . " is the promise of the Son of God and the Word of God. Jesus Himself said, "Watch therefore. . . . " We are to continually watch.

Other things will doubtless take place because of the weaknesses that we now see, because of the undermining of the security of our nation, so evident today. Other things may happen. But the one thing we can know for a sure thing is that Christ will come. The Bible, the infallible, inerrant Word of God, points to His coming. The Old Testament points to the first and second coming. The New Testament outlines what will happen when Christ comes the second time.

There are eight momentous events ahead. I'm not going

HOW TO PREPARE FOR THE COM[ING]

into these, except to mention them.

First, the coming of the translation of believ[ers] comes, the dead will be raised, the living will be changed, caught up into His presence.

Second, the Great Tribulation, which we studied in our Sunday school lesson this morning - that terrible time upon the earth, with tragic suffering, an awful time for seven years.

Third, the revelation of Christ at the close of the seven-year period, when He comes out of the heavens and down to this earth.

Fourth, the battle of Armageddon, which is fought by our Saviour against the enemies of God upon this earth.

Fifth, the thousand-year reign of Christ upon the earth - the setting up of the kingdom.

Sixth, the last rebellion of Satan comes - at the end of the thousand years.

Seventh, the Great White Throne Judgment.

Eighth, the new heavens and the new earth.

These eight things will certainly take place according to the Word of God: seven of them, making the number of completion, then, the new heavens and the new earth (number eight), the new beginning, described in the book of Revelation.

The future is bright for the child of God. It is in the Lord Jesus Christ. Our job is to be faithful, to be ready to meet Him in the air, to be ready to stand before Him without shame.

There are three things we can say about the fact that He is coming.

I. A COMFORTING FACT
"Wherefore comfort one another with these words."
— I Thess. 4:18

The words of His coming. He is coming. The resurrection of the saved, the translation of the saved, and we are caught up in the air to meet our blessed Lord.

HOW TO PREPARE FOR THE COMING CRASH

A lot of things come out of that; and of course, a beautiful and assuring fact that the resurrection of the dead in Christ will be at the time of His coming.

> *Now this I say, brethren, that flesh and blood cannot inherit the kingdom of God* . . . .
> —I Cor. 15:50

> *Behold, I shew you a mystery; We shall not all sleep, but we shall all be changed,*
> *In a moment, in the twinkling of an eye, at the last trump: for the trumpet shall sound, and the dead shall be raised incorruptible, and we shall be changed.*
> —I Cor. 15:51,52

This speaks of the coming of our Saviour, the resurrection of the dead, the translation of the living, and being caught up into His presence.

That means reunion. The second word in this first thought that I have in this idea is of reunion, a joining with those who have gone before, when the dead are raised, the living changed and brought together in the presence of our Christ.

That, of course, brings us to the fact of rejoicing - rejoicing in the coming of Christ. Heartaches are over, eternity is before us, and we are in the presence of God.

We should do some serious thinking about the second coming. In this day when things are shaky, troublesome, dark in some portions of the world, we need to think on the coming of our blessed Saviour. Trouble for the rest of the world, but for the Christian - we're to be in the presence of our Saviour! A comforting fact.

A lot of people get worried, are troubled and distressed, wondering what is going to happen next. One thing you can rest on if you are a child of God: one day we will be in the presence of our loving Saviour.

HOW TO PREPARE FOR THE COMING CRASH

II. AN EXCITING FACT

The fact of His coming - when we'll see the fulfillment of prophecy. The amazing prophecies of this Book will be fulfilled, every single one, as they were fulfilled in the first coming of our Saviour. When He was born of a virgin, when He walked on the earth, when He died upon the cross, all were prophesied in the Word of God in the Old Testament. His resurrection, His ascension, is given to us. So will the prophecies regarding His return. The establishment of His kingdom upon the earth shall be fulfilled in the minutest details. He is coming to receive us unto Himself.

I will never forget what Hyman Appelman said:

> "I have preached in so many places. Some people laugh when I talk about the coming of Christ and the rapture of the saints [the snatching away of the saints of God into the heavens], but I'll say this: You can laugh at me if you want to, but when Jesus Christ comes and the dead are raised, when the saved are changed and we are caught up into the air to meet Him, as I go up in the air I'm going to stick my tongue out at you and say, "I told you so!"

Here is the coming fulfillment of prophecy. He's coming again. We can rest upon this. We will see our Saviour face to face. We sing, "One day He's coming - oh, glorious day!" We think about His coming again. We sing, "Behold, He Comes!" and rejoice when we sing it. But one day we shall see the Saviour face to face. We are going to look at the face of the blessed Son of God, the One who died upon the cross for us, the One who bears the marks of nails in His hands and feet and the spear thrust in His side. We shall see the Lord Jesus again. One day we will see the realizations of our fondest dreams. In this world? No, but in His coming. Then will be the fulfillment and realization of our fondest dreams. All that we have ever thought of having will be brought to pass in Him.

In Christ the future means fellowship. Fellowship is a lost item in our day, but in Christ we have it. In Christ we have freedom from sin, freedom from the awful treachery of

HOW TO PREPARE FOR THE COMING CRASH

things of this life.

In Christ we see the accomplishment of all things in Him - blessed things. Mothers dream, fathers dream, children dream about what will happen one day, what will take place. The dreams of a lifetime will become a reality as we come into the presence of our blessed Saviour.

I can speak on a thought like this because there are so many things that I have had. I'm a dreamer. I try to think things out. I try to pray them through. I'm concerned about progress. I'm concerned about doing things for the glory of God. I'm concerned about new buildings for Tennessee Temple University. I'm concerned about the future of our schools, if our Lord tarries. I'm concerned about our church and what should happen here. I continue to think of the things God wants us to do.

I realize that perhaps my time of working is not very long. I have just a short time. He may come today. He may come tomorrow. He may come before next Sunday. But if He tarries, I do have just a short time to work. I think of so many things I want to see, so many dreams I want to realize. I believe it will all be accomplished in the coming of my Saviour, when I stand before Him.

That's not the end, just the beginning, the beginning of all beautiful things, the beginning of work. I rejoice in the fact that in Heaven, in the presence of God, in the thousand-year reign upon the earth, there will be something for us to do.

III. A DISTURBING FACT

The coming of our blessed Saviour. That He is coming is disturbing to folks who set their affections on earthly things. I refer to Christians now.

In Colossians 3:2, the apostle said, "Set your affection on things above, not on things on the earth."

The Lord Jesus said, ". . . . seek ye first the kingdom of God and his righteousness; and all these things shall be added

HOW TO PREPARE FOR THE COMING CRASH

unto you."

Today there is a dread, an awful clinging after the world by the children of God - those who are saved, those who are redeemed, those who are going to Heaven and know it. But at the same time, there is a desire for more, a desire for an acquiring of things around us. This fact of the coming of Jesus Christ is disturbing to those who are acquiring <u>things,</u> holding onto <u>things,</u> who want more of this world's goods. They have a desire to hold onto more, to keep more for themselves and their families. Yet Jesus is coming. We shall be caught into His presence, then all of this must be left behind.

Christian friend, look up! The coming of Jesus draweth nigh. Keep your affections set upon the Son of God. This is a disturbing fact to you as a Christian if you are <u>unprepared for His coming,</u> and to the lost who do not know the Lord Jesus Christ, who are lost in sin.

> *Then shall two be in the field; the one shall be taken, and the other left.*
>
> *Two women shall be grinding at the mill; the one shall be taken, and the other left.*
>
> *Watch therefore: for ye know not what hour your Lord doth come.*
>
> — Matt. 24:40-42

"Watch therefore," said the Lord Jesus Christ, "for ye know not what hour your Lord doth come." This is the fact of His coming. When Jesus comes, the saved are caught up into the air to meet Him, while the lost are left. How sad! The unsaved are not ready for this time; therefore we must point them to the Lord Jesus and urge them to accept Christ so they will be prepared when He comes again.

I read about a couple who had been studying in their Bibles about the second coming. One night they put their family to bed, then went to bed themselves. They had been

HOW TO PREPARE FOR THE COMING CRASH

talking about the separation and what is going to happen when Jesus comes.

During the night one of the children in the next room began to cry. Mother got up and went to check on the baby. When she got up, her husband was fast asleep on his side of the bed. After a while he suddenly awakened. He turned over to see if his wife was there - she was gone! He exclaimed, "This is it - the separation, the great separation!" He was quite alarmed. He thought she had been taken and he had been left.

Wait a minute! Jesus is coming. The dead in Christ shall be raised. The living shall be changed and the lost will be left.

Sinner friends here tonight, you need to recognize that without Jesus Christ you are unprepared, but in Him you are ready for the day that will take place for all events of the future. He is coming, coming in a bodily fashion, and visible to every saved person (Acts 1:10,11).

The time is uncertain, but not the event. The Bible warns us to be ready for His coming. "Watch therefore...," said the Saviour. Paul said the same thing in urging people to be watching. Peter said the same thing in warning about the coming of our Lord Jesus Christ. John warns us, also, that Christ is coming again.

This is the one hope for a troubled world - the coming of Jesus Christ.

I am not criticizing our President. I'm in no position to do that. But it is rather pitiful to hear him often say: "I think we're now near to having a warless world and a world of peace."

I have news for him. There will never be a world of peace until Jesus comes. He is our only hope for the world - all that we have. We can say to others that Christ is our hope. Serving God daily and living for God daily is real. One day we shall stand in His presence.

Let's think for a while about how to prepare for His coming.

HOW TO PREPARE FOR THE COMING CRASH

The first thing to do is receive Him as Saviour. If you have never been saved, then it is your business to receive Him now. "But as many as received him, to them gave he power to become the sons of God, even to them that believe on his name."

To receive Him as Saviour guarantees the future. When you put your faith and trust in Jesus, that guarantees all future days. It guarantees your safety in every single event that may take place. All is safe and secure in Him. One day we shall stand before Him.

Second, live for Him devotedly. Separated from the world. "Come out from among them and be ye separate, saith the Lord, and touch not the unclean thing." Live for Him devotedly hour after hour.

Third, serve Him faithfully. Be fervent in spirit, serving the Lord. To serve Him faithfully is so important. To serve Him lovingly is so important. To serve Him patiently is so important. Serve Him all the time! Why? Because He is coming again. We shall be caught up to meet Him in the air!

Are you serving God that way? Are you seeking to get people saved? Is that the aim of your life? To serve Him with all of your heart, to so live that others might see Christ in you - is that your heart's desire?

An old man, unsaved, had been mean, wicked and evil. When people spoke to him about Christ, he would curse them. If they tried to come to his home, in his anger he would order them away.

One day a little boy came to him and said, "Please sir, may I give you something?" The little fellow was so innocent about what he was doing, how he was doing it, and so concerned about the old man. "Please sir, I want to give you something. I would like to ask you to read this, if you will, sir. I would appreciate it so much if you would, please, sir." He put a gospel tract into the hands of the old man who had been so vicious and vile toward others.

The man took the gospel tract, read it and was saved.

HOW TO PREPARE FOR THE COMING CRASH

Later he stood to give this testimony: "I accepted Jesus Christ as my Saviour because of the warm and friendly word of a little boy who said, 'Please, sir, would you read this? I will give it to you if you will read it; I want you to have it.' Because of that, I turned to Christ and received Him as my own personal Saviour."

My dear friend, what a joy it is to point someone to the Lamb of God, to make someone else ready for the coming of our blessed Saviour! Christ is coming! Are you ready? Can you say, "I know Him"?

Do you have lost loved ones and friends who are away from God, out in sin? Are you concerned about them? Then ask God to help you do your best to help get them ready for the coming of the blessed Saviour. He's coming again. Do your best to get people to Jesus.

I read of a man over in Shanghai who had a very unique way of winning souls. A well-dressed Chinese gentleman was watching four men push a cart up the street. They came to one of the little raised bridges built over the stream running through the city. The men had difficulty pushing the heavily loaded cart over it. The well-dressed Chinese gentleman went to them and began to help push. He got hold of the rope and pulled. He brought the cart to the top of the little bridge. When he finished (he was talking to them all the time), they turned and went down the other side.

A missionary saw him and said, "Sir, I saw what you did. Why did you help the men, dressed as you are? Why did you run out to the street and help them push?"

"This is my way of witnessing," he replied, "I watch people. When they come to a difficult place, I jump in to help. While I am out there helping, I witness for Christ. I tell folk of Jesus who died on the cross. I have won hundreds to the Lord Jesus Christ this way. This is my method, my plan, my way of witnessing."

Some of you businessmen might adopt some method of telling people about Jesus. Some of you in offices could do

HOW TO PREPARE FOR THE COMING CRASH

likewise. Some of you could in various places of society. All can witness for Christ; all can tell how He saves sinners. This is it - getting folk ready for the coming of Christ, for He is coming.

Will it be a world crash? Will it be a crash in this nation? I do not know. Tragic things are happening. Amazing things have happened in the last few weeks. If you have read very much, studied very much, you know this is true. But one thing we are sure of: Christ is coming! And when He comes, we shall be caught up into His presence.

Are you ready? Have you accepted Jesus Christ? Have you put your trust in Him?

Sinner, if you are not ready, you can be by simple faith in Jesus. Let God have His way. Let Him have His way in the light of all that Jesus Christ has done for you. Let Him have His way in the light of the unchanging promises of God. Let Him have His way in the midst of all the fluctuating circumstances of life. Let Him have His way.

Chapter 3
The Episode of the Fifth Rib

And when Abner was returned to Hebron, Joab took him aside in the gate to speak with him quietly, and smote him there under the fifth rib, that he died, for the blood of Asahel his brother.
II Sam. 3:27

The Bible revolves around personalities - some good and some bad. It's the tendency of the world to picture those who are departed from us in the fable way and to say the best, the nicest things that we can say.

I'm reminded of one funeral service. The pastor spoke in such glowing terms about the man who had departed, whose body was in the casket. The mother turned to her eldest son and said, "Son, slip up there and see if that's our old man in the casket."

The Bible always speaks the truth. The Bible presents men as they are. I never lie at a funeral. But I do avoid saying things that ought not be said. I try to avoid being hurtful to anyone in time of sorrow. But the Bible tells it all.

I remind you of the Bible's frankness about Abraham - his misdemeanors as well as his greatness; about Moses, Elijah, Simon Peter, John Mark and many others. The Bible presents the strength of men and the weakness of men.

The story of the death of Abner illustrates the Bible pattern. Abner was a leader in the army of King Saul. I'm not going into the whole story, only enough to let you see some of it here in chapter three of II Samuel. He was a

THE EPISODE OF THE FIFTH RIB

capable man but devoid of any character or religious devotion, as far as we can find.

There are two characters to notice in this chapter before us. One is Abner, head of King Saul's army; the other is Joab, head of David's army.

Joab and Abner fought, and Joab won. The Word of God tells us that Abner killed Asahel, the brother of Joab.

Turning against his own king, King Saul, Abner was endeavoring to turn the kingdom over to King David, which meant it was a very underhanded, traitorous thing.

Joab came and killed Abner, smiting him under the fifth rib.

Notice this: after the death of Abner, King David, in sorrow, "followed the bier" (II Sam. 3:31) out to the graveside. He cried, "Died Abner as a fool dieth?" (II sam. 3:33). How did this man die? Did he die as a fool dies?

There are some lessons here. I'll come back to a portion of it in just a moment.

First of all, the danger of instability, wavering from side to side. The Bible says, ". . . for he that wavereth is like a wave of the sea driven with the wind and tossed" (James 1:6). Some people are always shifting, first to one church, then to another. First in one kind of business, then to another kind.

This past week I was listening to a newscast about a man I knew quite well years ago, Charles Templeton, or Chuck Templeton. Everybody from Canada would know him. A lot of folks in this country would, also. I knew Charles Templeton in Toronto, Canada. They knew what he was, what he could do. He was a Nazarene pastor in Toronto. He was famous, noted everywhere as an outstanding man of God.

I had a revival meeting in Evansville, Indiana, at the old Evansville Rescue Mission. Just a few blocks away, in the city auditorium, Chuck Templeton was conducting a city-wide revival campaign. Six and seven thousand people were packing the building every night. Chuck Templeton had resigned

THE EPISODE OF THE FIFTH RIB

the Nazarene Church and was then employed by the National Council of Churches of America. Later I read that he had gone to Princeton University or Princeton Seminary for three years of study.

Then trouble came. Doubts entered in. His wife left him, and he married again.

This past week, he appeared on television advertising a book. He said that he now calls himself an agnostic. Once a fundamentalist, once a believer in the Word of God, once steady in preaching, winning souls, calling people to repentance and to faith in Christ, he turned away from all of this and wrote a book declaring himself as to what he now is - an agnostic.

I'm saying, my dear friend, get established with the Word of God. Oh, the danger of instability!

<u>Again, the evil of self-seeking</u>. This fellow Abner very definitely was looking out for himself. He was seeking for himself. He wanted to leave King Saul and go with King David because he felt there were more advantages in that place.

You have to watch the man who is always looking out for self, who is always asking, "How much does it pay? What do we get out of this?"

Some years ago I brought a man here for a Bible conference. One day I was standing in the old church building when he came in. I met for the first time this famous, outstanding man. He said, "I'm here for the conference. Glad to be with you." We had a few words together, then he turned to me and said, "How much do I get for this conference?"

"What do you mean, Sir?"

"Well, what do you pay me?"

"Sir, we don't say anything about that. We give a love offering when it's over; and our people are generous. But I don't know how much you'll get."

"I must have $100.00 per day - or $500.00 for the five days I'll be here. Unless I get that, I'll have to go."

THE EPISODE OF THE FIFTH RIB

I said, "You may go right now. You're through," and I wasn't joking.

He turned, walked out the door, then came back and said, "I've changed my mind. I'll take the chance. I'll stay."

I should not have allowed him to stay. I should have said, "Sir, you are through. I don't want your kind around here. You're self-seeking, wanting something for yourself. I don't believe in your kind." I should have said so, but I didn't. I let him speak and we gave him a generous offering for the five days.

Oh, the evil of self-seeking! Whenever one is seeking for himself, danger comes. That man was later discovered in a motel room in Los Angeles, California, with another man's wife, and was shot to death.

Now I'm talking about self-seeking. Whenever you're seeking for yourself, you are in danger, my friend. Young man, mother, father, you're in danger when you're thinking only about how much you can get for yourself.

There's the plague of low standards. Abner had low standards. They plagued his life - standards of honesty, of truthfulness, of purity. All were missing in his life. See the danger of low standards, the plague of low standards today.

You get your standards way up high! You stand for something! Determine, "I'd rather die than be dishonest! I'd rather die than cheat my fellow man!" Get hold of that, and don't you vary.

We dismissed a boy from school some years ago for dishonesty, lying, cheating and stealing. His name came up in our staff meeting only yesterday. What's he doing? Back to the same old tricks, but in another field of service. The report has come back to us. It won't be long before he will be behind bars and begging for someone to get him out. You see, there is the plague of low standards.

Set your standards high! It matters not what it may be - whether in the paying of your bills, or simply in the living of your life - live so that others can see Christ in you. Don't

THE EPISODE OF THE FIFTH RIB

try to cheat!

If someone overpays you, go back and say, "My friend, you made a mistake. I want to return this to you."

If you feel that you haven't paid what you should have paid for something, simply go to the cashier and say, "I want to make this right. I want to always be right in my life."

Here's some practical things I want to put upon your heart.

I. PUT YOUR LIFE UNDER GOD'S X-RAY

Let the Word of God reach into your heart and search it out. Don't shun the truth. Watch your own life, your own soul, your own heart. Let God speak to you.

Does the Bible show that you are selfish? Face it, confess it, then turn from it.

Have you refused to do the simple thing of tithing? To me that is no little thing. A christian who will not tithe, who is too selfish to tithe that which God is asking of him, causes me to wonder if everything is all right with him. Watch it!

Does the Bible show that you are a selfish person? Do you seek for self, no matter whom you may hurt? Are you looking out for self and desiring things of this world?

Does the Bible point out laziness? Does the Word of God point out that you are looking for something for nothing, without expenditure of any energy? The Apostle Paul condemns laziness. He said in II Thessalonians, 'Unless you work, you're not going to eat.'

Are you weak morally? Are you seeking after the things of the flesh? Are your thoughts and actions wrong? I love young folks and I love to talk and pray with them. How many have come to me and said, "Oh Brother Roberson, I'm having a battle. My mind, my thoughts are killing me. Can you help me? Can you tell me what to do?"

I try to help them from the Word of God. I come back to the same old things I've said thousands of times: "You can have only one thought at a time. If it's a bad one, it's a

THE EPISODE OF THE FIFTH RIB

wrong one. If it's a good thought, it's a good one. But you can have only one at a time - just one. So center your mind upon God. Read your Bible. Pray. Seek the face of God. Make sure that you keep things right between you and the Lord."

Face your sin! Do something about it. Says I John 1:9, "If we confess our sins, he is faithful and just to forgive us our sins, and to cleanse us from all unrighteousness." Put your life under God's x-ray, the Word of God. Television can't do anything for you. Neither can the books of the world. Radio doesn't do anything for you. You've got to come back to the Word of God. Let the Bible x-ray be put upon your heart and life.

II. BUILD YOUR CONVICTIONS

Build them early in life. Young people, get strong convictions. Get them so strong that no matter what comes or goes, you're going to stand by those convictions.

Get your convictions and keep building on them. Make sure that you're building on that which is solid and substantial and according to the Word of God. Build on the solid Rock, Christ Jesus. Not upon the sand, but upon the Rock. Say, "Here I stand. I'm building my convictions upon Christ Jesus, my Lord and Saviour."

Build your convictions on the Word of God, this solid unchanging Word. "Heaven and earth shall pass away, but my words shall not pass away" (Matt. 24:35). The Word of God stands forever and ever! It never varies, never changes!

I read something quite interesting in a paper this past week. They have developed some new names, some new life styles for these seven deadly sins: pride, covetousness, lust, anger, gluttony, envy, and sloth.

For example, "pride's" new name is <u>success</u>. "Covetousness" has assumed the label of <u>law suit</u>. "Lust's" new title is <u>expression</u>. "Anger's" designation is <u>indignation</u>. "Gluttony" has become <u>good life</u>. "Envy" calls itself <u>regulation</u>. "Sloth" has a new name called <u>freedom</u>.

THE EPISODE OF THE FIFTH RIB

The author of this interesting discussion of the changing characters of the seven deadly sins points out that with the changes there is a comforting theory: one can commit all of them, provided he avoids hypocrisy. Are you listening? Do I commit adultury? Sure! Do I lie and cheat? Sure! But whatever I do or am, there is one thing I'm not - a hypocrite! That guy is a nut! He is a fool!

My father was a gracious man of God, and this happened when he was still a sinner and I was a boy attending Henry Clay school. We went to church in Louisville, Kentucky, this time and there some fellow made a statement that we were hypocrites. Dad got up and stalked out. He was angry. "I'm no hypocrite! I do cuss, but I don't lie about it! I do this and that . . . . " He thought "hypocrite" was something big. Later, he knew better, after he got saved.

Build your convictions. Turn away from the sinful things of this world, the things that hurt people, and ask God to help you be right.

First, put your life under God's x-ray. Second, build your convictions. Get some strong convictions and hold to them.

III. DIE TO SELF

Selfishness will wreck one's life. Here is the picture from this story. You didn't notice this while ago, but here it is: David's unselfishness. His friend Abner had been an enemy of David. But when Joab, David's general, killed Abner, David mourned as for a dear friend.

Listen! You can best judge a man on his treatment of his enemies. Are you listening? David was kind toward King Saul.

David was gracious toward his son Absalom when he turned against him.

David was kindly toward Abner when Abner turned against him. Though this one was wrong and seeking to undermine what he had, David was still standing. What was David doing? Dying to self.

Now, my friend, your life can never know the success, the

THE EPISODE OF THE FIFTH RIB

joy, the peace that God wants you to have, if you don't come to reckon self to be dead.

I read this last week: *"No one has ever committed suicide so often as I."* Do you know what he is talking about? Dying to self. Dying daily, every day. Paul said, "I die daily. Every day I die to myself, to my ambitions." Suicide every day - reckoning self to be dead.

Poor Abner was thinking only of self. He died at the hand of Joab. Joab killed him because Abner had killed his brother. David was mourning the whole thing, walking after the casket weeping; yet, the whole thing had a strange touch to it. There was no reason for David to be moved, except that David had a heart. He understood. He was concerned, even about enemies.

That brings a lesson to me. We must love our enemies. "Pray for them which despitefully use you."

I learned a lesson a long, long time ago. Every morning I pray for certain people. I pray for folks (excuse me) who hate my guts! I pray sincerely, for God to speak to them and make them right. I want my heart right toward those who are opposed to that for which I stand. Jesus said, "Love your enemies. . . . pray for them which despitefully use you. . . " (Matt. 5:44).

This is what David exhibited in this story, when he was dead to self, when he went out even to mourn the death of this man Abner, killed by his own general, Joab. He was simply doing the thing that I'm talking about here - dying to self.

IV. GUARD YOUR INFLUENCE

First, your influence should glorify God. Live so that others can see Christ in you. Somebody, somewhere, should think that you are Christlike. Some beautiful little child should think, "Oh, my mother and daddy are just as much like Jesus as I can think of anyone being." Your influence should glorify God. It should make people think of God

THE EPISODE OF THE FIFTH RIB

because of how you live and how you conduct yourself. Guard your influence. Don't let anything change it!

One little bitty, old dirty, insignificant sin (as the world looks at sin) can wreck your life and take away that purity, take away what you need for your life. So guard your influence.

Second, your influence should daily help someone else. The power of influence: ". . . . none of us liveth to himself, and no man dieth to himself" (Rom. 14:7). Live a positive life. Live so others can see Christ in you. Use your strength to strengthen others.

When somebody comes up to you and says, "I want you to pray for me," that's good. When our folk come in and say, "Brother Roberson, would you mind praying for me?" I feel like I'm getting somewhere. It is bad when no one has enough confidence in you to ask you to pray. You are just one of the crowd. Live so that others can be blessed by your life and influence.

Third, your influence should point to Christ. Every step you take should point to Christ the Saviour. Every word you speak, every business deal you ever make, should point to Christ. If you are engaging in some crooked, doubtful or dishonest business, get away from it. If you're engaging in something with a question mark, get out of it. I promise you that God will bless you and take care of you abundantly.

Your influence should point to Jesus Christ. Let no one look at you and say, "That fellow says he is a Christian, but look what he did. That man said he was a Christian, but look how he cheated me." "Look, that man says he is a Christian, but listen how he talks, the speech he uses."

Point to Christ when the whole world criticizes you. Point to Christ when loved ones are taken from you by death. And keep on pointing to Christ and rejoicing.

Have you got what I have been saying tonight out of this unique story in the Word of God? A man was killed. I know it is something you haven't read very carefully in II Samuel

THE EPISODE OF THE FIFTH RIB

chapter three, but read it and underscore some of the verses, as I have done in my Bible. That's a strange story, yet, here it is - something that helps us put our life under God's x-ray.

See yourself as God sees you.

Build your convictions.

Die to self.

Guard your influence and keep your influence right.

I picked up a book on yesterday. It had a sermon written in 1898. You know what the sermon was about? About William E. Gladstone, Prime Minister of England for many years. It went on to talk about William E. Gladstone. I read it all. He was great. He was gentle. He was energetic. He had moral courage. Most of all, Gladstone was a Christian.

Here's what it had to say about his Christian faith. *(1) His faith was simple.* He believed in Christ. He believed in the Bible. He believed in the Holy Spirit - William Gladstone, Prime Minister of England, one of the famous men of all time.

(2) His faith was sentimental, not cold and formal, but alive and moving. He could shed tears - William Gladstone, the Prime Minister of the country.

(3) His faith was sublime. For years, over his bed hung the motto, *"Thou will keep him in perfect peace, whose mind is stayed on thee. . . "* Every morning William E. Gladstone spent time with Bible study and prayer. He worshipped every Lord's day in the house of God - never missed. He led his family to Christ - all of them.

There was an outstanding man, a man of worldly fame that time cannot erase. Yet, here was a man who believed the simple old faith in the way we believe it and preach it in Highland Park Baptist Church. It meant something. His name is still revered to this day by those who respect honesty, uprightness and decency.

Listen to me tonight! Let your life count for God! Get on the right side, young man! Get on the right side, young lady! Get on the right side, Mother, Father! Get on the right side,

THE EPISODE OF THE FIFTH RIB

student! Get on the right side, young businessman! Say, "O God, help me to live a life that will honor God and will show forth Christ. I'll not do wrong. I'll not be dishonest. I'm not going to be a cheater. I'll not be a dope head. No; I'm going to be right with God."

An old pilot passed away in Boston, Massachusetts. He had piloted little ships around the Boston area for some seventy-five years. All of the time people knew him as a faithful Christian.

This dear old man came to the time of dying. As he was passing away, his face brightened. In a moment of sudden alertness he said, "I see a light!"

A friend standing by thought his mind was wandering, so he asked, "Is it the Highland light?"

The old man replied, "No, it's not the Highland light."

Another asked, "Is it the Boston light?"

"No, it's not the Boston light."

Still another said, "Is it the Minot light?"

"No, it's not the Minot light. It's the light of Glory! The light of Glory!" Then he said, "Let the anchor go." And in a few moments the old pilot slipped out to the other side to stand in the presence of the Lord.

My dear friend, that's where I want to stand some day. And I don't want to be ashamed when I get there. I don't want to have to hang my head and say, "Lord, I messed up. I didn't do it right when I was at Highland Park in Chattanooga. I failed You!"

Rather, I want to stand with head upright, eyes open, and look into the face of the Lord Jesus Christ and say, "Lord I tried. Yes, I did fail at times, but I did try. I did my best. I tried over and over again. Sometimes I was weak, sometimes I was unstable, sometimes I was unfaithful, but Lord, I tried."

I want to look into His face and let Him know that I love Him and that I did my best for Him here. I want my life to count for Him.

Chapter 4
The Hourglass Sermon

> *Go to now, ye that say, Today or tomorrow we will go into such a city, and continue there a year, and buy and sell, and get gain:*
> *Whereas ye know not what shall be on the morrow. For what is your life? It is even a vapour, that appeareth for a little time, and then vanisheth away.*
> *For that ye ought to say, If the Lord will, we shall live, and do this, or that.*
> *But now ye rejoice in your boastings: all such rejoicing is evil.*
> *Therefore to him that knoweth to do good, and doeth it not, to him it is sin.*
> — Jas. 4:13-17

The Bible says that man should be aware of the brievity of life. "For what is your life? It is even a vapour, that appeareth for a little time, and then vanisheth away."

Some fail to see the uncertainty of life. David said, ".. there is but a step between me and death." And James 4:14 reminds us: "Whereas ye know not what shall be on the morrow."

Most people fail to see the eternal significance of life, that life is eternal, that it is Heaven or Hell. You are an eternal soul who will spend eternity with God or will spend eternity in Hell. Your life touches others. By your life, you are pointing people to Christ in Heaven or to Satan in Hell. Paul said, "For none of us liveth to himself, and no man dieth to himself."

THE HOURGLASS SERMON

In answer to the question, "What is the true picture of your life?" someone has said, "Imagine an hourglass before you. Connecting the bowl at the top with the bowl at the bottom is a tube so thin that only one grain of sand can pass through at a time." This hourglass is before me. See the slender portion between the two bowls as the sand drips through ever so slowly.

Here is a picture of your life, even on the busiest day. So many of us are busy. We have things we must do. But even the crowded hours can only come one moment at a time.

Difficulties come one at a time. Heartaches come one at a time. The trials of life, the strains of life, are invariably in single file as that coming from the top to the bottom of an hourglass, depicting the passage of time. Just a grain of sand at a time, just one single portion at a time - this is life. This is part of life.

Someone has said, "Take care of the minutes and the hours will take care of themselves."

Another said, "If you want to become a man of the hour, first learn to make every minute count." Oh, the importance of time!

I want you to see a three-point outline.

I. THE WORTH OF TIME

Psalm 90:12: "So teach us to number our days, that we may apply our hearts unto wisdom." Time is precious. Why?

It is precious because it is God-given. God gives us the time we have. All we have tonight belongs to Him. Our being in this service, our life here is a gift of Almighty God. Some might question this a bit and say, "Well, so what? We go on, we live our life out, and we come to the end."

Let me give one simple illustration. King Hezekiah was a sick man. He turned his face to the wall. He was troubled, distressed, dying. And when he prayed to God, God said, "I will add unto thy days fifteen years," and fifteen years were added to his life, to be used for God's service in the

THE HOURGLASS SERMON

kingship of Israel.

This is only one picture. Life is God-given, this we know; so we must ask Him for our day-by-day needs.

Second, it is precious because it is short. The Apostle Paul said that the time is short.

The time is short for suffering. I wish I could sometimes say that to people. I'm afraid that they might misunderstand. There is a man in the hospital now who is past eighty. Why he is suffering so much, I do not know. He spent his useful years in service; now he's confined to his hospital bed, covered with sores. The doctor said the same type sores are on the inside of his body. Certain medicines he had taken reacted on him the wrong way, so now he is suffering so much.

The time is short for suffering. This means we must be patient. This means we must await the coming of our Lord and know that He will deliver us in that day.

The hospitals and sanitariums are full. The mystery of suffering is all around us. But we must trust God.

The time is short. One day we shall be in the presence of our Lord. Then we shall be like Him - without the suffering and the agony of this life.

The time is short for service. Be willing to serve. Be ready for God to take and use your life in the finest and best way.

Oh, so many Christians are trying to avoid the place of service. So many are trying to get by without doing anything. They sit on the sidelines and refuse to serve God, refuse to get into any place of activity. Be willing to serve.

Be enthusiastic in your service and ask God to take your life and use it for His glory. Put your whole soul and life into what you are doing.

I like the little text I preach on quite often in Romans 12: ". . . fervent in spirit; serving the Lord." That means to be enthusiastic.

I came here in 1942. A few weeks later Homer Rodeheaver was with us leading the music for a meeting. He was the great singer for Billy Sunday. He carried his big trombone on his

THE HOURGLASS SERMON

his arm. He sang so beautifully, so gently, and so smoothly. I was having a good time preaching the Gospel. People were getting saved. I was a young man, kicking the slats out of everything I could, and having such a good time doing it.

One day Mr. Rodeheaver got me aside and said, "Young man, I'm afraid you are going to go too far. Some of your members have come to me about the way you work and preach. They think you're too enthusiastic. I recommend that you take it easy, that you not work and preach quite as fast. Relax a little more. Take a little more time in what you're doing.

When he finished talking, I simply said, Mr. Rodeheaver, you take care of the music and I'll take care of the preaching."

He said, "Well, thank you, sir. (He was so gracious.) Brother Roberson, I shouldn't have said a word. You know, I was brought up under Billy Sunday's ministry. There was never a man as enthusiastic as he was in his great preaching across the big platforms. I saw all of that. But when some of your members came to me and said what they did - 'We wish our pastor would take it easy; we prefer quiet talks, a little easier type of message, not quite so enthusiastic,' I came to you about it. You're right. If I were you, I'd just go on and do it the same way I'd been doing it." And I have for all these years. God helping me, I'd like to keep it up!

Listen, be enthusiastic in what you do!

Then again, be faithful. Souls are fast sinking into Hell. We must be faithful. This matter of time is precious because it is short.

<u>Third, it is precious because the decisions of this life settle eternity</u>. "What shall I do then with Jesus, which is called Christ?" Here is a question that has to be answered. When you answer it, then you decide whether you spend eternity in Heaven or in Hell.

There are decisions that touch eternity in what we do with our lives. Then how careful we should be in making the right decisions.

THE HOURGLASS SERMON

Write down, please, the worth of time. I want you to see this and hold to it - the worth of time.

II. THE WASTING OF TIME

Most people are prodigal in their waste of time. Young people waste time. How wasteful are so many in this day and hour, without thinking about the seriousness of life. Some say, "Brother Roberson, you can't scare us. We are young. We have plenty of time."

That's not true. You don't have plenty of time. Time is short - very short.

Middle-agers waste time. They feel like they have plenty of time to waste and to use for what they desire.

The aged waste time. I am disturbed about this. When people retire, they sit on the sidelines and do nothing, as though they had plenty of time, when actually, they have only a few short years, should the Lord tarry.

The waste of time - watch it carefully. Watch it, please!

First, time is wasted when Christ is excluded from my life. If you leave Jesus on the outside, you are wasting time. Unless Jesus is in the center of your life, you are wasting time. Christ said, "I am the way, the truth and the life. . . " It must be in Jesus that we have life. Yes we are wasting time when we leave the Son of God outside.

Second, time is wasted when I worry. Worry is sin. The life of faith excludes worry. The child of God must not worry, must not fret, but he must simply trust God every step of the way.

I like the words of Philippians 4:6,7:

> *Be careful for nothing; but in everything by prayer and supplication with thanksgiving let your requests be made known unto God. And the peace of God, which passeth all understanding, shall keep your hearts and minds through Christ Jesus.*

This is for us.

Time is wasted when I worry. Many of us are wasting time.

THE HOURGLASS SERMON

Gather up those thoughts and say, "O God, help me to live so that I am not throwing away these wonderful days You have given me."

Third, time is wasted when I enter into worthless and sinful activities. The world seeks to lead you to do that which is worthless, that which is meaningless. Thousands are spending years in penitentiaries, wasting what time God has given them. Why? Because they went after the world and after sinful pursuits.

Fourth, time is wasted when I turn from His work. Many do this. Many fall and turn away from the work that God has given them to do. They turn from the task that God has appointed for them. They fail both in heart and life because of this.

Time is precious and time is wasted. Maybe I can illustrate this.

Here is a young man called of God. He has been trained for the ministry. He becomes a pastor, and a good one. After pastoring maybe months, maybe years, he suddenly becomes a bit dissatisfied. He has a wife and children. He should be happy in the Lord and rejoicing in what is given to him. But he turns away from the work of God and leaves his wife and children and goes off with a young woman in the church. He goes away a few hundred miles to live.

The sad part is, he has thrown away a whole life. He was saved by the grace of God; he was called to preach; and he was rejoicing in his life. Suddenly he turns away, throws his life into the gutter, into the waste of sin and Satan. Now, the whole thing is gone, and in a few moments' time.

The husband of that young woman who ran away with the preacher came to see me this past week. He was a heartbroken young man. He said, "I love God. My wife said she was saved. She even taught a Sunday school class. We loved the pastor. Now, to think that he - a man we have trusted and loved so much - would run off with my wife and both leave their own families."

THE HOURGLASS SERMON

This young fellow sat before me this week and shed his tears. He said it was an awful waste of life. And he was right. But, oh, how foolish are people! My friend, watch that you, too, do not turn from what God wants you to do!

I was one time conducting meetings in another state. It was a beautiful church. The building was packed and jammed the two nights I was there. The pastor was working, it seemed, in a wonderful way. Souls were being saved, and I rejoiced in it. I couldn't see how a church could be any happier and more harmonious in spirit than that church seemed to be.

Suddenly I was called and told that the pastor had left his place of duty, had left his wife and family and had gone to another state with his secretary. He called back home and stated, "It's all over. I'm through. I've given up the ministry altogether."

Oh, what an awful waste! Now, after all this, he has tried to come back to his family.

What I'm trying to make you see is that time is wasted when we turn away from the work of God, when we depart from the place of full-time service God has given us.

But some of you turn away from God's Sunday service. You're not faithful in Sunday school, not in your teaching, not in your training of young people. You quit the choir, you quit the Sunday school, you quit the ushering, you quit everything and turned aside. Why? "Well, I don't want to go ahead."

Oh, my dear Christian friend, let God have His way. Don't waste the time God has given you. Spend every day, every hour, in the finest and best way. One moment at a time, as the hourglass illustrates for us, living for God and serving Him.

III. THE WISE USE OF TIME

We have talked of the worth of time, of the waste of time; now, we talk of the wise use of time. What is the wise use?

<u>First of all, I'm using time wisely when I worship God.</u>

THE HOURGLASS SERMON

We cannot worship God too much. It is ordained by the Word of God that we come together for singing, for preaching, for worship, for meditation. It is a holy hour when you come to the house of God on Sunday night, or Wednesday night, or Sunday morning. This is using time wisely.

Here is the other part: these are the hours when God can take hold of your soul, build you up, strengthen you, and give you added courage for all the duties of the day. Hour by hour, day by day, God will bless you.

When you come here for services, some of you say, "O Brother Roberson, so many hours. And I don't get much out of it." Don't worry. Come Anyway. You can never tell what God may do for you. He may drop a single thought by a song. It might be a thought by reading one verse of Scripture. It might be by a single sentence by the minister. God might use anything to strengthen your heart while in His house.

Worshipping God is holy, blessed, good, wise. God has so ordained by His Book that we worship Him. It is a wise use of time when I come here to worship Him. I come to smile. I come to sing. I come to enjoy the hours.

The other day someone spoke a little critically of us because we occasionally applaud in the services. It is more or less spontaneous. It is more or less an expression, like you say "Amen." We don't intend to be out of line when we applaud. It is just to show we appreciate someone or something that has been said or done. We are here to worship God in the freeness of our hearts and souls with liberty God gives us through Christ Jesus. We worship Him.

<u>Second, it is a wise use of time when I study His Word.</u> My dear friend, you are not wasting time when you study His Word. If you don't know much about it, read it anyway. And keep on reading it. God will open your heart and mind through the Holy Spirit. He will cause you to understand what is in this Book. So spend time in reading and studying the Word.

Let me challenge you this year to read your Bible through.

THE HOURGLASS SERMON

Shame on you if you haven't done that. It's very simple to do. About four chapters a day, perhaps taking fifteen minutes or less, and you can read through your Bible in less than a year. That means every portion of it, from the first of the Old Testament to the last of the New. I'm not wasting time when I study God's Word.

Third, it is a wise use of time when I pray and seek His face. We can't pray too much. There's no way you can come so much before God that you tire Him. He invites us to come - in season, out of season. "Pray without ceasing," says the Word of God. Pray in times of trial. Pray in the hours of happiness. Pray when you are failing. Pray when you are succeeding. Ask His help in everything. He understands. He knows your heart. And He is there to help you every time.

There was a woman who was quite a prayer warrior. She had a habit of playing the piano and singing. In the little community where she lived, the houses were close together. So all the people could hear her when she played the piano and sang. No one was offended. They liked it, because they believed in her sincerely.

Then, she had a sorrow. Tragedy came in the home. Her heart was broken. She still came back to the piano the next day. But this time she thought, *I'll begin with the song, "I must tell Jesus all of my trials, I cannot bear my burdens alone."* So she sang and played that. As the people again listened, they knew she was still in touch with God, she was a woman of faith. So must it be for all of us.

Pray! Pray for yourself, then pray for others. Make praying a part of your life.

Samuel said, "God forbid that I should sin against the Lord in ceasing to pray for you." It's a sin not to pray for others.

Let's pray for others, as did praying John Hyde.

Let's pray for others, as did old Earnest Reveal up in Evansville, Indiana.

Let us pray for others, as Hyman Appelman does.

THE HOURGLASS SERMON

I can go on and on talking about people who spend much time in prayer. The wise person prays. Read your Bible, pray and worship God. Keep God first.

Fourth, it is the wise use of time when I live for God. "Let your light so shine before men, that they may see your good works, and glorify your Father which is in heaven (Matt. 5:16). I must not compromise. I must live a positive life. There must be no shifting from side to side. I have to be wholly and completely on God's side.

Remember what Elijah said to the people of Israel? "How long halt ye between two opinions? If the LORD be God, follow him: but if Baal, then follow him." He called them out. He had the contest on Mount Carmel. The fire came down from Heaven and consumed the altar of sacrifice. The people fell upon their faces and cried, "The LORD, he is the God."

Watch yourself. Do not get into the habit of profanity, evil speaking and dirty talking. Don't allow yourself to be led into lying or cheating. So live for God that others can see Christ in you. It matters not where you may be, stand for God and, uncompromising, let your light shine.

Fifth, it is the wise use of time when I witness for Him, when I tell the story of Jesus Christ. I never make a mistake when I talk about the Saviour. I never make a mistake when I witness for Him. Souls are lost and dying. We have the message. We have what they need. "He that believeth on the Son hath everlasting life." Men are saved by simple faith in Jesus Christ.

Someone has said, "Our main business is not to see what lies dimly at a distance, but to do what is clearly at hand." The thing that is always at hand is to witness to people everywhere, to tell them of Jesus and of His power to save. The wise person wastes no time when he witnesses for our blessed Saviour.

The queen selected an artist to paint her picture. He was famous, and he was good. She notified him that she would be

THE HOURGLASS SERMON

ready at a certain time for the first sitting of the painting.

When the message came to the artist, so excited was he that he ran out in the streets and started telling his friends. He rejoiced in his good fortune. He talked here and he talked there, then after awhile he went on his way. He hadn't noticed the time.

When he arrived, there was no queen. She had waited for a while, but when he didn't arrive, she had gone on her way. What an opportunity he lost because he did not value time! He was not availing himself of his opportunity.

Child of God, be busy for the Saviour. Use your time in the best way for witnessing. Don't let the weeks and months go by, but serve God now.

There is worth of time, the waste of time, and the wise use of time.

What can we say to you unsaved tonight? Are you here without Jesus. Oh, the uncertainty of life! You have no promise of tomorrow. "For what is your life? It is even a vapour, that appeareth for a little time, and then vanisheth away." Make no plans without God. "Boast not thyself of tomorrow."

Sinner friend, think of it - the certainty of death if Christ tarries. "And as it is appointed unto men once to die, but after this the judgment." Every man is on his way to the cemetery, if He tarries. We are coming to death, every single one of us.

Doctors in hospitals may help for a while, but it will be all over after a while and we step out into eternity. Prepare to meet thy God. Friend without Jesus Christ, there is only one thing to do: repent and believe. Be saved right now. Give your heart to Him now.

Christians, get ready. The judgment seat is just ahead, when we must stand before our Saviour to give an account of ourselves.

I want to be ready. I want God to help me. "O God, don't let me waste my life. Don't let me waste my time. Let me

THE HOURGLASS SERMON

use wisely all that I have and all that is given me."

Christian, tonight think of your life. Think of the time that God has appointed to you.

And sinner, get ready. The time is short.

Consider the amazing grace of God. How good the Lord is to us - looking down from Heaven's glory, so concerned about each one. He knows our tendency. He knows our sin. He knows our will. He knows our rebellion. Yes, He knows all about us, but loves us still. We should redeem the time because the days are evil. Let us give our best to the Saviour.

Chapter 5
Fireworks Don't Last

For now we see through a glass, darkly; but then face to face: now I know in part; but then shall I know even as also I am known.
And now abideth faith, hope, charity, these three; but the greatest of these is charity.
— I Cor. 13:12,13

For our light affliction, which is but for a moment, worketh for us a far more exceeding and eternal weight of glory;
While we look not at the things which are seen, but at the things which are not seen: for the things which are seen are temporal; but the things which are not seen are eternal.
— II Cor. 4:17,18

And I suppose "temporal" in verse 18 is the one and only time it is found in the translation, from the original in the King James Version.

Go to now, ye that say, today or tomorrow we will go into such a city, and continue there a year, and buy and sell, and get gain:
Whereas ye know not what shall be on the morrow. For what is your life? It is even a vapour, that appeareth for a little time, and then vanisheth away.

FIREWORKS DON'T LAST

> *For that ye ought to say, If the Lord will, we shall live, and do this, or that.*
>
> *But now ye rejoice in your boastings: all such rejoicing is evil.*
>
> *Therefore to him that knoweth to do good, and doeth it not, to him it is sin.*
>
> — James 4:13-17

I can still recall quite vividly the occasion back in Louisville, Kentucky when, as a young man, I would go out to the fairgrounds on July 4 and watch the display at night of the fireworks given by the city for the people to enjoy.

Some Roman candles would shoot high into the air, then burst into ten thousand glittering stars, which would quickly fade away as they fell toward the ground.

At the state fairgrounds, the displays were always elaborate, as I can recall them now. Some in this city, in years past, have indeed been very elaborate.

The American flag was often pictured in fireworks, in beautiful color. The crowd would stand, the band would play - a very patriotic moment. Ofttimes we would see some historic places pictured by fireworks, such as Mount Vernon or "Ole Kentucky Home." Sometimes it would be the display of a galloping horse, a barking dog, or something else, each with special sound effects.

These displays always created great excitement. The people who had gathered watched with wide-open eyes. The children covered their ears when the firecrackers were too loud. You can almost see the scene, can you not?

There was always a strange unity of the people as they watched. Every eye was fastened upon the scene in front of them - the exploding machines and the building up of the pictures as they came on little by little. There was no dozing, no sleeping, but a wholesome concentration as everyone looked, marveled and expressed pleasure.

But after a while it was all over. The fireworks ceased.

FIREWORKS DON'T LAST

The last Roman candle had been shot into the air; the last sparkler had made it's beautiful color; the last firecracker had sounded off; and the last glowing ember on the great display turned black. Then, the field became dark and dead as all the people walked away.

I can still recall that many would exclaim, including myself, "Wasn't that beautiful! Wasn't it something wonderful to see!" Then it was all over. We saw it for just a few moments, not to see it again for perhaps another twelve months. Some of the display might be given next July 4th.

Now I use that to illustrate things that fade away, things things that change, and things that stand. That brings us to the portion of our message I want to emphasize this morning - the things that abide.

There are some things that do last. The fireworks of this world are gone. The firecrackers and the sound - these are over. The light made by these inventions of men have disappeared. But there are some things that stand.

I. GOD'S ETERNAL WORD STANDS

Heaven and earth shall pass away, but my words shall not pass away.

— Matt. 24:35

But the word of the Lord endureth for ever. And this is the word which by the gospel is preached unto you.

— I Pet. 1:25

The Bible is the Book of the ages. The Word abides. The Bible is the world's best-seller, but it is also the most neglected Book in the world.

No one is smart, no one is well read without the reading of the Word of God.

The Bible endures. It is God's message to man. It speaks with authority. It has the answers to all our questions. And

FIREWORKS DON'T LAST

it is ever the same.

My son-in-law mentioned this morning about his first Bible. I can recall my first one from Sears and Roebuck in Chicago, obtained by mail order at $1.90 - a very nice buy back in that day.

The interesting thing about the Bible enduring is that the one I bought fifty-two years ago from Sears and Roebuck catalog is exactly the same in content as the one I hold in my hand now.

That leads me to say that I like the King James Version. I'm not much in favor of all the modernistic translations and the so-called interpretation worked into it by some men. The Old Bible endures.

The Bible enlightens. "The entrance of thy words giveth light..." (Ps. 119:130).

The way of salvation is clearly given. Christ, "... the way, the truth, and the life..." (John 14:6).

The Bible points the way from paradise lost to paradise regained.

The Bible gives us the beginning of sin and the result of sin. This penetrates the darkness of today. We see the trend of society, the behavior of men, and the behavior of nations. The Bible enlightens. We can see things from the Word.

The Bible encourages. There are rough places. There are steep hills to climb. There are shadows to face. There are deep waters to cross. And the Bible encourages us when we face all of this.

The Bible encourages us in the time of death and in times of sorrow, when loved ones go from us.

Sitting here this morning is our brother, Gene Payne, who sang so beautifully with Neil Queen at the funeral service for his father last Friday. Gene said, "I felt I had to sing. I wanted to sing."

The Bible strengthens in the time of suffering. How much the Word can do for all of us. In the hour of suffering, when these bodies will fail, when things are not quite the

FIREWORKS DON'T LAST

same, rest upon God's eternal Word. It's here to help and to strengthen when suffering is our lot. We all suffer. If you haven't, you will. That is a part of this body, the breakdown of the body, that comes to us after awhile.

From her sick bed Florence Nightingale organized the hospitals of England and of London especially. Her mighty work is still remembered.

Though Louis Pasteur was partially paralyzed and suffered all the time, yet he did a monumental work that still abides today.

Francis Parkman, an American historian, suffered endlessly. He could work only about five minutes at a time. He would write with letters so large that it would take almost a half page for one single word. He would write for five minutes, stop, then pick it up again when his eyes would allow him to do so, until he wrote twenty volumes which are among the best volumes of history produced in this nation.

The Bible came out of dark hours. The Psalms came out of dark hours. Read the Psalms. You'll find much to help you. Read the prison epistles by the Apostle Paul, the Apostle Peter, John on the Isle of Patmos, and others. Greatness comes from men who have gone through suffering. The Bible strengthens in the time of suffering. So rest upon the Word of God.

The Bible strengthens in the time of disappointment. My friends, I could not tell you how many times I have had to pick up my Bible, in hours when I've been disappointed in certain situations, maybe even in this church, or around this church, or maybe in Tennessee Temple University - situations here in the operation of our work. I had to come back to the Word of God. When I was disappointed - disappointed in people, disappointed in myself, disappointed in the situations surrounding me, I had to come back to resting upon the Word of God.

What am I saying? That the Bible comforts, that it strengthens, that it encourages - all this and far more.

FIREWORKS DON'T LAST

"The Word of God endures forever," says the Word of God about itself. You'll always find treasures in the Word, blessed things, things that you never thought you could find. Even though you may have read your Bible for a lifetime, there are still things to be found in God's holy Word because He wrote it. So rest upon the Word of God.

A man up in New Jersey had an aunt who passed away and left him some money in the will, perhaps $400 or $500. Then she left him some possessions that he could keep. He put them away. Then when he got older, he had to move from his home to his son's. He began picking up what he had. Here was the Bible left by his aunt. Carelessly, and somewhat thoughtlessly, he sat down and began turning through its pages. He discovered something. Inside the pages of the Bible he found bills which amounted to more than $5,000.00. Though he had been suffering a lack, suffering for needs in his own life, yet he had never stopped to look into the Word of God.

We may not find actual money, as he did, yet here are the promises of God, worth more than all the money of this world. You can rest upon what God has to say to you.

The Word of God stands. When all the firecrackers have displayed themselves, you still have the Word of God. Rest upon it.

II. GOD'S NEW TESTAMENT CHURCH

I may surprise you by saying that, but for this age, for this time until Jesus comes again, the New Testament church will abide. I don't care what the fanatics say; I don't care what the depressing remarks may be, or what people in some forms of churchanity might think when they say, "The church will be no more," the New Testament church will abide until Jesus Comes. It may be small, it may be large, it may have to go through all sorts of persecutions, but it will abide until Jesus comes to take us home.

Persecution may come, but the church will live. Modernism

may invade, but the church will live. Indifference may claim many, but the church lives. Sin may lay hold on many, but the church lives. Satan will fight and deceive, but the church lives.

This is what we want to see regarding the New Testament church. The church that stands for and preaches the pure holy Word of God is the church with the largest crowds. We see this around the whole nation. The New Testament church will stand. It will live.

Now what is our business? <u>First, to exalt Christ</u>, to preach Christ, to lift Him up. The world must see Him. The world must know Him. It is our business to preach Christ.

<u>Second, we are to obey His commands</u>. We are to do what He says. We are to win souls. The Bible says, "He that winneth souls is wise." We are to send out missionaries to the ends of the earth. We are to baptize converts. We are to do the job that God has given us to do. We are to obey His commands.

<u>Third, we are to live righteously</u>. Keep your heart right. "Abstain from all appearance of evil" is our business as members of the New Testament church. We are to live righteously. We are to live so that Christ may be seen by others.

Keep your emotions right. Ephesians 4:26, "Be ye angry, and sin not: let not the sun go down upon your wrath."

Listen; you may be angry for a righteous cause, and that is good. We ought to get upset about sin, about wrongdoing, until we express ourselves about it! Let trivialities, the meaningless things of life, pass by. But, about those things that are important, those things that are the meaningful, these are the things for which we must stand.

That is where we should always take our definite stand for righteousness.

<u>Fourth, we must worship God.</u> Our business in the local church is worshipping God. Our empty pews cry out against us. Whether on Sunday night, Sunday morning, Wednesday night prayer meeting, or whenever, this speaks against the

church, against the people of God. We need to worship God and be faithful in attending God's house.

Down through the years I've been driving home in all of my meetings, in all of my work, in every church where I've pastored, the matter of going to church Sunday morning, Sunday night, and Wednesday night prayer meeting. God has honored this. Here we've seen things happen because of the faithfulness of God's people in coming to church. That's the way it should be.

I recall holding a revival meeting years ago at the First Baptist Church in Ensley, Alabama. While there, I stayed in the home of a couple. I was put in a room near the front of the house. The bedroom for the man and wife was next to mine.

We went home after the Sunday morning service. The couple began talking. The walls were thin, so I could hear them. He said to his wife, "Now I went to church this morning, but I'm not going back tonight. I've never gone to more than one service in my life on Sunday, and that's all I'm going to now."

I heard his wife say to him, "But I think you might break the habit this time and go to church. We've got the evangelist with us. He is right next door, in the next room. He's preaching and I think you ought to be there."

"I don't care if he is there. I'm not going. Once is enough for me. That's all I can take. That's all I've ever had. That's all I want."

She talked on and won the battle. That night he sat with her. I can see them now sitting in front of me. Ordinarily I'm not a lengthy preacher, but that night I put together every sermon I could think of! I had him here and I would let him have it so he couldn't forget it. I preached something from almost every message I had. I wanted to get hold of that fellow.

Going to church and worshipping God is important. The New Testament church will abide, will stand in this age, until

FIREWORKS DON'T LAST

the coming of our blessed Saviour.

Some people say, "Well, Brother Roberson, you do so many unusual things in your Sunday school. Yes, and what we do at Highland Park will last, and it has for these forty years that I've been here.

Back in the first or second year when we started doing some new things, the folk were so fine. The Sunday school was growing and abounding. People were being saved in every service. A pastor in another Baptist church stood up on a Sunday morning and expressed himself about Highland Park, and Lee Roberson and all the rest, saying, "He's running a three-ring circus. I want to prophesy to you that it will soon be gone. A thing like that can never last."

His words came right back to me, within a few minutes after the service was over. That man was voted out of his church. Then he tried another church. After a while he failed there and then quit the ministry. He is dead now, and Highland Park is still going ahead. He was criticizing just the outward thing of attracting people to the house of God. He missed the whole point of what we are doing here - trying to get people to the Lord Sunday after Sunday.

III. GOD'S UNCHANGING PURPOSE

First, God's eternal Word; second, God's New Testament church; and third, God's unchanging purpose. The purpose of God is to redeem man, to take out a people for His name (Acts 15:14).

We have been called and commissioned for God's great purpose. Jesus said, ". . . as my Father hath sent me, even so send I you." We are God's messengers to proclaim the message of everlasting life through Jesus Christ, the blessed Son of God.

Our position and our job is to preach Christ. Paul said: "But we preach Christ crucified, unto the Jews a stumblingblock, and unto the Greeks foolishness" (I Cor. 1:23).

As we preach, we are to win souls. We are to press upon

FIREWORKS DON'T LAST

people the great need of the Saviour. We are to urge them to receive the Son of God!

This is what the Lord Jesus meant when He talked about bearing fruit. To be fruit-bearing Christians is what He demands of us.

On this day of July 4, we talk about the rights and liberties that we have in our country. This is the right given to us, and we express it.

God has some rights, too. He has the right to say to you that you are to bear fruit. You are to be a soul winner. You are to get people to Jesus. You are to so live daily that others can see Christ in you. You are to bear fruit. ". . . we preach Christ. . . "

We are to preach the abundant life through our Saviour. He said, "I am come that they might have life, and that they might have it more abundantly." This is ours. Not just a little skimpy life, but an abundant life in Jesus, a life that abounds, a life that brings joy and happiness hour by hour - living abundantly and living courageously.

We are to preach an eternity of joy in the presence of God. How many verses we could give on the joy in Heaven that we have through Jesus Christ our Lord.

The Christian abides forever. It's not a firecracker existence. It is a matter of knowing Christ. We shall be in the presence of our eternal God and eternal Saviour forever and forever. The things of this world pass away, but the Word of God abides. Yes, it abides.

Some months ago some fellow on a motorcycle was shooting himself up into the air. His name is Evil Kneivel. He was crazy. One can have the headlines for awhile, then it is all over. But, the child of God abides. The work that God has given us to do abides.

I remember reading this past week, in one of the books that I picked up, about Thomas Edison. At one time a fire destroyed his plans, his factory - everything he had. All of his inventions seemed to be gone in just a moment's time.

FIREWORKS DON'T LAST

Edison was walking through the charred remains and wreck of the buildings. As he came to the area of his office, he looked down on the ground and saw a picture of himself, a picture that had been placed on the wall in his office. Edison bent over, picked it up and looked at his picture, untouched by the fire. It wasn't even scorched by the flames which had destroyed the entire building. He took a pen out of his pocket and wrote across the picture, "It never touched me, so I must be fireproof."

I've got something better than that. If you are in Christ Jesus, you are fireproof. If you are in the Son of God, you have nothing to fear, for Christ is your Saviour and Heaven is your home.

Modern pleasures do not bring happiness. Most amusements and pasttimes are just miserable escapes from reality. Science brings no pleasure, no joy, no salvation. Death thrives on the jet planes. Education does not have all the answers. Mental institutions are full of college graduates. Religion is an all-time failure. Followers of Baal illustrate that to us.

Honest, sensible people are looking for that which will last. They are tired of the fast disappearing fireworks of this age. They look for that which will stand. My dear friend, I have it. It's in the Word of God, this Book the Bible.

God the Heavenly Father, Christ the Saviour, and the indwelling Holy Spirit - they are for all of us.

On this special day, as we think of our nation and of our needs, as we see what is happening all around us, we need to come back to the holy Word of God and rest upon its promises.

There are three things that I have given that never change: God's Eternal Word; God's New Testament church; and God's holy purpose. I trust this morning that you know Christ as Saviour and that you can rest in Him today. I know that all things are mine for eternity through my blessed Lord. Can you, too, say that this morning? If you are a child of God, you can. If you are a child of God, you abide. You have everlasting life in Jesus Christ. You can rejoice throughout

FIREWORKS DON'T LAST

all the days to come.

I trust this morning that God will speak to your hearts and that you will say, "O God, let me use my life in the best way possible. Let me see others and their needs. Let me see the unhappiness of people around me, that I might point them to Jesus Christ, that I might be a soul winner, that people might be saved through faith in the Son of God."

Marie Antoinette was made the queen of France. With the king, she was riding down the main boulevard of the city on the day of coronation. They say that the officials of Paris took all the poor, the beggars, the ill and afflicted and shoved them into the back streets.

As the queen rode down the street, she saw the well-dressed people, the beauty of their attire. She saw the culture of their faces. But she saw none of the people of the back streets.

With the king, she went to live in the palace. And she lived there altogether blind to the needs of the people until the beginning of the French Revolution, then came the awakening to the fact that she had not seen it all, just a small part.

This is what I want you to see. This is a needy world. Don't you try to hide a thing. This is an ugly, dirty, needy world. The only answer is Jesus Christ. My friend, try anything or anybody you want to. There is only one answer - Christ. He is the answer to all of the illnesses, all of the afflictions, all of the ugliness that this world has.

Do you know Him as your Saviour? Can you say, "He is mine"? Have you accepted Him but turned away from following Him? Would you come back this morning and confess to Him, "I want to follow Thee and do Thy will for the rest of my days"?

Chapter 6
One Tiny Conjunction

> *Surely goodness and mercy shall follow me all the days of my life: and I will dwell in the house of the LORD for ever.*
> — Ps. 23:6

John Lynn was working with children. He had a group before him on one occasion and said, "I wonder how many of you can quote the Twenty-Third Psalm." A number of hands were raised. One little girl who raised her hand was about four-and-a-half. He thought perhaps she could not do it, so he said, "All right honey, come up and say it."

She walked on the platform and stood before the audience. Somebody had told her what to do, apparently, for she bowed, then she began quoting: "<u>The LORD is my shepherd; that is all I want.</u>" She bowed again, and walked back and sat down. True, the child did not give the entire Psalm, but she said it all in a single sentence - *"The LORD is my shepherd; that is all I want."*

Psalm 23 is one of the best-known portions of the Word of God. In every nation, every tongue, every tribe where the Bible is read, the 23rd Psalm is memorized. It is taught to children and repeated by adults.

The Psalm gives the personal, individual testimony of a man of God. What David said by inspiration should be the heart-expression of every child of God.

Notice the location of the Psalm. Psalm 22 is a Psalm of the Cross. It begins, "My God, my God, why hast thou

ONE TINY CONJUNCTION

forsaken me?" and ends, ". . . he hath done this," which may be another way of saying, "It is finished."

Then, what about Psalm 24? That is the Psalm of Mount Zion. It is a picture of the King entering into His own. He says:

> *Lift up your heads, O ye gates; even lift them up, ye everlasting doors; and the King of glory shall come in.*
> *Who is this King of glory? The LORD of hosts, he is the King of glory.*
> —verses 9, 10

There you have the two mountains: Mount Calvary - the Cross - in chapter 22, and Mount Zion - the kingdom - in Psalm 24. In between you have the picture of the valley, a place of green grass, of quite waters, the Shepherd. Here is the Psalm of beauty and comfort, a message that increases with all the years - "The LORD is my shepherd, I shall not want." This story has been repeated often. A big banquet was in progress. At the banquet table were seated two special people - a pastor of some years, and an actor. When the master of ceremonies looked around at his crowd and saw them there, he thought, *I will have the actor come up and give a recitation of some kind.* So he nodded to the actor and asked if he would come, a man quite famous, well-known to everyone. As the M.C. introduced him, he said, "Will you say a word to us, or perhaps give some recitation, something that you have memorized?"

The actor just sat for a moment. The preacher by his side shoved his Bible into the hand of the actor and said, "Why don't you just read the 23rd Psalm?"

The actor left his place at the table, went to the platform, stood there with the Bible open, and read very carefully, very beautifully, Psalm 23. The people were solemnized as they listened. This actor said it so beautifully, then walked

ONE TINY CONJUNCTION

back and sat down.

Then, very strangely, the actor said, "I would like to have my friend, the pastor here by my side, say the 23rd Psalm for us, too."

The preacher left his place, walked up to the platform, stood before the crowd and began the 23rd Psalm. This time it was quite different. He quoted it in such an impressive way that some were even wiping tears from their eyes.

As the preacher took his place again, the actor turned and said to him, "Sir, I can see the difference: I know the Psalm, but you know the Shepherd."

Look at verse 6 again. Here is the tiny conjunction "and." Look at it again: "Surely goodness and mercy shall follow me all the days of my life: and I will dwell in the house of the LORD for ever." What is he doing? Connecting time and eternity, connecting this life - "Surely goodness and mercy shall follow me all the days of my life:" with eternity, - "and I will dwell in the house of the LORD for ever." This life and eternity.

I. THE CHRISTIAN'S CONFIDENCE

"Surely goodness and mercy shall follow me..." Psalm 23 speaks of the Lord, our Shepherd. Because we have the Shepherd, surely goodness and mercy shall follow us.

First, our confidence is in the unchanging God. "For I am the LORD, I change not..." (Mal. 3:6). That brings to mind Hebrews 13:8, "Jesus Christ the same yesterday, and today and for ever."

Now man changes. Everything changes. Everything around us is changing all the time. Our cities change, our state changes, our nation changes. Clothing is changing. Customs change, cars change.

People may disappoint you. They may change, too, but God - never. He said, "I am the LORD, I change not." "Jesus Christ the same yesterday, and to-day and for ever." Our confidence is in the unchanging God.

ONE TINY CONJUNCTION

Second, our confidence is in the unchanging Word of God. Listen to this: "For ever, O LORD, thy word is settled in heaven" (Ps. 119:89). The Bible never changes.

God's Word never changes on sin. My dear friend, what was sin a year ago is still sin now. What was sin a hundred years ago is still sin now. Sin does not change. We like to make out that it does, but not so. This is the Word of God: "The wages of sin is death." "The soul that sinneth, it shall die." God's Word never changes on sin.

God's Word never changes on salvation. "For by grace are ye saved through faith; and that not of yourselves: it is the gift of God: Not of works, lest any man should boast." Salvation through faith in Jesus Christ.

God's Word never changes on security. Paul said, "for I know whom I have believed, and am persuaded that he is able to keep that which I have committed unto him against that day." And Jesus said, "And I give unto them eternal life; and they shall never perish. . ." God's Word never changes on any of these things.

Now this is what we preach and teach at Camp Joy. Day by day the Word of God is given to the young people going there - 3,000 this summer, we trust.

These three things we set ourselves to do at Camp Joy. First, win boys and girls to the Saviour; second, make young people outspoken Christians for God; and third, give them a new standard of living - separation from the world - which is unheard of in most places.

II. THE CHRISTIAN'S PRESENT LIFE

"Surely goodness and mercy shall follow me all the days of my life. . ." says Psalm 23. The Apostle Paul said, ". . . The life which I now live in the flesh I live by the faith of the Son of God" - the Christian's present life.

A few words about this life.

A time of trouble. Look at Job 14:1, "Man that is born of a woman is of few days, and full of trouble." Listen to Paul:

ONE TINY CONJUNCTION

"We are troubled on every side, yet not distressed; we are perplexed, but not in despair" (II Cor. 4:8). This is the time of trouble.

A time of sorrow. Life is not one round of pleasure. Sorrows come to one and all. They come unexpectedly. They come upon us with shocking suddenness. We have to be prepared. Death may take a loved one from our side at almost any moment. We have to be ready. This life is a time of sorrow.

A time of change. The happiness of a wedding and the sorrow of a funeral; the happiness of a promotion and the anguish of a demotion; the joy of success and the misery of failure.

"Change and decay in all around I see;
O Thou who changest not, abide with me!"

This is a time of change.

A time of disappointments. Dreams are made, then broken. Businesses fail. Your children fail in what you want them to be.

Friends may disappoint you, those upon whom you have leaned so long. They became tired and turned away from you and refused to help you. But is there help? (This is the negative side.) A time of trouble, a time of sorrow, a time of change, a time of disappointment. Is there something else? Can we say something positively? Oh, yes. Listen to it. "If God be for us, who can be against us?" Here is the promise of God.

A time of opportunity. Opportunity knocks daily for us to serve God. He is saying, "This is the way I want you to walk. This is how I want you to serve Me. I want you to help others." Yes, a time of opportunity for all of us.

A time of preparation - getting ready for Heaven, preparing for the time when we stand in His presence.

A time of expression - a time to express our love for Him. Not to forget Him, but to live every day so that others can see Christ in us. He is near to us at all times: we should

ONE TINY CONJUNCTION

always be conscious of His presence. That is on the positive side.

The negative side we can see, but the positive side is that God is for us and God is with us in every trial, in every difficulty. He never fails.

He is here tonight. "Lo, I am with you alway, even to the end of the age." "God is our refuge, a present help in time of trouble." Always with us.

I was reading about a preacher - I think it was A. J. Gordon. The man who wrote this story did not give his name, but I think it was about Dr. Gordon. Dr. Gordon was a very fine preacher but was somewhat troubled about his church. He went home to his study to pray about what he should do. He was discouraged to the point of almost quitting.

In the time of his worry and anxiety, he went to sleep. In his sleep he had a dream (he relates the dream himself) of a Sunday morning worship hour. The people were there in great numbers.

One man came down the aisle and took his place in the center of the building. Dr. Gordon saw him bow his head in prayer when he entered. He also saw him nod to the people around him, greeting them in a very friendly way.

Then, Dr. Gordon said he began to preach. The people listened. But this man especially was intently listening, watching every thing and doing it in a sweet and sincere way.

When it was all over, in his dream the preacher went to one of his deacons and said, "Well, a good service this morning. But there was one person here I did not know - the man who was seated in the center of the building."

Don't you know him, Pastor?"

"I do not believe I do."

"Why He comes to every service. Pastor, that Man is the Lord Jesus Christ!"

The preacher said he awakened from his dream in anguish of soul because he had failed to recognize that Christ was with him all the time. In every single service He knew what

ONE TINY CONJUNCTION

was going on. Every song, every sermon, every word, every thought, was open to Christ and he, the pastor, failed to see this.

Ah, listen to me! This life is a time of expression. Here is the time when we feel the presence of God, when we can express ourselves in reality of life to Him. Express your life by your testimony. Express it by your gifts. Express it by your faithfulness. Express it by your stedfastness.

The thing that disturbs me in this day and time is shifting people. That annoys me! I can never understand it! Some people are never steadfast in Christ's service. They move so fast and so often that it would be difficult even for the Lord Himself to find them. Never steady, never in the work of God.

Now, let your life, this present life, be an expression of your love toward Him. Live so others can see Christ in you with a stedfastness of life, with a faithfulness in all of your service, in all of your duty to Him, always giving your best.

III. THE CHRISTIAN'S FUTURE LIFE

Look at your Bible again. "Surely goodness and mercy shall follow me all the days of my life, and" - "and" there is the conjunction - "I will dwell in the house of the Lord for ever."

"The LORD is my shepherd." When you can say that, then you can say the last part. If you can say, "He is mine - my Saviour, my Lord, my Master" - then you can say the last part: ". . . and I will dwell in the house of the Lord for ever." There is the tiny conjunction "and." This speaks of Heaven. Heaven is a home. "I shall dwell in the house of the Lord for ever" - a home. Jesus said, "In my Father's house are many mansions" - a beautiful picture of Heaven, many abiding places in Heaven.

Heaven is identified with a Person. He said, ". . . the house of the LORD. . . " God is there. He is with us now, and we are going to live and abide with Him forever. It is His house,

ONE TINY CONJUNCTION

His place.

Heaven is timeless - everlasting, eternal, forever. This is taught throughout the eternal Word of God. Everlasting life is God's gift to us.

Heaven is a place of revelation. "Now we see through a glass darkly, but then face to face" - a place of revelation.

One time the Apostle Paul was carried up into the third heaven. He was given visions of things that he said "I cannot tell about." He was brought back to earth to carry on his work and to do his ministry; but what glory he saw in the presence of our Lord!

Heaven is a place of revelation. One day we shall stand before our blessed Saviour.

Listen carefully. In this life we put great premium upon money, houses, cars, things of this world. But, my friend, when you come to stand before the Lord Jesus Christ, how much will it all matter? When you come to stand before Him at the judgment seat and give an account of yourself to Him, how much will all of this matter? "So that every one of us shall give account of himself to God."

Oh, how much premium we place upon things! I am as guilty as anyone else. But, when we get there, what will count? What is the thing that is going to count in the presence of our blessed Saviour? It may be a five-minute conversation with a man down the street about his soul. You may have talked to a person on the sidewalk, unknown to you, about Christ. Yet, that is recorded now in the books of God. This is important, the thing God has put us here for. What matters then will be souls. Souls only. "Ye are my witnesses," said our blessed Saviour. We are now to be at the job, night and day, witnessing for Him, as we prepare and think of the future, and of all that God has and will do for us - Heaven, Heaven's throne, the judgment seat of Christ, etc.

That is the reason we lay emphasis upon the work of Camp Joy. I may not be able to be up there much, but when I put my money, my time into it, I have part in every soul that

ONE TINY CONJUNCTION

gets saved. And so have you. Every single person making an offering has a part in every soul saved.

Five or six hundred boys and girls may be saved in a single summer. When they go out of there, saved and with a testimony for the Lord, they will go home to tell the story of the Saviour. Over and over again they will repeat it. Then when in Christ they come to die, they will ascend into the presence of God to be with Him forevermore. That is the joy of it all!

That is what we are doing. These are things that count. The rest is secondary. The job you have, the money you possess, the position you hold in life - this is all secondary. I am not saying you should not attain the things. They are all fine. But do not neglect that which is of primary importance - the salvation of a soul.

"Surely goodness and mercy" - God's goodness and mercy. God's watchdogs after all of us. God's goodness, God's "mercy shall follow me all the days of my life: and I will dwell in the house of the LORD for ever."

What a beautiful conclusion to this brief message as it comes from the heart of David and from the hand of God to us! How magnificent it is! All this belongs to the person who puts his trust in Jesus Christ. If you have neglected Him, or turned away from Him, or ignored His claims and His call, then this is not yours. You cannot say, "The LORD is my shepherd; I shall not want." Nor can you say, "Surely goodness and mercy shall follow me all the days of my life: and I will dwell in the house of the LORD for ever." You have missed it all unless you know Jesus Christ as Saviour, unless you can say, "He is mine. He is all I need."

Many of you have heard the name of F. B. Meyer. He was a great English preacher. He preached in London a lot and preached in this country quite a few times. Dr. Meyer was a very unusual man. I have many of his books, *"Back to Bethel"* and other sermons by this great English preacher and Bible teacher.

ONE TINY CONJUNCTION

Dr. F. B. Meyer used to speak to men on Sunday afternoon in London, back in the days when you could have a crowd on Sunday afternoon. These men would come and fill up the building for a simple Gospel service. Hundreds came. They would sing, they would testify, and they would hear a simple, Bible-teaching message every Sunday afternoon.

One Sunday afternoon Dr. Meyer was seated on the platform. The choir was singing, the orchestra was playing, in preparation for the sermon. Dr. Meyer looked out over the audience and thought, *What can I say to this crowd? I have said about everything I know to say.*

About the time Dr. Meyer was getting ready to bring his message, the violinist, sitting over in the midst of the orchestra, suddenly had a string to snap and break. The fellow pulled the violin down to fix it. He took out the broken string, dropped it on the floor, pulled another out of his case and began putting it on, preparing to go on with his music. But he dropped the string on the floor. Dr. Meyer knew that he now had something that would help. When he was introduced, he walked from his place over to the orchestra, bent over, picked up the broken string and walked to the pulpit, then he said, "My friend, here is a broken string. It is not good for anything. It can never again make music. There is no manner of way that this can be joined together, put back together to create beautiful music, such as a violin can produce. It is only a broken string. And this is the way some lives are broken - completely." The great Dr. Meyer continued: "This broken string cannot be used on the violin again. But, when your life is broken, there is One who can mend it and make it whole again. Though sin may come and break your life and ruin it, Jesus Christ can take that broken life and bring it back together again!" And with that Dr. Meyer went on to preach one of his masterful sermons, a simple message to the men on that given Sunday.

He did not then know it, but in the service sat a man who had come there so discouraged, so blue that he thought of

ONE TINY CONJUNCTION

suicide. When Dr. Meyer held up that broken string of the violin, this discouraged soul thought, *That is my life. I am just like that - broken.* But when F. B. Meyer tossed the string down and said, "But, my friends, Jesus Christ can come and mend the broken hearts, restore the broken lives, give you a zeal for living, a joy in life and a home in Heaven," he determined that was what he wanted. And the man who thought of suicide turned and accepted Jesus Christ.

O my dear friend, it can be so in your life. Christ can put together broken pieces. Your life may be broken, a lot of things may be wrong, but I know One who can put it all together again.

I talk to so many folk, I listen to so many, both in person and on the telephone. I get calls from everywhere day after day, long-distance calls from every part of the nation. In most cases these people have not stopped to think that Jesus Christ has the power to put it all together again if they would but let Him. But the tragedy is, they will not do it. They want somebody else to tell them what to do.

My dear friend, I have just one other thing to say: Jesus Christ can satisfy the soul. He can mend the broken pieces, Jesus can make you what He wants you to be and what you should be.

"Surely goodness and mercy shall follow me all the days of my life: <u>and</u> I will dwell in the house of the LORD for ever." That tiny conjunction "and" joins this matter of time, this present life and eternity. ". . . <u>and</u> I will dwell in the house of the LORD for ever." Do you know Him tonight? Is He your Saviour?

Chapter 7
How to Change Your Life in Thirty Minutes

That ye may be blameless and harmless, the sons of God, without rebuke, in the midst of a crooked and perverse nation, among whom ye shine as lights in the world;

Holding forth the word of life; that I may rejoice in the day of Christ, that I have not run in vain, neither laboured in vain.
— Phil. 2:15,16

But grow in grace, and in the knowledge of our Lord and Saviour Jesus Christ. To him be glory both now and for ever. Amen.
— II Pet. 3:18

Every thinking Christian desires a change in his life, no matter what. If you are a soul winner, you want to win more souls. If you pray, you want to pray more. If you read the Bible, study the Bible, you want to know more about it. You never get through. There is always a moving forward. It may be that you know something of the power of God. But you want more of God's power upon you. Every thinking Christian, every honest Christian, wants this.

It is sad that some people come to the place where they say, *Oh, I am saved; so now what? That is all of it.* No, No! Every Christian, every honest Christian wants to grow and go forward. For that reason I am saying that you can change your life in thirty minutes so you will never be the same again.

HOW TO CHANGE YOUR LIFE IN THIRTY MINUTES

I would never be the same again, if I would do the thing that God wants me to do.

The sinner, too, can change his life in thirty minutes by the power of God, by his decision, by his acceptance of Christ. He can change his destination - where he is going when he dies or when the end comes - to Heaven or Hell; but he can change it only through Christ Jesus to the place called Heaven.

I want a greater sense of the presence of God. I want a greater hungering and thirsting after righteousness. I want a greater knowledge of His Word. I want a greater evidence of His working through me in witnessing.

I am praying that as I speak to you - and I speak to myself - our hearts and lives might be so tender and so moved by God's power that we will not be the same.

What a shame when some people, saved twenty-five, thirty, forty years, never change, unless they change to go backwards. They become backslidden, get away from God, and from the things of God.

This evening I want to point out how to change your life in thirty minutes.

I. BY RECEPTION OF JESUS CHRIST

But as many as received him, to them gave he power to become the sons of God, even to them that believe on his name.

— John 1:12

The first point is that of knowing Christ as Saviour. This is the imperative. I cannot offer you a single thing, I have nothing for you, unless you know Jesus Christ as your Saviour. There must be a reception of the Son of God. By relationship you are in the family of God. You must know Him by fellowship in walking with Him, if you are to grow in grace and be what He would have you to be.

Sinner, eternal life depends upon what you do with the

HOW TO CHANGE YOUR LIFE IN THIRTY MINUTES

Son of God; not upon your works, not upon your church membership, not upon your baptism. It depends upon what you have done with the blessed Saviour. Jesus said, "I am come that they might have life. . ." Jesus said, "I am the way, the truth, and the life." This life is in Jesus Christ, the Son of God, not in anyone else, not any place else.

There may be things that trouble you at times, but you come back to the simplicity of seeing that you are a lost sinner and repent of your sin and receive Christ as your Saviour. You can be saved. I cannot explain it all - I do not have to; it is a mystery. You must be born again.

Praise God, I know that I am saved! I was saved as a boy in high school, in Louisville, Kentucky in my home; then I made my public profession at the Cedar Creek Baptist Church. I knew very, very little about the Bible, but, I knew that Christ died for me and I received Him as my Saviour. It was all settled by my simple faith in the Son of God, settled and established forever and ever.

I am a strange person. I have never had a doubt about my salvation from that day until this. I may some day, but not up to this time, and that has been a long time ago. I know that Christ is mine. I am resting in Him, and I rejoice in what I have in the blessed Saviour.

So, if you are to change your life, there must be a reception of the Son of God.

J. Wilbur Chapman, the great Presbyterian preacher, was holding a meeting some years ago in one of the big northern cities. Folk were coming by the thousands to hear him. One lady came, a very prominent woman of the city, a society leader and quite wealthy. She listened to him for awhile; then, like any poor old sinner, she came down the aisle and said, "I want to be saved," and she was happily saved.

About a week later, Dr. Chapman said this same lady came to him and said, "I want to tell you something. I have entertained at my table the royalty of England and other countries. I have had the presidents and leaders of this nation in

HOW TO CHANGE YOUR LIFE IN THIRTY MINUTES

my home. But, I have had more fun, more pure enjoyment, more peace of heart in the last week than I have had in all the past."

Why? She had Christ! We must know Him as Saviour! We must receive Him. Earnestly, simply, as a child, we must come to the Son and receive the gift of everlasting life.

What a sad story of a famous movie star, known to most of you by name. She was so famous that anywhere she went the crowds came. Multitudes would turn out to see her. Her picture was seen in all the movie houses and on television. Her voice was known in many places.

One night she gave her testimony in a big hall. Thousands were there to hear her. They called her back again and again by their applause. She kept coming back, bowing to the crowd. Finally, she came out no longer.

Some of the friends left the auditorium and went back to find her. She was down in the corner, in the back of the stage, sitting on the floor crying and stating, "My heart longs for something better than this!"

My dear friend, there is something better than all of that - Jesus, the Son of God. This star did not have Him, so she died a suicide. She went out of here because there was no peace, no joy, no happiness in what she was doing.

My dear friend, money cannot satisfy, education cannot satisfy, prominence cannot satisy! You must have Jesus.

The first step in "How to Change Your Life in Thirty Minutes," is to receive Christ. That is as plain as ABC. One of the problems of Chattanooga is that we have heard it so much. The Gospel is preached here in many places. You have heard it so much until it has become "old hat." But no, you come forward tonight and you say, "Christ is what I need. I have never received Him." You may be a church member, you may have been baptized, but you have never been saved. Then come and receive Christ as your Saviour.

HOW TO CHANGE YOUR LIFE IN THIRTY MINUTES

II. RECOGNITION OF YOUR PLACE IN THE FAMILY OF GOD

Of whom the whole family in heaven and earth is named.
— Eph. 3:15

The family of God is made up of the saved in Heaven and upon the earth. If you are a child of God, then you are in the family of God. Here is your responsibility: "So then every one of us shall give account of himself to God" (Rom. 14:12).

You can change your life. You are saved by faith in Jesus Christ, and a child of God through your simple faith in Him. Now you have to recognize your place in God's family.

There are no money problems, if folk recognize their place in the family of God. There is no problem in church attendance, no problem in Sunday School, no problem anywhere, if you recognize what you are through faith in Jesus Christ.

You say, "Because of this, there are certain things I must do."

First of all, recognize your responsibility as a member of God's family. You belong to the family of God. We are a family here tonight, a family of believers. We have come together to worship Him on Sunday evening. Others may turn aside, some churches may be closed, but we are here to worship God. You have a responsibility to tithe and to go beyond a tithe. You have a responsibility to daily live for God.

If you are a child of God, you really have something. That you have to recognize. This can change your life. A lot of folk do not get it. A lot of poor people come down the aisle, join the church, maybe I baptize them, then they walk out of here and that is all of it!

One puny fellow came the other day and made a profession of faith on a Sunday morning. I mean a "puny fellow" - without any mind, any thought to what it was all about. I suppose

HOW TO CHANGE YOUR LIFE IN THIRTY MINUTES

I made a mistake when I baptized him. He was a married man. I baptized his wife, too. Somebody said, "You will be in church tonight, of course." "No," he said, "We are going some place else."

Oh, my dear friends, excuse me! The child of God is seeking for opportunities to serve God. You are not running after the world; you have left that crowd altogether, or should have. This man failed to get it. If he was saved, he failed to see his responsibility.

As a member of the family of God, you have something to do. I belong to this church; therefore, I am obligated to tithe. I am obligated to give of my best in this place. If you do not intend to do that, then do not join this church. If you are going to play around, mess around, then don't do it around here. We have enough of that kind. We need folk who mean business for God, who will take responsibility of living for Christ as a member of God's family and a member of this local New Testament church.

<u>Second, there must be a recognition of your responsibility to give the Gospel</u>. We must give the Word of God. We must not shun it. There can be no happy change in your life unless you have the desire to give the message of Jesus Christ to someone else. Perhaps the first mark of any person's salvation is that mark of wanting to see someone else saved. This is your responsibility. You have to assume this when you come into the family of God.

You say, "I am concerned about others. I do want my family and loved ones saved. I want my friends saved. I want the whole world saved and I will do my best to give the message to people everywhere, that they might come and be saved." This is part of it, your responsibility.

You can change your life tonight. Some of you are not tithers. Shame on you! You have missed the blessings of God. Some of you are not concerned about missions. Shame on you! You haven't got it!

Some of you are not too concerned about anything that

HOW TO CHANGE YOUR LIFE IN THIRTY MINUTES

goes on around you. You simply take things as they are. My friend, recognize your responsibility of giving the Gospel to the ends of the earth by home witnessing and by foreign missions. This is God's work, this is His calling for all of us, and we must never get away from it.

Some of our folk miss it. A lot of our people have it, praise God! This is one of the greatest missionary churches in the world. We support over 500 missionaries. Thousands of dollars every month go to missions alone out of this one church. We are not going to slow down but will keep on. We have discovered that the more we give, the more God gives to us. The larger offerings we have for missions, the more the offerings come in for all the work here.

Do you think Camp Joy is a burden? My dear friend, I wish all the work was as easy as Camp Joy. God blesses it and supplies the need. It takes thousands of dollars, but God supplies because people care.

How much do you care? How much are you concerned about getting the Gospel to the ends of the earth? That is important. Recognize this responsibility.

Third, a recognition of your responsibility to show forth Christ. It is important to show forth the Son of God to a lost and dying world. That is what the apostle is talking about here, "Holding forth the word of life," showing others that you are in the family of God and living for Christ. It is important that you have this. We are to be showing forth the Son of God. This is important to you and to me.

Somebody said that a watch set accurately is efficient for the setting of many watches. That is true. If I set my watch accurately, then you can set yours by it, though there may be 5,000 to 6,000 in this service tonight. I can set all of these right, every single one.

This simply means that multitudes can be changed by your life. Amen? If you do that which is right, then your life can bless other lives. But a setting of the life must be right or the whole thing fails.

HOW TO CHANGE YOUR LIFE IN THIRTY MINUTES

One watch can set many watches; one life can set many lives. "Holding forth the word of life;" doing the thing in a real way, understanding what it means to be a child of God, recognizing your responsibility, doing what God wants you to do.

Are you real? Some Christians, I am afraid, are artificial. I know some of them.

Remember the story of the Queen of Sheba? She came to see the wise man Solomon. She sent him flowers. She challenged the great king to tell her the difference between the real flowers and the artificial. The artificial ones were perfumed and beautiful.

Solomon simply told the servant to open the window. He did, and in a few moments when the bees came they went to the flowers - to the real flowers. You can always tell the difference, can't you?

You can always tell the difference in Christians, too, by how they act, how they behave themselves, what they say. It is always evident if you are a child of God.

Recognize this second point: your place in the family of God. This can change your life. You do not ask, "Do I do so and so?" If God says it, you do it! Obey the Son of God. Why? Because you belong to the family of the eternal God.

III. RESIGNATION TO THE WILL OF GOD

This is the thought that never escapes me. I pray daily. "Father, I want Your will done in my life. If it is Your will for me to be the pastor of the Highland Park Baptist Church, that is what I want. If it is Your will for me to be Chancellor of Tennessee Temple University, that is what I want. But if it is not your will, then I do not want it. And take me away from it all together." I want the will of God to be done. If it is His will for me to suffer, I will take that, too. I am not complaining about suffering, not finding fault with God in the slightest. Keep that in mind. Some ask me a lot of questions about this. No! No! I never complain. I am taking God

HOW TO CHANGE YOUR LIFE IN THIRTY MINUTES

at His own word and telling Him, "Lord, if this is Your will for my life, then this I receive. This I accept without any complaint."

That is not easy. Sometimes it is human to complain. It may sound easy to say it, but sometimes there are difficulties. The world, the flesh and the Devil crowd in and try to keep you away. But you are to pray, "Lord, this is it - resignation to Your will for my life."

What does this mean? <u>First, resignation to His will is revolutionary</u>.

A man came to see me Friday morning. He sat down before my desk and said, "Dr. Roberson, God has called me to be a missionary in Haiti."

I said, "That is a French-speaking country."

"Yes it is."

"How old are you?"

"Forty-six."

"Do you speak French?"

"No, I do not."

"Do you speak a word of French?"

"No, I don't."

"Well, that is going to be a big job."

"I know it is, but God has called me."

Wait a minute! I did not argue with him. If God has spoken to the man about going to Haiti as a missionary and to learn the French language, that is up to God and him. It may be difficult, almost impossible for him. But I am saying, resignation to the will of God is often revolutionary.

When God called me to preach, I had already had two years in business school, had finished and had gotten a diploma. My mother had already set it up for me to be a worker in the office of L & M Railway. I had applied for a job. Although I was not then old enough, she made the application so that I could go ahead and work. But God said to me, "That is not for you. I have something else for you to do." Perhaps God would call me to be a preacher, an evangelist,

HOW TO CHANGE YOUR LIFE IN THIRTY MINUTES

or whatever. I said, "Lord, I am ready." He changed everything. It was revolutionary. He will do that for your life, too. Your whole life can be changed in a moment's time, during thirty minutes of this service.

Second, resignation to His will is comforting. The fighting is over. The peace of God comes in. There may be fightings without but peace within. If you are surrendered to His will, resigned to His will, then the peace of God will be yours, though outside there may be conflict, trouble, heartaches, discouragements and disappointments. In the heart, when surrendered to His will, there will be peace.

This is why so many are always troubled, always distressed. We are always trying to help people because they have not surrendered fully to the will of God. Their inner heart is troubled and upset; their whole life is disturbed. They fail to have the peace of God.

Third, resignation to His will is directive. If you resign to the will of God, He will always guide you to the place of service. If you are not being guided, somehow, some way, some time, then it simply means you are not surrendered.

If you have no place of service, then surely God is holding off and saying, "Wait a while. You are not ready." God wants to guide you. And when you resign to His will, He will direct your life and show you the service that He wants you to render.

There are some things that I want to suggest quickly:

Look at your life. You have my three main points. Hold to them, if you will, please. But now, look at your life. Are you saved? Can you say tonight, "I know I am saved. I know Jesus Christ is mine, and I am not worried about that"?

Are you satisfied with Christ?

> "I am satisfied with Jesus,
> But the question comes to me,
> As I look at Calvary
> 'Is my Master satisfied with me?'"

Are you satisfied with Christ? Are you satisfied with your

HOW TO CHANGE YOUR LIFE IN THIRTY MINUTES

life? Don't answer too quickly. Paul never was. He said, "So fight I, not as one that beateth the air." He said, "I am fighting . . . this one thing I do . . . I press toward the mark for the prize of the high calling of God in Christ Jesus." He was never content. He was always pressing on. So are we to press on.

Look at your life, Christian. Sinner, look at your life! Are you satisfied with what you see?"

You say, "Brother Roberson, you mean to tell me that in a service like this, on a Sunday night at twenty-five minutes of nine, my whole life can be changed?" Oh, yes!

R. L. Williams was the head of the Northwestern Railway. Mr. Williams became a very wealthy man, of course, in a big position. He said.

> I learned a lesson one day in just about half a minute that taught me something I never got away from.
>
> As a boy, I got a job as the ticket man, as a clerk at a counter in the railroad. I was taking the tickets and selling the tickets, of course, at the counter. Then I got to the place just as a boy, when I was rough and mean-spirited.
>
> As a lad I criticized people. I called them names and made fun of them. I thought I was a big shot because I was taking tickets at a window of the railroad yard. I got so big I could not stand myself.
>
> I kept on going and doing the same thing, until one day I sold a ticket to a salesman; and when I did so, I gave a harsh remark. I turned my back on him.
>
> As I looked back around, the salesman was bending over the counter. He had his face all the way over the side of the counter where I was standing. He had his arm down on the counter looking at me. He said, "Sonny, if you are going to amount to anything, you had better change your attitude. If you are going to get anywhere in this world, you will have to change the way you are doing. You are going to be a failure if you go on as you are. Get wise to yourself." The salesman pulled his arm back and walked away.
>
> After that salesman left, God spoke to my heart. Something snapped inside me I had never seen before. I saw what a fool I was making of myself as a young man, being so mean, so harsh to people, feeling that I was bigger than

HOW TO CHANGE YOUR LIFE IN THIRTY MINUTES

anyone else.
   I changed. I said, "O God, I am going to change," and I did from that moment on.

R. L. Williams became the president of his company and a famous businessman. And he says, "It all dates back to that one talk, that one vow to God."

Look at yourself. Where have you failed? Where are you failing? Come on, you businessmen. Come on, you housewives and young people. Where are you failing in your life? What is the thing that is wrong tonight?

Let this hour change you so that you can walk out of here determined, "This has been a new day for me, a new beginning. Monday is going to be a day of blessing because I am putting my faith in Him."

Look at the offerings of Christ. He offers pardon and salvation. He offers peace; "My peace I give unto you." He offers power. "But ye shall receive power after that the Holy Ghost is come upon you."

Look at the invitations of Christ. He invites you to come. "Come unto me all ye that labour and are heavy laden, and I will give you rest." He said, "Whosoever will, let him take the water of life freely." He urges us to come. He invites us to come and to receive all that He has.

If we are living in a poor, dying state, it is our fault, not God's. We are not taking what He has put upon the table for us. Here it is on the table: walk up and receive it. It is for you and for me. You can change everything in this brief moment we have together.

Oh, the patience of your Saviour! How tenderly He cares for us!

Oh, the persistence of our Christ! He does not give up. He keeps on working with us all the time.

Oh the purpose of our Saviour! His purpose is to be glorified in us, that we might glorify the Father. Sometimes we walk away from Him and we fail. He said, "I want to give you pardon and peace and power. All of this can be yours

HOW TO CHANGE YOUR LIFE IN THIRTY MINUTES

if you will simply come and take that which I am offering you." It is for you. Receive it for your own. This should be the change of your life and my life.

I am not just preaching. I am not just concerned about preaching tonight. I am concerned about something deeper and richer than we have ever known. I am concerned about a sense of the blessed Lord in my life. A concern for others around me. A recognition of the indwelling Holy Spirit in my life so that my life might be changed, might be made like unto the blessed Lord.

"More like the Master, I would ever be,
More of His meekness, more humility."

Do not refuse His invitations. He invites you to come and take all that we have talked about tonight. Do not turn your back on Him. If you do, you have hurt yourself.

For many years George W. Truett was a great preacher of the First Baptist Church of Dallas, Texas. I can still recall with clarity the hours when I stood or sat in his presence. What a man of God! I sat with this great man in a banquet hall. He never once smiled in the years that I saw him. They say that he had not smiled in years. And he never smiled in public.

He never told a joke. I never saw him laugh. I sat by his side over and over again - in Birmingham, Alabama in a meeting; in Nashville, Tennessee in a meeting - the great Dr. George W. Truett, an amazing person.

When Truett went to Dallas years ago, (he stayed almost fifty years in that one church), he began holding funeral services, as a pastor must. One day he met an unsaved undertaker. When he started witnessing to him about Christ, the unsaved man turned him away. Dr. Truett kept on talking to him, but the fellow kept saying, "No."

When Dr. Truett would stand to speak at a funeral, sometimes the undertaker would sit in a chair over to one side and wipe the tears from his eyes as Truett spoke to him and to the family. Because of the conviction upon his heart, he was

HOW TO CHANGE YOUR LIFE IN THIRTY MINUTES

greatly troubled; yet, he refused every time.

After years had gone by, Dr. Truett still had the funerals and the undertaker was still working, and had become quite prosperous. One day the undertaker stopped him and said, "Dr. Truett, I want to ask you something. How is it that I used to listen to you and like it? I thought you were a good preacher. As I listened, sometimes I wiped away a tear. Now for years I have listened and nothing moves me. I am not stirred at all by what you say. Your sermons do not get next to me. Your illustrations do not help me. Something is wrong."

Dr. Truett said, "Yes, sir, something is wrong. It is not my message. I am preaching the same message - the message of Jesus Christ, the Saviour. But the thing wrong is that you have listened so much and have shaken your head and refused so much that now your heart has become as hard as stone. What I say now simply passes you by. Nothing happens at all. Nothing convicts you. I can do nothing to help you. And God cannot either, unless there is a breaking up of your heart. You have refused too long; you have gone too far."

My friend, that can be true of sinners, but it can also be true of Christians, if you turn away from the better things of God.

What have we said? The reception of Christ; recognition of your place in the family of God; and resignation to the will of God, that His will might be done in your life.

Chapter 8
The World's Greatest Ordination Service

> *Ye have not chosen me, but I have chosen you, and ordained you, that ye should go and bring forth fruit, and that your fruit should remain; that whatsoever ye shall ask of the Father in my name, he may give it you.*
> — John 15:16

There is something sacred and strange about an ordination service - a service when a young man is ordained to the Gospel ministry.

I remember so vividly my ordination in Louisville, Kentucky, at the Virginia Avenue Baptist Church. I had been called to the little Germantown Baptist Church in Memphis, Tennessee. I knew that God had called me to preach. The church in Tennessee had requested my ordination at the hands of the church in Louisville.

Rev. L. W. Benedict, a gracious and godly man, was my pastor at Louisville. He arranged the details of the ordination. First, there was the examination in the afternoon. Some fifteen ministers were present. Some were professors at the Southern Baptist Seminary; others were pastors of the city.

The examination was difficult - not because of the professors but because of my first pastor, Rev. J. N. Binford, the man who had shaken my hand the morning I came forward and professed my faith in Christ, also the man who baptized me. He had also baptized my mother and father. A great man but mighty tough on me when I came to the ordination.

THE WORLD'S GREATEST ORDINATION SERVICE

Brother Binford had never been to college or seminary, but he knew his Bible. He threw the questions at me hard and fast. The seminary professors were kind, but the old pastor at Cedar Creek was not so kind. However, I passed the examination.

Rev. J. N. Binford, Rev. L. W. Benedict, and others took part in the ordination service. I remember the ordination prayer, but especially I recall the laying on of hands. This touched my heart. I had been called to a small church. I felt that God would use me in that place. In my heart I felt very much what I am sure Barnabas and Saul felt when the leaders of the church in Antioch laid hands on them and sent them away.

I had a strange burden upon my heart after the ordination. There was no lightness, no flippancy. Instead, I felt I had assumed a load. I had a responsibility, one that I could never escape.

When I drove out of Louisville to my first church, the burden remained, and it was there when I arrived in Memphis. It was there when I preached. It was there when I quit preaching. It is there today. It will be there, I am sure, as long as life shall last.

An ordination is sacred, solemn and sweet. There is something about it in the realm of the holy. It is more than a funeral, a wedding, the observance of the Lord's Supper, or the act of baptism.

The burden of my message is this: you Christian, have an ordination, and you cannot escape it, neither should you try to. I wish that every Christian would accept this ordination so plainly pointed out for us in John 15:16.

Charles Hadden Spurgeon was never ordained as we ordain ministers from this church, but he was ordained by the hand of God. D. L. Moody was never ordained as we ordain ministers from this church, but he was ordained of God.

This is a great ordination service. In this hour I pray that every Christian will assume the place God expects you to occupy.

THE WORLD'S GREATEST ORDINATION SERVICE

I. WE HAVE BEEN ORDAINED TO FRUITFULNESS
Ye have not chosen me, but I have chosen you, and ordained you, that ye should go and bring forth fruit, and that your fruit should remain...

Yes, we are to bear the fruit mentioned in Galatians 5:22,23:
But the fruit of the Spirit is love, joy, peace, longsuffering, gentleness, goodness, faith,
Meekness, temperance: against such there is no law.

It is my conviction that the fruitbearing mentioned in this place is that of one Christian winning a lost one to the Lord Jesus Christ. This is the fruit we are to bear.

Allow me to break down this thought. If we are to be fruitful, three things must be true.

<u>First, there must be faith.</u> We must have faith in God for overcoming difficulties. You will never be a soul winner unless your faith is of such proportions that you can overcome disappointments, discouragements, ill health, sorrows, economic burdens, and the general worries of life.

Faith overcomes mountains.

Faith in God is a builder of character. Man cannot live in fellowship with God unless his character is built and he becomes like God. It was so with the martyr Stephen. He emerges as one of the finest characters of the first church. He is described as a man full of faith and the Holy Spirit. The eyes of this one were fixed upon the Lord Jesus.

Faith will lead you to undertake great enterprises for the winning of souls. The Apostle Paul had faith. By his faith he went from country to country proclaiming the Gospel and winning men to the Saviour.

You will never be successful in winning others unless you have faith.

I like the story given by Dr. Howard Kelly, the great

THE WORLD'S GREATEST ORDINATION SERVICE

Christian physician of Baltimore. He told it like this:

> In my hospital I had a nurse in training who was a lovely young lady, beautiful of face, pure in heart. She was a happy Christian to adorn the Gospel of Christ. Every patient who came under her care loved her dearly. Not only the patients, but one of the finest young doctors, who was interning, fell in love with her. They planned to be married when she finished her training. They say that "everybody loves a lover," and everybody loved these two and smiled when they saw them standing together in the corridor. They were married just after she was graduated.
>
> A little over a year they lived in complete contentment. Then one day they brought the young doctor into the hospital with an incurable disease. It broke the hearts of all of us. She nursed him lovingly until the Lord took him Home. About a month later she came back to work on our staff. I dodged her. They had been in my home to dinner, and I felt very close to them. I just didn't want to meet her. I knew that anything I tried to say to comfort her would do no good. So I stayed away from her, but suffered with her.
>
> Of course, it was inevitable that I should come face to face with her. When I did, she slipped her arm through mine and said, "You've been dodging me." I said, "Yes, I have. I didn't know what to say. I couldn't think of anything to say that would help heal your broken heart."
>
> To my utter amazement, she stood there smiling. Then she said, "Dr. Kelly, I have no bitterness in my heart. I am very grateful to God. God gave me more than He gave any other woman. He gave me two years, two beautiful years - the one before we were married and the one after we were married. I had the love of the finest man who ever lived for two whole years, enough to last me a lifetime. Dr. Kelly, you are all wrong. You don't need to say a word. I say a prayer of thanksgiving every day. I have faith in God."

Second, there must be a vision. The Bible says, "Where there is no vision, the people perish." We will never be much in soul winning unless we get a vision. We have been ordained by the Lord to bring forth fruit; and to do this, we must see the world lost and undone, without Christ, without God, without hope.

Some years ago the Los Angeles Chamber of Commerce

THE WORLD'S GREATEST ORDINATION SERVICE

offered a prize of $500 for the best slogan submitted for the city. Mrs. Harry C. Malry, the mother of three children, submitted the prize-winning slogan. It read, "Vision to see, faith to believe, and courage to do."

This is what we must see - the need for a vision. We must see the thousands and millions of this earth without Jesus Christ. We must see our failures in trying to win souls. We must give ourselves to the great task of reaching more with the Gospel.

Third, there must be a concern. A concern for the souls of others should mark our lives. I say this to the young Christians, I say it to the older Christians: there must be a concern for the masses who are outside the doors of our churches, a concern for the lowly, a concern for the privileged, a concern for all men who know not the Saviour.

The Son of God expects the individual Christian and the church to bear this deep concern for the redemption of souls.

> Have you looked for the sheep in the desert,
> for those that have missed their way?
> Have you been in the wild, waste places,
> where the lost and the wandering stray?
> Have you trodden the lonely highway,
> the foul and the darksome street?
> It may be you'd see in the gloaming,
> the print of My wounded feet.
>
> Have you folded home to your bosom
> the trembling, neglected lamb?
> Have you taught the little lost one
> the sound of the Saviour's name?
> Have you searched for the poor and the needy,
> with no clothing, no home, no bread?
> The Son of man was among them;
> He had nowhere to lay His head.

THE WORLD'S GREATEST ORDINATION SERVICE

> Have you wept with the brokenhearted,
> In their agony of woe?
> You might, whispering beside you,
> "Tis the pathway I often go."
> My brethren, My friends, My disciples,
> Can you dare to follow Me?
> Then wheresoever the Master dwelleth
> There shall the servant be.

We have been ordained to bear fruit, and the Lord expects us to be deeply concerned for others.

The story is told of a poor woman who was a faithful Christian. She was a member of the First Baptist Church of Dallas, Texas. Her son was unsaved and she was concerned about him. He was breaking her heart with his drinking and other sins. He refused to go to church with her.

One afternoon, as the boy was asleep, the mother felt impressed to walk softly into the room and kneel beside the bed and pray. She prayed that God would let her take her boy to church that night. Soon she became so disturbed about him that she began to sob. The boy woke up and said, "Mother, what are you doing?"

"Son, I didn't mean to wake you. I just came to ask God to let me take you to church with me tonight."

The boy replied, "I will go with you tonight if you promise never to ask me again."

"I can't promise you that. I'm going to follow you like a mother, down to the grave." He finally consented to go.

They arrived late and took the last two seats on the back row. Dr. George W. Truett preached. God's power, in answer to the mother's prayer, got hold of the boy. When the invitation was given, he wept his way to the foot of the cross and salvation.

After the benediction that night, the mother kissed her boy over and over again. Then she fell down before the preacher, hugged his knees and said, "Pastor, it was through

THE WORLD'S GREATEST ORDINATION SERVICE

you that God saved my boy tonight!"

Dr. Truett said that he would rather have that testimony than to wear the crown of England.

My friends, this can be your joy each day. Here is the greatest work committed unto man: it is the task given to each one. You have been ordained to be a soul winner! You have been ordained to bear fruit!

II. YOU HAVE BEEN ORDAINED TO PRAY

. . . whatsoever ye shall ask of the Father in my name, he may give it you.

God has ordained that you, Christian, touch Heaven. God has ordained that you, Christian, get answers to your prayers.

I have been ordained to preach. Shame on my life, if I fail.

I have been ordained to preach this holy, infallible Word. What a shame if I turn away from it!

I have been ordained to preach that Jesus was born of a virgin, that He died upon the cross, that He is ready to save all who will repent and believe in Him. Shame on this preacher if I fail!

I have been ordained to preach that Jesus was buried in the grave, and rose on the third day. Shame on me if I fail!

I have been ordained to preach that Jesus Christ is coming again. One day we shall see Him face to face. Shame on this preacher if I fail!

I have been ordained to preach.

But, I have also been ordained to pray, and pray I must. You, too, my friend, have been ordained to pray. Jesus said, "I have chosen you, and ordained you . . . "

First, we must pray about everything. Paul said: "Be careful for nothing; but in everything by prayer and supplication with thanksgiving let your requests be made known unto God" (Phil. 4:6).

If a matter concerns you, it concerns your Heavenly Father. Therefore, pray about it. Jesus tells us to pray about

THE WORLD'S GREATEST ORDINATION SERVICE

our "daily bread." This means that the minutest details of life can be brought to God in prayer.

There is a strange attitude on the part of some people. They think that they should not pray about small things. But God has ordained that we pray about everything.

Second, we ought to pray earnestly about big matters. Jesus said, " . . . all things are possible to him that believeth." Jesus said, "And all things, whatsoever ye shall ask in prayer, believing, ye shall receive" (Matt. 21:22).

Pray about everything. Believe the promises of God. I mentioned in the first part of my message about L. W. Benedict, pastor of the Virginia Avenue Baptist Church in Louisville, Kentucky. I remember so well when Brother Benedict felt impressed that God would give him a radio station. He found out where one could be purchased and what the cost would be to have it erected in Louisville for the use of his church.

After fervent prayer, he went to one of the big office buildings in that city. He studied the register of names on the board in the foyer of the building. He prayed about what he should do. After prayer, he caught an elevator and walked to a certain door and asked for the president of the company.

After some delay, he was admitted to the big man's office. The pastor sat down and simply told the story. "I have been praying for a radio station. I felt impressed to come to this building. I studied the register downstairs. I took your name as the one that God wanted me to speak to regarding this matter."

The outcome of it was, that businessman, an unbeliever, gave Rev. L. W. Benedict more than $100,000 for the erection of a radio station, on which I had a part for two years.

The matter of God answering prayers is pretty well established here at Highland Park. All that you see today in the church, the schools, the mission program, the chapels, Camp Joy - all of this is a matter of prayer. God answers prayer. He exhorts us to pray about everything. We should

THE WORLD'S GREATEST ORDINATION SERVICE

not hesitate to pray for big things in the name of our God.

Third, we should pray for others. We are called to be intercessors. We have been ordained to pray. This ordination means that we must pray for our fellow man.

We must pray for fellow Christians who may be going through dark times. We must pray for those who are experiencing financial difficulties. We must pray for those who are beset by sins of the world. Yes, we must bring before God the needs of our fellow Christians.

But especially, we must give ourselves in prayer for the lost. We must pray that conviction will settle upon the hearts of those lost in sin, that they might be brought to the Saviour and to life everlasting.

There is a beautiful little story, a true story, that I love to tell. It tells of a dear mother who attended a revival campaign. The evangelist had preached on prayer and the necessity to pray for loved ones. The mother had an unsaved son.

When the service was over she went back to her home. Impressed of the Lord, she returned to the church. It was then past midnight. The building was dark, but she cared not. She was not afraid. She entered the building, knelt at the front of the auditorium, and in fervent prayer she poured out her heart to God, praying that God would save her son.

When the morning light was breaking, she returned home, did the housework and took care of the chores. At the morning service time she returned to the church.

A little while after she had left for church, there came a car to the front of the old home place. The young man got out and went inside. He called for his mother, but she was not there. He checked with the neighbors and they said, "Your mother is at church." The young man got in his car, drove to the church, entered the building, and sat down at the very rear of the auditorium.

The pastor preached. The invitation was given. The young man, in tears, walked down the aisle, and on his knees received Jesus Christ as his Saviour. The mother did not

THE WORLD'S GREATEST ORDINATION SERVICE

know he was there until he passed her on his way down to the front.

He was saved that day. As he stood in the church, the pastor asked him, "How does it happen that you are home? I thought you were some distance away and could not get here."

The young man replied, "I was awakened past midnight. I could not sleep. I felt that something was wrong at home and that I should come and see Mother. I arose, dressed, got in my car, and drove as fast as I could to see if there was anything I could do for her. When I arrived home, I found she was at church. So I came here at once. I heard the message. Now I am saved. I know why I awakened - God wanted me to come and get saved."

The only thing the boy didn't know at that time was that his mother had been upon her knees in the church from midnight until morning, praying for the salvation of her son. Now Mother's prayer had been answered! God had awakened the boy and brought him home so he could hear the Gospel and be saved.

God grant that we might pray for others, that we might pour out our hearts for people to come to the Lord Jesus Christ and to salvation.

I read about a restaurant owner who put a placard in the window reading: "Free Meal Tomorrow." A man passed by the window, saw the sign, and decided that he would come back the next day. He returned the following day and asked for the free meal. "Oh," said the proprietor, "that's tomorrow."

Remember: tomorrow never comes. It is today that you should settle the matter of your salvation. It is today that you should give your best to the Lord. It is today that you should determine to be an intercessor and pray for others. It is today that we should say an eternal "yes" to Christ and surrender our lives to His control. God grant that it might be so.

Chapter 9
God and A Worm

> *But God prepared a worm when the morning rose the next day, and it smote the gourd that it withered.*
>
> *Then said the LORD, Thou hast had pity on the gourd, for the which thou hast not laboured, neither madest it grow; which came up in a night, and perished in a night:*
>
> *And should not I spare Nineveh, that great city, wherein are more than sixscore thousand persons that cannot discern between their right hand and their left hand; And also much cattle?*
>
> — Jonah 4: 7, 10, 11

I read about a seminary professor who, visiting in a certain church, was called on to give a certain message. He did a rather strange thing. He walked up on the platform and read chapter 1 of Jonah without stopping. He read chapter 2 without stopping. He read chapter 3, and, without stopping, he read chapter 4, then sat down. The people listening to him that day said it was one of the greatest sermons they had ever heard.

You see, when you mention the name "Jonah," most folks think only about a whale, a fish. They have missed the rest of the story. And quite often we miss the last part, given in Jonah, chapter 4, which I want you to see tonight.

This is an amazing story that God has given to us. The outline of the book is very simple.

GOD AND A WORM

Jonah 1 — Running away from God; Jonah's disobedience.
Jonah 2 — Running to God; Jonah's prayer.
Jonah 3 — Running with God; Jonah's preaching.
Jonah 4 — Running ahead of God; Jonah's complaints.

Then, look at it again, please, and think of it once more:
Jonah 1 — Jonah and the storm.
Jonah 2 — Jonah and the fish.
Jonah 3 — Jonah and the city.
Jonah 4 — Jonah and the Lord.

This little book of Jonah has 13,028 words in the English language. It presents a beautiful picture of God's love for both Jew and Gentile. Jonah was a Jew, a Hebrew. He was sent to a heathen nation for the preaching of the Gospel. Of course, you know the struggle that came and how he finally got there.

We will center our thinking upon Jonah, chapter 4. Jonah preached and the people turned to God. Back in chapter 3, in the last portion, we see revival coming; and Jonah was displeased. He complained about it. The only preacher in the world to get mad because he had a revival.

Jonah went outside the city and made himself a booth. God prepared a gourd to shelter him. Then God prepared a worm to cut down the gourd. Jonah was left in the hot sunshine. He prayed to die. God spoke to him in a very positive way, as we find here in verses 9, 10, and 11: "You are angry, troubled about this matter? What about these people of Nineveh? What about the folks that I want to spare - the adults and the children, even the cattle?"

So God prepared a fish, as we find in this book. In chapter 4 He prepared a gourd, He prepared a worm, then He prepared a wind, a hot wind to blow upon Jonah.

What am I getting to? God has a hand in all things, large and small. We should never leave Him out of our lives. We should pray and consider the will of God about everything we do. The largest matters to the smallest matter - all come under the hand

GOD AND A WORM

of God.

There are three things that I want you to see in the lesson this evening.

I. THE LIMITED VISION OF MAN

When revival came to Nineveh, Jonah was displeased. This shows his limited vision. One very fine commentary said, "Jonah cuts a sorry figure," and he does. He was displeased, angry, and he prayed to die. The commentary stated: "Jonah, the rebellious prophet, trying to run from God."

We have Jonah, the harsh prophet. Notice one sentence in his message: ". . . Yet forty days, and Nineveh shall be overthrown" - eight words. That's all he preached as far as we know. He repeated those eight words again and again, and revival came.

Jonah, the proud and selfish prophet. I used to think Jonah was a weak fellow, but I don't believe that now. I believe he was strong. Yes, he was weak at certain moments, weak like Elijah was weak. But Elijah also had strength. He was God's chosen man for a certain time, a mighty man who was taken up to Heaven in a wave of the hand of God. Elijah was a great man, but he had weak moments, as when Jezebel pursued him and he prayed to die.

The Apostle Peter had some weak moments, when he denied the Lord and turned aside; but he also was strong. He preached a sermon on the day of Pentecost when God blessed with thousands saved.

Abraham Lincoln had some weak moments. I read something this past week in the story given by John Gilmer Sneed that I had never read about Lincoln. Lincoln at one time (in 1841) was engaged to be married. On the day of the wedding, he left his bride at the altar. Abraham Lincoln failed to show up. He was scared half to death. For twenty-two months he ran. For twenty-two months he escaped the altar. Finally, like it always does, he got caught and married.

GOD AND A WORM

I'm trying to point out that Jonah had some weaknesses, but don't think he was an entirely weak man.

What is our task? To see the lost world as God sees it. Jonah failed in this. "The fields are white unto harvest," lost and undone; people are all around us, yet we don't see them as God does.

Our task, our aim, is to love the lost as God loves them. We cannot be complete unless we love people and want to see them brought to the Saviour.

Our task is to do as God commands. Sow the seed and let God give the harvest. We are to sow the seed continually. We are to go into all the world and preach the Gospel.

Will you have opposition? Of course you will. Will people fight you? Certainly. They've been fighting us here in Chattanooga for all these years I've been here. They fight the Gospel, these mean, wicked people who have no understanding of the Word of God. Some church people also will fight what we do because they think it is foolishness, this matter of preaching and giving invitations and getting people saved and baptizing converts. They will talk about it and criticize us.

One Baptist preacher said some years ago that we run a 'three-ring circus" at Highland Park Baptist Church. That was the year I baptized 555 people in a single year and he baptized only five in twelve months.

You'll have some opposition. It will always come upon any church, upon any people doing something for God, but we have to stand. We stand by the Word of God. We have a job, a task to be carried out. But, opposition may come. It will come.

A man went to Montana some years ago. He made a lot of money in the mining operations, so he decided to build a city. He put up a city on one thousand acres of land in Montana and made it quite beautiful. He put in the streets and the sewers, and fixed it all exactly right. He built the houses and the schools - everything except a church. He

GOD AND A WORM

hated the church and said so.

He invited the outside people to come there. Many did come to the beautiful city in Montana, built on a thousand acres of land. But, when some found there was no church, they would not come. For example: Women school teachers were hard to find; they just wouldn't come with their children since there was no church. They were afraid of the sin and the wickedness.

In five years time the wealthy man was bankrupt because no one backed his city. They wouldn't come to it. Opposition? Oh, he cursed. I read some of the statements written about what he had to say. Since he opposed the Gospel, his city failed. He found he could not go ahead without taking God into his plans.

Get a vision, Christian people, of the foreign fields, of home fields. Get a vision of your home and its needs. Let God have His way.

This man Jonah missed it for a while. He did not see it. The rest of the story is not given in his book, ending with chapter 4. The last words are the words of God. There was more to follow, I'm sure.

Get a vision of the need of your field, the need of this world, the need of people.

In the State of Ohio a family has a church built at the side of their home. It is a beautiful building. Inside the church are two pews. In the center is an altar. Two pews and the altar - just enough seats for the family. That's all they have and that's all they want.

What's wrong? Selfishness. That's not a church! A church reaches out to the whole world. The church has the doors open to all who will come.

There was also a selfishness reflected on Jonah's part as he looked on the job and disapproved of the thing God had done.

God uses instruments. In this case he used a common little worm to teach the prophet a lesson. Jonah was proud and he

GOD AND A WORM

was pouting. God had to teach him. The worm gave him the lesson that he needed. He brought down the gourd so that Jonah couldn't have the shelter from the storm and from the hot blast of the air. Jonah complained, but God used just a simple thing.

God used the boy David to humble the giant Goliath.

He used timid Jeremiah to speak to Judah.

He used the rustic Amos to give a message to the court of Israel.

He used Alexander Cruden to give us the concordance. Someone has said that Cruden's Concordance is worth more than a billion books. Sometimes I'm almost tempted to agree. I check the concordance for what I want.

Alexander Cruden had to spend some time in a mental institution because of the weakness of his own mind at times, yet giving us this mighty work. The hand of God was upon him.

He used a shoe clerk to bring Moody to Christ.

Let God use you. Get a vision. Get a vision of the task. Get a vision of the job, and say, "O God, use my life in the best way Thou canst for Thy glory for all times to come."

This man Jonah had a limited vision, and this is bad.

II. THE HEART OF GOD

Look again at Jonah 4:10,11. Here is the heart of God pictured:

> *Then said the LORD, Thou hast had pity on the gourd, for the which thou hast not laboured, neither madest it grow; which came up in a night, and perished in a night:*
>
> *And should not I spare Nineveh, that great city, wherein are more than sixscore thousand persons that cannot discern between their right hand and their left hand; and also much cattle?*

How beautifully pictured! God's expression here is as

GOD AND A WORM

beautiful as John 3:16: "For God so loved the world, that he gave his only begotten Son. . . " This portion of Jonah, chapter 4, and the expression of God's love, is as beautiful as Luke 15 telling of the parables and the seeking Saviour after the lost.

The second point of my message is the heart of God.

First, we see God's tender patience with the resentful prophet. How patient He was with this man who turned away. God is always that way. Jonah cried unto God and God had to speak back to him. Then Jonah said, "Therefore now, O LORD, take, I beseech thee, my life from me; for it is better that I die than live." Jonah was saying that he could not go on because of what God had done, what had happened in that place. But God had tender patience with the resentful prophet!

Second, we see God's loving concern for the Ninevites. We must see that the people of Nineveh were wicked. That was the city that had just gone all out for sin, according to history. But God loved them. He had a concern for their children, concern for the adults. He even had a concern for the cattle. An amazing picture of the love of God!

Jonah was more concerned about himself and about his own comfort than he was about the people of Nineveh. Jonah wanted his own way.

I do not have time to discuss the fact that this was a Jewish man being sent into a heathen nation to preach the Word as God had directed. God had a loving concern for the people of Nineveh. And He has a desire for all of us. He wants us to care for souls. He wants us to preach that "whosoever will, may come," inviting sinners to the Saviour. The compassion of God is revealed through His Son, Jesus Christ.

Christ cares. The blind man was saved and had his eyesight restored by the Lord Jesus. The woman at the well was saved out of a life of sin. The woman taken in adultery and cast down before the Lord Jesus, was saved. Zacchaeus, the

GOD AND A WORM

rich publican was saved. Nicodemus, the leader of the Jews, was saved. So was the thief on the cross - all because Christ cares.

You've got to catch a vision. You have to ask God to help you not limit your vision; not be like Jonah, but to let you see the love of God, the heart of God, and how He yearns over sinners.

A group of young people had a meeting of counsellors and leaders of Christian organizations in a certain college town. Many different schools were represented. They met together on Friday night and had a glorious time, then again all day Saturday. After the Saturday night service, they had to go back home, back to their own school and work. Quite a few spoke up and said, "This has been so beautiful. The fellowship on this campus and the fellowship of our meetings here have been so wonderful that we regret we have to leave."

When they all had finished speaking, one fellow jumped up. "Hold it! I've just been saved through the meetings. I've come to know Jesus as my Saviour. I don't feel like you do. I want to go back to my campus, go back to my school and tell others what Jesus has done for me!"

This is to be the attitude every child of God should have. We should be hungering always to give the message to people everywhere so they, too, might know of God's love and desire to save and to give peace and joy to the heart.

III. THE SHADOW OF THE CROSS

First, you have the limited vision of man; second, you have the heart of God; now, the shadow of the cross.

Jonah was three days and three nights in the belly of the fish. Jesus said in Matthew 12:40, "For as Jonas was three days and three nights in the whale's belly; so shall the Son of man be three days and three nights in the heart of the earth." He could have been caught up by the fish and expelled on the shore in a day's time, but not so. Here is a picture of the resurrection of the Lord Jesus Christ. Here is a picture of the

GOD AND A WORM

death of Christ upon the cross.

And may I say this: Some people believe Jonah died inside the whale, inside the fish. I don't think that is necessary at all for the completion of the story. Some commentaries make a little statement about Jonah dying in order to give the picture of Jesus dying, the body being placed in the grave, then the resurrection. Jonah pictures our Saviour, pictures the grave, pictures the resurrection - all of this is given in the book of Jonah. The shadow of the cross is stretched out across the entire ancient scene of Jonah. Here is the picture of Jesus, the blessed Son of God. Here is the picture of the loving God. "But God commendeth his love toward us, in that, while we were yet sinners, Christ died for us." Here is the picture of Christ's death upon the cross. "Christ died for our sins according to the scriptures." Here is the resurrection from the grave - Jonah being vomited out of the fish's mouth onto dry ground. Here is salvation offered to all men, both Jew and Gentile. All is pictured in this one single story of Jonah.

I want you to see the shadow of the cross. From the first of Genesis to the last of Revelation, the Lord Jesus Christ is given. Jesus is in every part of the Bible - in all the prophets, major and minor; in every single word all the way through. Christ is in the center of it all, even in this tiny book of Jonah.

Jonah is a strange book. It concerns God and man, and it mentions a city and the people of the city, but that's all. Other minor prophets are entirely different from that. But here is the shadow of the cross; here is the death of the Son of God; here is the resurrection; and here is salvation offered to all men.

The same God who loved the people of Nineveh, also loves us. The same God who loved Nineveh, also loves Chattanooga. The same God who loved Nineveh and sent a prophet to that town to preach unto them, also loves this city. All of us are here for a definite purpose. If we are saved, we are here to

GOD AND A WORM

give the Gospel to a lost and dying world and to help Christians. The sinner must understand that God loves him, that God is concerned about him, that God is eager to help him.

God now is looking down from Heaven's glory and is seeking ways whereby He can ferret his own way into your heart and cause you to see His love and His sacrifice, His blood shed on Calvary's cross so that you might be brought unto life eternal. That God loves you is pictured so beautifully in the story given here. It shows God's greatness. It shows God's interest in all people. It shows His interest in one lonely man - Jonah. It shows God preparing the fish, the gourd, the worm, and the wind.

It gives me a lot of joy and peace to know that God is everywhere, that He controls everything, that I can pray about my every need. It may be so small that I would not talk to you about it, nor Dr. Faulkner nor Dr. Cliff Robinson, but I can talk to God about it. And I can say to Him, "Lord, I'm sorry but I just don't feel I can make it," and know He is listening. And I have the assurance from His Word that he cares, that He is concerned. We can pray about everything that troubles us - everything, it matters not what it may be.

Praise God that He is with us! That He is ready to help us! Ready to bless us! This is pictured so beautifully in the story given here in Jonah.

Sinner friend, as God loved the people of Nineveh, that wicked city, so He loves you in this city. If you have never been saved, know that God loves you and cares for you and is doing all He can to show you that love.

That is why this church. That is why this preaching. That is why this singing. It is for your sake, so that you might hear the Gospel, repent of your sins and be saved.

There is an old story which dates back before the days of automobiles. It tells about a young couple engaged to be married. The girl decided to marry someone else and ran away. The young man's heart was broken. He went on living his life, but he never married. People wondered why, but his

GOD AND A WORM

answer was, "I can't do it."

After some years had gone by, the girl who had left him returned. Her husband had left her and went back to his home. After her return, some thought the young man to whom she had first been engaged would rise and say, "I told you so. You made a mistake. And I'm glad you're suffering." Instead, he went to her and said, "I want you to know that I do still love you." She wouldn't listen. She couldn't believe he could after all that had happened.

The days went by. The story goes that one day when she was riding down the street in a buggy, suddenly the horse was scared by something and began to race down the street. This young man, now older, saw what was happening and rushed into the street, grabbed the horse and stopped it from running away. In so doing, his body was trampled by the horses' hooves. She got out of the buggy, grabbed him in her arms and held him. In almost his last breath, he said, "Now, do you believe me? I do love you. I do love you. Do you believe that I do, in spite of all that has happened?"

You say, "Brother Roberson, that's a strange story. Would a person really do that?" That's what God did.

When man had turned away from Him because of sin - sin, the transgression of the law; when man had refused all that God had offered to him; when man had despised everything, God sent His son, Jesus, to die. He said, "Now do you believe that I love you?" "For God so loved the world, that he gave his only begotten Son. . . " God wants us to see His love. He wants us to know that He loves and cares for us.

Jesus, the Son of God, is concerned that we see and understand that He died in our place. "Don't you see it?" He said to the thief on the cross, "Today shalt thou be with me in paradise."

Salvation is yours and for all men who will repent, believe, come to Jesus Christ and be saved through faith in Him.

Chapter 10
Please, Please, No Flowers, No Telegrams, No Cards, No Sunshine Baskets, No Family Visitation Hour

For Christ is not entered into the holy places made with hands, which are the figures of the true; but into heaven itself, now to appear in the presence of God for us:

Nor yet that he should offer himself often, as the high priest entereth into the holy place every year with blood of others;

For then must he often have suffered since the foundation of the world: but now once in the end of the world hath he appeared to put away sin by the sacrifice of himself.

And as it is appointed unto men once to die, but after this the judgment:

So Christ was once offered to bear the sins of many; and unto them that look for him shall he appear the second time without sin unto salvation.
— Heb. 9:24-28.

There are some passages in the Word of God that are not too popular for use at funeral services. For example, Luke 12:16-21. This has to do with the rich fool, his full barns, his own self-sufficiency. He talked to his own soul and said, "Soul, take thine ease, eat, drink, and be merry." God said unto him, "Thou fool, this night thy soul shall be required of thee." This would not be a popular portion for any funeral

PLEASE, PLEASE, NO FLOWERS...

service.

Neither is Luke 16:19-31. This is the story of the rich man and Lazarus. The picture of Hell is graphically given to us. The man "lifted up his eyes, being in torments, and seeth Abraham afar off. . . " This is not a picture that you would like to draw for the average person, a picture of a man suffering in the awfulness of Hell.

Also in John 3:18 and 3:36 are some words that are not too popular. "Comdemned" is not a popular word to use at a funeral service; neither would be the words "wrath of God," found in this portion.

Hebrews 9:27 is a verse that wouldn't be too pleasing to many people: "And as it is appointed unto men once to die, but after this the judgment." This verse speaks of three things: God's thought for man; the sureness of death; the judgment of the time when men shall stand before God.

Notice that in the verses before and after Hebrews 9:27 are two blessed thoughts. First, you have the cross of Christ given. Jesus and His death upon the cross of Calvary for us is mentioned in verse 26. Verse 28 states, "So Christ was once offered to bear the sins of many; and unto them that look for him shall he appear the second time without sin unto salvation." Hebrews 9:27 has some connotations of sadness in this matter of death and judgment, but the cross of Christ and the coming of the Lord Jesus are mentioned before and after it.

A few months ago while visiting in Nashville I picked up the newspaper and began reading the death notices. I saw the death notice of a young man, and his picture. I have it before me now. Here is how the write-up began: "Please, please, no flowers, no telegrams, no cards, no sunshine baskets, no family visitation hour." Then followed a write-up of 380 words.

In the entire write-up, starting with the words that I am using as the title of my message this evening, there is nothing about the man's salvation. There is nothing about his local

PLEASE, PLEASE, NO FLOWERS . . .

church membership or his church affiliation, though the names of families, friends, associates, and the place where he worked were given.

When I read the article, certain questions came to me. Did that young fellow know Christ as his Saviour? If so, did he have a clear testimony for the Lord Jesus Christ? Did someone ever speak to him about being saved? Was he prepared for death?

I began thinking about this one and all that was said about him in this 380 word article. Was the sting of death removed by his faith in Jesus Christ? The Lord died that we might have life everlasting. He died to take away the sting of death.

I remember Dr. M. R. DeHaan telling a story about his sons when they were small. Dr. DeHaan had a hobby of raising bees, so he had a beehive in the backyard. One day his boys went into the backyard. As they stepped into the yard, one bee headed straight toward one son and stung him on the forehead. The little fellow jumped up and down, fell on the ground, kicking and screaming in pain. After the bee had stung the older brother, it swung around and started for the younger one. He also began screaming and crying.

Dr. DeHaan said to the younger son, "Son, you don't need to cry. There's no use in shouting and jumping up and down. When your brother was stung by the bee, that was the end of his stinger. Now he cannot hurt you. He is now no more than a fly flying around through the air. He has no stinger."

Then Dr. DeHaan took his two boys, sat them down, turned to I Corinthians 15, and began to show them what it is that we have in Jesus Christ. The sting of death is sin, but in Jesus Christ the sting is gone. You are free from that because the Son of God bore the sting in His own body.

He found the stinger of that bee in his older son's eyebrow. "This bee can hurt one time only, just once," he said. Then he told them, "Jesus, the Son of God, came to die upon the cross of Calvary for sinners. He took the sting of death upon Himself. He died that we might be free from the awful sting of death."

PLEASE, PLEASE, NO FLOWERS...

That is a beautiful picture of what God has done for us.

When I read the story in the newspaper of this one who died in Nashville, I thought of his record. What kind of record did he leave? This write-up gave nothing at all - just a bunch of words about people, situations and working conditions. The introduction says: "Please, no flowers, no telegrams, no cards, no sunshine baskets, no family visitation hour."

It went on to say that they didn't want anyone to call or anyone to come see them. They did not want a thing from anyone. It simply stated that he died and they were going to have the funeral service at a certain hour.

What kind of record, my dear friend, will you leave when you are gone?

Apparently that is all that he had to leave, all that the family could write in 380 words of the obituary. That was the end. Nothing was said about salvation, what he had done, or what he had accomplished.

If you were to depart this life tonight or tomorrow and they were to write up your notice in the newspaper, what kind of record would you leave? What would it be? I have tried to put down a few things:

I. I LOVED THE SAVIOUR

I would want my record to show that I loved the Saviour. I would want folk to know it, too. I would want that listed somewhere, if I were to pass away. I would like it written down specifically that this one believed in Jesus Christ, loved Him, and followed Him.

You see, we must testify and speak of the faith that we have in the Lord Jesus Christ. Not only so, but we must so live that no one can doubt our salvation, not for a single second. People must know that we are saved by the way we live. This record of living for the Saviour should be manifested for all to see. My friend, do you love Him? Do people know that you love Him?

Do you recall me telling about the man who came to see

PLEASE, PLEASE, NO FLOWERS...

me and I lead Him to the Saviour in my office? With the Bible open before him, in prayer he accepted the Lord Jesus Christ and was happy in his salvation.

I said, "Sir, I want you to come to church next Sunday, walk down the aisle, take your stand, and be baptized."

He said, "I shall do so."

"Sir, where do you work?"

"At a certain company here in Chattanooga," and he named where.

Oh, a lot of our men work there. What division?"

He named me the division of the company.

I said, "Fine. One of my fine men works there in that division."

"What is his name?"

I gave the name.

He said, "Excuse me, Sir. If that man belongs to your church, then I am going elsewhere. I don't care about coming here if you have that kind of members. I have been working there for many months and that man has never mentioned Jesus Christ or the church or anything to me. I had a hungry heart and wanted to be saved, yet no one said a word to me. He has told filthy jokes, filthy stories and said some wrong things. Sir, if that is the kind you have in your church, I'll go somewhere else."

The man who was guilty of those things is not a member of our church now. If got a little too hot for him here. He didn't like that because his life didn't bear right. He didn't have the right record.

I want my life to count for Jesus Christ. So should you. I want others to see Christ in me and know that I belong to the Saviour. Let it be written of your life that you are one who has been redeemed by the precious blood of the Lamb.

II. ONE WHO SERVED GOD

I want my record to show I served faithfully. I want this written about my life. I think you want it about yours, too.

PLEASE, PLEASE, NO FLOWERS...

You do not want just a meaningless group of words put together, do you? There should be something about your Christian life, your service for God, your faith in Jesus Christ.

And it should show more than just a name on the church roll book, more than just a part-time interest in the things of God. There should be an interest that will stand and be established and will last forever.

I want my life to encourage others by my faithful service. I want to encourage those around me to speak some words that will lift up, help, and guide someone else along life's way. Their words can give added strength for the work that God has called others to do.

An outstanding English preacher told his story about his young years. He said he had great difficulties. He was guilty of doing things that were wrong, and he knew that. His family called him in often and talked to him and prayed with him and tried to help him, but they didn't get through to him.

One night when he was in his teens they had a long conference with him. When they tried to reason with him, he got up and walked away. As he walked out of the room and down the hallway, he walked by a door that came open and there stood Grandmother. Grandmother walked up, put her arm around him and said, "John, I believe in you."

He walked on to his room. He said that was the first time anyone ever said that to him. He thought, *If that is the way it is, then my life is going to change.* As an introduction to his salvation and to other good things in his life, he said it was when his grandmother said, "I believe in you."

I wonder sometimes if we fail to help others because of the words we speak and how we speak them. Perhaps kindness of speech could encourage someone. We can serve God faithfully by encouraging others and by so living that they can see Christ in us. The record of your life and mine should not be a meaningless jumble of nothing, but a life that is established and accomplishing something for God. I want to be found faithful. Do you?

PLEASE, PLEASE, NO FLOWERS...

Have you heard the story of Paul Schneider? It was back in the days when Hitler was doing his evil works against Jewish people. Thousands and thousands were killed. Hitler issued anti-Jewish decrees around his nation from time to time, doing it to destroy all the Jewish people.

Paul Schneider was then a pastor in Germany. When Hitler put out his first decree, he preached against it. He said, "This is wrong, entirely wrong to hate and to desire the deaths of God's chosen people." Then he went on to say what else he wanted to say.

In a few days Paul Schneider was arrested and put in jail. After staying in jail a short time, he was released (a trick of the German government). He came back to his church and went on preaching. After a short time, there came another anti-Jewish decree. Again Paul Schneider stood up and said, "I am against this. This is against my Bible and against all that I believe. I cannot stand without saying something against this thing."

Of course, he was in trouble again. That night after the service, when Paul Schneider and his wife were walking home, they walked over a little raised platform (or bridge) built over a little brook of water. When they came to the top, they just stood there for a moment. Mrs. Schneider turned to her husband and said, "Paul, can't you hold back a little? Isn't there something else you can do? Why do you have to say what you say? Why do you have to open up the way for trouble Sunday after Sunday? Isn't there some way you can avoid this and get by?"

Paul said to his wife, "I must speak out, even if it means my life. I must speak for your benefit, for the children's benefit, for my church, and for my people. I must be honest. I must be truthful."

She could say no more.

In a few days, another decree came out. (They were coming faster, now.) Paul Schneider stood again and took his stand for Christ and for the Word of God. Again trouble came.

PLEASE, PLEASE, NO FLOWERS...

He was put in prison. And in a few days, he was led before a firing squad and shot.

Listen to me! Consider this matter of faithfulness, this matter of standing for Christ, this matter of being found faithful. What a blessed word "faithful" is! "Moreover it is required in stewards, that a mán be found <u>faithful</u>."

What about your life? If a record were written about you, what would it say? Do you believe in Jesus Christ? Have you been found faithful in the work of our Saviour? Or have you neglected the most important things that God has for you to do?

III. I HATED EVIL AND LOVED RIGHTEOUSNESS

I must know what is right and what is wrong. Then I must stand for the right and against the wrong. There must be a separation from the world and a separation to the things of God. This must be established in my life. There must be no grayish matter; it has to be right or wrong. And I must stand for right at all times.

<u>First, keep your testimony spotless</u>. Watch it day by day, hour by hour. Don't allow anything to come in to taint or to destroy the beauty of a testimony for Jesus Christ. Keep it spotless.

<u>Second, let others know of your faith in God and your desire to live for Him</u>. Say it so they can hear it. Say it so they can understand that you are a child of God and that you are seeking to live for the Saviour.

<u>Third, hate all evil, whatever it may be</u>. Don't compromise! Stand your ground and say, "This is what I believe! This is how I stand on righteousness. I want to live righteously and I want others to live righteously. I am opposed to evil, to sin, to shadowy things of the world, and to Satan." Such a position, such a stand will cost you something every once in a while.

One of our deacons has taken a stand for a number of years against the liquor traffic. I've heard what he has said;

PLEASE, PLEASE, NO FLOWERS...

he has told me the things that he believes in his heart. He is active in civic affairs in Chattanooga. He has been trying to get memberships of certain companies, certain businesses, certain individuals in some of the organizations in this city.

One man who runs a liquor store in Chattanooga spoke up: "If Mr. So and So is on your committe, then I will not join. That man has been against our liquor business through the years!" Praise God!

Stand, my dear friend. It may hurt sometimes, but hate the liquor traffic and the business of sin. Be against all sin so you can live for God. Hate all evil - profanity, gambling, or whatever it might be. Hate it! Hate evil! Love righteousness!

The other day I was starting my message about scenes of what sin can do. We see them quite often. A lot of our men were here that morning from our downtown mission. Some were here who were saved through the fine mission in Dalton, Georgia. I see the men. I love them. They know that I love them. I see so many people who are under the influence of Satan's power.

I can think of one man. I would speak to him often and witness to him about Jesus Christ as he sat alongside one of the store buildings. My church was located just down the street. I would see him often when I went to the post office. He would be sitting there with a red face, a red nose, potbellied, weak, breathing hard, full of liquor most of the time, and foul-mouthed. His family was ashamed of him. What a shell, what an impossible individual he was! You ask, "Can Jesus do anything with someone like that?" Yes, the Son of God can save him, transform him, and make him into something. He cared nothing about Christ. He wouldn't listen to me. He wouldn't even have a conversation with me about the Lord Jesus Christ.

So it is with many people like him. They turn away and refuse the very message. But, we still take our stand for righteousness and against evil.

Did you see this in the paper: "Sinning is legal only in

PLEASE, PLEASE, NO FLOWERS...

churches in New Orleans," by Paul Harvey? Paul Harvey said that he went to New Orleans and discovered that the only games in town were in the churches. He said that a taxicab driver said that all the places in the city had been cleaned up and there was now no gambling at all except in Roman Catholic churches! Every Friday night the churches of the city have bingo, with prizes going up to $1,000. Paul Harvey said, "I thought you ought to know before you go there that sinning in New Orleans is only in the churches."

Take your stand against sin and evil. Stand without compromising. Say, "This is what I believe! I cannot change! This is my conviction and my stand for righteousness!"

IV. ONE WHO FOUND THAT GOD NEVER FAILS

God comforts. God strengthens. God sustains. God guides day by day. God never fails. I do not want an empty mass of words or something meaningless on my record. I want my record to show I have done something that is worthwhile, to let people know that I have found in my experience of life and ministry as a preacher of the Gospel that God never fails, that He does all He promises to do, and that I can rest upon Him and His Word.

I was reading about a preacher in Washington, D.C., a Dr. Elson. He said that when he was a boy, he and some others were out swimming and jumping in a little creek, having a good time.

It came to the close of the day. When they arrived home, it was discovered that Elson's nine-year-old brother was not with them. They began a search. Finally that boy's dog discovered the boy's clothes by the side of the creek where they had been swimming. When the rest of the boys had started toward home, the nine-year-old had jumped in again and something happened to him. His body was found in the creek and was brought out.

Dr. Elson said that when they went home that night, they sat there stupefied. "We didn't know what to say or how to

PLEASE, PLEASE, NO FLOWERS...

say it. We all sat there in a family circle. I can recall the entire scene. No one knew what to say so no one said a word."

The family pastor came to the home and read from the Word of God: "God is our refuge and strength, a very present help in trouble. Therefore will not we fear, though the earth be removed, and though the mountains be carried into the midst of the sea." He read on through Psalm 46 to "Be still, and know that I am God: I will be exalted among the heathen, I will be exalted in the earth." Dr. Elson said, "That Psalm stayed with me all of my life. I have never forgotten the beginning verse: "God is our refuge and strength, a very present help in trouble."

My dear friend, have you discovered that? He is our present help in time of trouble. He never fails.

I want to leave in my record that I have a God who has never failed and a Christ who has never forsaken me all these years of my life and ministry. The Lord has been with me every single step of the way.

My favorite verse is Romans 8:28: "And we know that all things work together for good to them that love God, to them who are the called according to his purpose." It wasn't always Romans 8:28. Once it was I Peter 2:21: "For even hereunto were ye called: because Christ also suffered for us, leaving us an example, that ye should follow his steps."

In a time of darkness, when our baby died, and I felt I couldn't go on, God said, "Here is a verse for you for the rest of your life," and He gave me Romans 8:28. I held on to it then, and I am holding onto it now.

In the midst of every trial, every tragedy, every suffering, every sorrow, every pain, every difficulty, I hang onto this verse: "And we know that all things work together for good to them that love God, to them who are the called according to his purpose."

I want to leave a record that God has never failed and will never fail those who put their faith and trust in Him!

PLEASE, PLEASE, NO FLOWERS...

V. ONE WHO DESIRED TO SEE THE SALVATION OF SOULS

There is one thing more: I want to leave a record of one who desired to see the salvation of souls. I want that to be written down about my life. I hope you, too, will have it written about your life that you wanted to see people saved. "He [Andrew] first findeth his own brother Simon... And he brought him to Jesus" (John 1:41,42).

I may fail to win many. I often fail in my services here in the church. Yes, I may fail. But above all, I do want to see folks saved. I do want to see someone come to the Lord Jesus Christ. Here is one burden that God wants me to carry - a burden for souls. I must not be burdened about money. I must not be burdened about criticisms by the world. But I must be burdened about souls. I should endeavor to daily get people to Jesus.

We have given an invitation in this church since 1942 and we have had responses all through these years. In 1942, when I first came as your pastor, we started out on Wednesday night inviting people to be saved. I have had people say to me, "Why do you give these invitations? Why not give them just one a week? That is enough." Some have even criticized our baptizing on Sunday morning, Sunday night, and Wednesday night. "Why not baptize only one time a week?" they ask.

I am trying to emphasize that our business, our desire, is getting people saved. And this is the record that I want to leave: Lee Roberson believed in getting people to the Lord Jesus Christ and he believed that Christ is able to save to the uttermost all who will repent and will come to Him.

Listen to the verse, "And as it is appointed unto men once to die, but after this the judgment." What a verse! There is not much light in that; there is not much brightness there, unless you look at the first part where you see the love of God in the death of Jesus Christ on the cross, and unless you look

PLEASE, PLEASE, NO FLOWERS...

at the last portion where you see the second coming of Jesus to receive us unto Himself. "And as it is appointed unto men once to die, but after this the judgment." Built into this is the love and care of God. Built into the verse is the sacrifice of Calvary. Here is the blood of the cross - Jesus dying for us. Built into that single verse is the offer of salvation to all who will repent and believe.

The verse itself may be severe if you leave out the other things. But when you take that verse with the rest of the Word of God and with all God has promised, you can see that we have life everlasting through Jesus Christ, and that all who will repent can be saved.

Think of the uncertainty of life. ". . . For what is your life? It is even a vapour, that appeareth for a little time, and then vanisheth away." And think of the certainty of death. ". . . it is appointed unto men once to die. . . " If Jesus tarries, all of us will be dead in a few years, even the youngest one here. See from the Word of God the need to be prepared. He said, "Prepare to meet thy God."

Oh, repent, believe, come and receive Jesus Christ as Saviour. Know that He has promised us great and glorious things beyond. Heaven is ours through our faith in the blessed Lord. O God, help us to lay hold upon what we have heard tonight. Let your life be meaningful, my friend. Don't live an empty life. That is what some are living.

You could die tonight and not one soul would miss you. No one would say a kind thing about you. You have never done a good thing. You have just been a negative force. You have accomplished nothing positive for God. Your life wouldn't count.

But it can, if you will put God first and live for Him and serve Him, and read your Bible, and seek His face, and try to get people saved. This is what I want, and I hope what you want. Whether young or old, keep on the firing line for God.

Do you know Christ? Have you put your faith in Him?

PLEASE, PLEASE, NO FLOWERS...

Are you trusting Him tonight? Can you say He is yours?

An old minister had been preaching a long time. He had prepared many sermons in the study at home. Then the home was sold and he had to move into another house. Perhaps he didn't have much longer to preach. He was a bit disturbed about it all. He had never quite become accustomed to this matter of dying and to talking to people about death. Funeral services bothered him some. He was not too well acquainted with the words to use in time of death. All of this troubled him.

His moving day came. Carpets, rugs, furniture were soon moved from the house. He was wandering from room to room and looking at things again. His servant came in and said, "Sir, you may go now. Everything is gone. The new house is much better. Let's go this way."

Listen! It taught him a lesson that he never got over. The new house IS much better. What we have in Jesus Christ is a thousandfold better, ten thousandfold better than anything we could ever have here.

Is He your Saviour tonight?

Chapter 11
The Verse That Jumped From the Page

And the same day, when the even was come, he saith unto them. Let us pass over unto the other side.

And when they had sent away the multitude, they took him even as he was in the ship. And there were also with him other little ships.

And there arose a great storm of wind, and the waves beat into the ship, so that it was now full.

And he was in the hinder part of the ship, asleep on a pillow: and they awake him, and say unto him, Master, carest thou not that we perish?

And he arose, and rebuked the wind, and said unto the sea. Peace, be still. And the wind ceased, and there was a great calm.

And he said unto them, Why are ye so fearful? how is it that ye have no faith?

And they feared exceedingly, and said one to another, What manner of man is this, that even the wind and the sea obey him?
— Mark 4:35-41.

I was passing through a storm. Some people might not confess this, but I was fearful. I was somewhat disturbed. My heart was distressed. I was not resting fully upon God as I should have been.

I was reading in the Word. As a matter of fact, during that time I had read much of the Word of God. I had read almost

THE VERSE THAT JUMPED FROM THE PAGE

all the Psalms. I had read through the Book of the Acts and made outlines of every chapter. And I had gone through other portions of the Word.

In my distress of heart I came to verse 40, quoted above. It seemed to jump out of the page into my consciousness: "And he said unto them, Why are ye so fearful? how is it that ye have no faith?"

When I first read that verse, I was somewhat disturbed. I thought, *The Lord's not very kind. That seems a little bit sharp to say to the people in that day.* I thought it was sharp to my own heart. "Why are ye so fearful? how is it that ye have no faith?"

As I thought of that, I thought of the loving Saviour. Could I ever find any place where the Son of God was unkind? No! Do I recollect any spot where Jesus would have been thought unlovely in action, or in word, or in deed? No! Then, I had to come back and say that this is said in love: "And he said unto them, Why are ye so fearful? how is it that ye have no faith?"

That shocked me! I thought of my lack of faith, of my doubting heart, of my distressed mind. I looked at it again. I kept reading that portion of the Word until I could not get away from it. I know that I am saved. I know that God called me. I know He answers prayer. I have no doubt about any of that. I know, too, that I am expressing what comes from your heart.

There are times when you are beginning to doubt, when you are fearful, when you have little faith. If this could happen to one who has been preaching almost fifty-five years, forty in one single church, then it might happen to you.

Now, I know I am saved! Not a question in the world about that. But there was a fearfulness that I had to settle, and the Word of God helped me. This single verse meant so much to me! "Why are ye so fearful? how is it that ye have no faith?"

THE VERSE THAT JUMPED FROM THE PAGE

I. CONSIDER WHY MEN FAIL

They fail because of lack of faith. They fail because of fear. Fear is the thing that sabotages our lives. "Sabotage" comes from the French word "sabot" which means "a wooden shoe." I read where back in the early days when people in factories got mad at the employer, they would pull off the wooden shoe, throw it into the machinery and tear it up. From that we get the word "sabotage."

Well my dear friend, in the same way, fear will sabotage your faith, will sabotage your life and keep you from having what you need day by day.

Fear comes from blindness, failing to see what God wants us to see. Failing to see the Word of God. Refusing to see what God has done and is doing. Fear comes from blindness.

Fear comes from selfishness. Look at these disciples. Jesus was asleep in the ship. They awakened Him saying, "Master, carest thou not that we perish?" Selfishness, thinking of self. They said, "Now Master, what's wrong? You are not caring for us. We are perishing." They were thinking only of themselves.

Now in our own lives fear comes from selfishness. We think of self and consequently we fear. We are afraid of what may happen to us, to our families, to our loved ones. Cast out selfishness! Pray about it. Ask God to help you be concerned for others. Mighty things have been done by people who have cast out selfishness.

I was reading this week about a little boy who came to a great man who was making violins. The boy said, "Sir, I can't sing. I can't play an instrument. What can I do? What do you think I can do with my life?"

This fine, humble man, but still famous in life, answered the boy, "I don't know what you can do. But you let God have your hands, your mind, your body - all you have - and surrender to Him. Leave everything in God's hands." With great unselfishness he talked to the boy for a long time. That boy became the great Antonio Stradivari, the man who

THE VERSE THAT JUMPED FROM THE PAGE

made the famous violins of the world.

I was reading this week also of Demosthenes, who just about lost everything because of his stupidity and because of his inability to speak. A man who heard him speak said, "Why, you speak all right. You speak like Pericles." An Athenian statesman said, "Why, you can do it! Keep going!" I don't know the names of the two men who were used to help Demosthenes. In the same way we can help others, unless we are beset by selfishness.

You speak to some people and within moments they are talking about self, of that which has happened to them, about what they want to do, never thinking of anyone else. Oh, may God help us! Fear comes out of selfishness.

Fear comes from deafness. We do not hear what God wants us to hear. Hear the Word of God: "Faith cometh by hearing, and hearing by the Word of God." Are you listening, child of God? "Faith cometh by hearing, and hearing by the Word of God." Hear this Book, then say, "God has spoken to me and I rest upon the promises of God's Holy Word."

Fear will come when you refuse to listen. I wish I didn't feel this way; I wish somehow I was wrong, but I don't think I am. When I speak at funeral services and read John 14:1-6, I am aware that some folk sitting out there have never even read that portion of the Word of God. I can quote John 3:16, and they will be ignorant of that, also. They do not read the Word, do not study the Word, do not know the Word. They have not heard what God has to say to them. Even some professing Christians have turned away from the Bible. Read the Word of God and let it speak to you.

Notice here in the first part of chapter 4 of Mark, Jesus gave the parable of the sower and the seed and how many refused to hear what God had to say to them.

II. CONSIDER WHAT FAITH CAN DO

<u>First of all, faith gives peace of heart in the midst of a storm</u>. This is what faith can do. Your life and your heart

THE VERSE THAT JUMPED FROM THE PAGE

can be quiet in the midst of all your anxiety and your troubles, if you are resting in God.

I do not say that it is going to be an easy or pleasant thing to have an operation that you have pending a few days from now. I am not sure how I would feel if I had to go to the hospital again for an operation. But, I know this: when you have faith in God, there can be peace and rest when the storm is raging.

I do not believe that Stephen was troubled when the stones were falling upon his body, putting him to death. When he prayed to the Father to forgive the people around him, I think he had peace of heart.

I don't think the great Apostle Paul was troubled when they brought him to the chopping block to chop off his head with a Roman sword. He, too, had peace of heart. So it must be for every child of God. Faith will give that peace!

Second, faith will give purpose to your life. When you have faith in God, there will be a purpose.

I am amazed at some folk. I get so many interesting letters. I had a long letter of ten pages on my desk this morning. Strangely, most ten-page letters I get are written by women, but this was from a young man twenty-three years old. He wrote, "This is a rather long letter, but I want you to read it." He told all about his troubles. He said, "I have no purpose for living. I am twenty-three. I believe I am saved. But I have lost all purpose for living completely!" He told me about his mother and father, about his church, about his pastor, about how disappointed he was in people. He had lost his purpose for life.

Wait a minute, my friend! You will lose the purpose, too, when you look at people. That's what that boy was doing. Rather, look up toward God and say, "God, I want to glorify Thee. I want to satisfy Your purpose in my life."

Faith will give a purpose to your life. Men need direction. I need direction! You need direction! Every one of us in the same way. And it is faith that will give that purpose.

THE VERSE THAT JUMPED FROM THE PAGE

Third, faith gives power to achieve. By faith we lay hold upon the power of the Holy Spirit.

Have you ever heard me quote, "Be filled with the Spirit?" It is one thing to say, "I know that's in the Bible, and I would like to have the fullness of the Holy Spirit." But somehow, you never lay hold upon it. You never achieve because there is no power to achieve. You are resting wholly and completely upon self.

I noticed an amazing thing several years ago. You folk will bear me witness to this. I sat on the sidelines for six months. Not because I wanted to, but because there was nothing else I could do. And in the strangest kind of way, God kept blessing this work more and more. The offerings were up to the top. Praise God! Every single portion of our missions - Camp Joy, Union Mission, World-Wide Faith Missions, everything - up on the very top! Tennessee Temple Schools - the very finest and best. The best enrollment in the Summer School we had ever had. The largest number of new students coming to Tennessee Temple we had ever had in all the school's history. Everything was moving! That just showed this little preacher something. It didn't depend so much on what I was doing; it depended on the working of the power of God through our lives. When we rest upon God's power, then we have power to achieve.

Consider what faith can do. Hold to the three words: peace, purpose and power.

III. CONSIDER HOW TO GET FAITH

First, faith comes by a Person - Jesus Christ. This brings us back to the Word of God and back to the unfailing One, the unchanging One - Jesus Christ, the same yesterday, today, and forever. Faith comes by a Person. O God, make us conscious of Your presence all the time.

The disciples (in John 20) were in an Upper Room. It was a strategic time, a time of fear. They were scared to death. The Bible says they were fearful. Behind closed doors, locked

THE VERSE THAT JUMPED FROM THE PAGE

doors, all of a sudden Jesus walked into their midst. "Then came Jesus, and stood in their midst." He will do the same for you and me.

Faith comes by a Person. I must practice feeling the presence of my blessed Lord all of the time - in sickness or in health; in darkness or in the sunshine.

Second, faith comes by a practice. What is a practice? The practice of believing. Faith comes by practice, by believing the Word of God, resting upon what God has said to us. If God says it, we believe it. This is what we have been doing in this church for forty years. We do this on tithing. We obey and God blesses. We do this on witnessing, on soul winning, in missions, and in every other way. We obey God. Skepticism is the Devil's way. He will try to make you doubt everything. But if you rest upon God, faith comes by practice, the practice of believing that if God says it, that is all we need.

Third, faith comes by a partnership, a partnership with our blessed Lord, with Christ. He is ready to guide us. We sing so often, "And He walks with me, and He talks with me." He said, ". . . Lo, I am with you alway, even unto the end of the world."

When we link our lives with the Son of God, we cannot fail. But there must be a linking of ourselves in partnership with our blessed Saviour. We must rest upon Him to get the job done. When we do that, then we can win others to Christ. We can be soul winners. God can then take our lives and use us.

Someone asked Dr. Lyman Beecher many, many years ago, "What is the greatest thing a man can do?" Beecher, a highly educated, fluent preacher, famous in his day, answered, "Well, being a theologian is a pretty big thing. Being a scientist is great, too. But the greatest thing a man can do is to introduce another to Jesus Christ." This is what we can do in partnership with our Saviour. We can introduce others to the Lord Jesus.

Look at your story again. First of all, Christ is saying,

THE VERSE THAT JUMPED FROM THE PAGE

"I am watching over you. I am with you in times of heartaches, sickness, distress, confusion; when your home is torn up; when your business is gone; when reverses come. I know your needs. So pray and seek My face."

Second, Christ is saying, "I have complete control over all things." I like that! "I who have complete control over the winds and the waves, have control over all other things." "And we know that all things work together for good to them that love God, to them who are the called according to his purpose."

Third, Christ is saying, "I am with you, fear not." His presence is enough. He will be with you every hour you come to Him.

Some sitting here this morning have gone through some hours of difficulty. You have wondered what to do. Maybe God can bring this single verse out of the Bible to speak to you. Or it might be the words of Jesus, "Peace be unto you." He may be exhorting all of us this morning, "Why are ye so fearful? How is it that you have no faith?" You are saying, "Lord, I claim Thy presence that you are with me all the time. I have faith in You. So I shall not faint or fail because of that faith."

A little boy became quite ill. The doctor told the father, "He will have to have an operation. You can tell your son." The father said to his boy, "Son, the doctor said you have to have an operation."

The boy said, "All right. But Daddy, I want one thing and that is for you to be with me all the time."

The father said, "Son, I will come to see you every day that you are in the hospital."

"Daddy, I didn't mean that. I want you with me all the time."

"Son, I don't think I can do that."

"Yes, Daddy. I have got to have you with me all the time."

"Son, if that's what you want, then that's what you will have."

THE VERSE THAT JUMPED FROM THE PAGE

The boy went to the hospital with his father. He had the operation. He was brought back to the room after about six hours. His father was sitting in the chair beside the bed. The little boy opened his eyes and saw his daddy, smiled, closed his eyes, and went back to sleep. A little later he opened his eyes again and looked up. There was his father sitting in the chair. He weakly said, "Daddy, this is wonderful!"

The father said, "Why son, what's so wonderful - being in a hospital and having an operation?"

"No - wonderful that you can be here by my side."

My dear friend, that story of the little boy is nothing compared with what we have through Jesus Christ. "Lo, I am with you alway."

You are not alone, my Christian friend. You are not alone when you have faith in Jesus Christ. You can rest upon Him and know He is with you in this hour, in every hour. We can trust our Saviour for all things. "Lo, I am with you alway, even unto the end of the earth."

What does He want us to do? He wants us to witness. He wants our nearness - and not for selfish purposes. He wants us to be near Him, not just so we can say, "I have peace because I am near Him," but because our lives can reach out to others.

The Great Commission has been given. In that we are told to go and be witnesses of Him in all places. This commission is from the Heavenly Father, from the Saviour. We must not fail Him. That pays off most of all.

My Christian friends here this morning, let me exhort you to get a sense of His nearness. Stand up against Satan and the wiles of the Devil, then you say, "God is mine, Christ is mine, Heaven is my home, and I fear not. I am in Him and He is mine." When you have that, then begin speaking to others about Jesus Christ. Witness for the Saviour and rejoice in the opportunity.

Not many of you know the name of Dr. Willard Jenkins.

THE VERSE THAT JUMPED FROM THE PAGE

Dr. Jenkins was a great pastor in Texas at one time. Once he was preaching in a two-week revival in North Carolina. One soul was saved, one little boy nine years old. And that was all.

After the meeting people went away saying, "Not much of a revival; only a little boy nine years old was saved." Dr. Jenkins thought the same thing.

Then when Dr. Jenkins was pastor of the First Baptist Church in Athens, Georgia, where the University of Georgia is located, one Sunday morning a young man came down the aisle and said, "Sir, I have come to join the church. I am saved. Sir, do you know me?"

Dr. Jenkins said, "No, I don't know you."

"I'm the one little boy who was saved in that revival up there in the country."

He joined the First Baptist Church in Athens and became a faithul member. He finished his work in the University of Georgia. He went on and got a Ph. D. degree. Rockefeller Center hired him for a job for awhile, then to another big job. Next, he became President of Mary Hardin-Baylor College at Belton, Texas. The president of it!

Dr. Jenkins said he watched that boy - one day a boy and now a man - a man of experience. One day he came to Dr. Jenkins and said, "Dr. Jenkins, I want to thank you for leading me to Christ when I was a boy nine years of age. That changed my whole life. That has given me peace and happiness and purpose for my life through all these days. Thank you for it."

The greatest thing you can do is to live for the Saviour, rest upon the promises of God and point someone else to the Lord Jesus Christ.

I was holding a revival meeting in the small town of Dumas, Texas, in a beautiful, new church. A young man came to me (he had been here at Tennessee Temple Schools) and said, "I want you to go to see my dad."

I said, "I am just here Monday and Tuesday, but I will go Tuesday afternoon."

THE VERSE THAT JUMPED FROM THE PAGE

On Tuesday afternoon we drove out in the country. Around Dumas, Texas, it is just flat, level ground. No trees, no bushes - nothing, just flat. We came to a humble home in the middle of a field. It was pouring down rain. We got out of the car and went inside. In a few moments I led the boy's father to the Lord, then his mother. After prayer, I went back to the church and preached that night. When I gave the invitation, the two of them came down the aisle. Both said, "We know we are saved. We were led to Jesus in the home by Brother Roberson."

My dear friend, that's worth everything! The greatest joy you can have is to win someone to the Saviour. All of it depends on our soul winning, our work, our witnessing, our nearness to the blessed Lord Jesus Christ.

Christian friend, let Him have His way with you.

But sinner friend, you need the Saviour. And you need Him now.

Chapter 12
The Wrap-Up On The Second Coming

And I heard a great voice out of heaven saying, Behold, the tabernacle of God is with men, and he will dwell with them, and they shall be his people, and God himself shall be with them, and be their God.
And he that sat upon the throne said, "Behold, I make all things new. And he said unto me, Write: for these words are true and faithful.
— Rev. 21: 3,5

Behold, I come quickly: blessed is he that keepeth the sayings of the prophecy of this book.
And, behold, I come quickly; and my reward is with me, to give every man according as his work shall be.
— Rev. 22: 7, 12

Years ago, I was pastor of the First Baptist Church of Greenbrier, Tennessee. I was there for a period of three years. I lived in the back of the church in a tiny room about eight feet wide and twelve feet long. A small monkey stove was used to heat in the wintertime, but it did not do much good. In the summertime I had plenty of heat in the back of the church building. It was quite a place. I carried water from my neighbor's well, which was some distance away, but I didn't object. For three solid years I lived in that place and enjoyed my ministry in that church. I am saying this just to

THE WRAP-UP ON THE SECOND COMING

let you know of the existence I had. It might have been a little bit lonely, but I made no complaint.

There were no telephones or televisions. I did have a very small radio set. It was very inadequate, but I got by.

During this three-year period I began to study my Bible. After having been in Louisville Seminary and then finishing my work at the University of Louisville, I studied the Word of God. I discovered something that I had missed on the second coming of Jesus Christ.

I recall when I first read with interest and understanding John 14:3 where Jesus said, "I will come again. . . " I had read it before and passed it by, except for a matter of comfort for those who were in sorrow.

I took my Bible and began marking in the New Testament every single verse that I thought referred to the second coming. I used two letters - "SC." I finished all the New Testament, then went back to the Old and began to re-read and search for all the verses on the second coming.

Watch very carefully! I had never owned a Scofield Bible. Back in my days you did not carry a Scofield Bible into the classroom. I thought it was poison, so I did not own one. I had never seen the little book *Jesus is Coming* by W.E.B. or any books by Dr. W. B. Riley, or Dr. H. A. Ironside, or any of the other men of the past who did such a marvelous job in preaching and teaching on the second coming.

One Sunday morning I stood before the audience and announced, "Today, I want to preach on John 14:3. This is my text: Jesus said, "I will come again." And I preached on the second coming of Jesus Christ.

A little later, after I had mentioned the second coming, a man came up to me and said, "Sir, I appreciate what you are saying. You must be a premillennialist." (I did not know anything about premillennialists, postmillennialists, or hardly anything else.)

I said, "Is that all right?"

"Well, that's good."

I said, "Well, I am for it then, whatever it is." That word was

THE WRAP-UP ON THE SECOND COMING

not used in the seminary, and amillennialism had not come into being as it is today.

What I am saying is this: whenever one takes the Word of God and studies it, he will come out believing the same thing every time. He will look for the return of Jesus Christ.

After I began speaking on the second coming of Jesus Christ, I found a friend in Springfield, Tennessee, W. R. Petagrew, pastor of the First Baptist Church. Later, he became a pastor in Louisville, Kentucky, at the Old Walnut Street Church. He was very highly educated and a very fine preacher. He believed in the second coming of Jesus Christ. He had made many notes on this, so he gave me a stack of mimeographed notes on the second coming. I began to read and study all he had to say in this matter.

From that, much of my ministry began. I knew that I was saved and that God had called me. But after I got hold of the great truth of the second coming, everything changed. My attitude changed, the atmosphere of the church changed, my attitude toward my work changed entirely. I began doing things in the light of the return of Jesus Christ.

Every person should have an interest in the second coming of Jesus. The lost man cares little about this. His heart has never been touched by the Spirit of God. He can know nothing about the second coming of Jesus Christ, so he turns away.

The mere professor of religion is not interested. I said "mere professor," not possessor. He may profess, belong to churches, but he has no interest. He may be a Methodist, Baptist, Episcopalian or Catholic, but if he knows not Jesus and does not possess salvation, then he has no interest in the second coming.

This afternoon I answered a letter from a young man from Rome, Italy. He had written,

> Brother Roberson, I am writing you to let you know that I have now been saved. I used to belong to your church, but I was never saved. My mother comes to your church now.

THE WRAP-UP ON THE SECOND COMING

> I went to see a friend in this city, a missionary supported by your church, and he led me to the Lord Jesus Christ. All the time I had been a professor but not a possessor. I belonged to the church, but that was all. I had no interest in anything. I was not saved. I lived for the Devil. But since the Lord has saved me, everything has changed completely. I want to come back to Chattanooga and Tennessee Temple Schools. I have got some friends from the Marines that I want to bring with me. They have an interest in this, too.

A mere professor is not interested in the coming of Jesus. Neither is the worldly Christian. Why? Because his mind and heart are absorbed with the things of this world.

With that as an introduction, let me quickly give an outline.

I. BEHOLD HE COMETH

Revelation 22:12 says, "Behold, I come quickly." One verse in every twenty in the New Testament refers to the return of our Lord Jesus. Every book of the Bible has some mention of the second coming with the exception of one of the minor prophets, as far as I know.

He is coming again. There is one second coming. The second coming has two stages: the rapture and the revelation. The rapture means the snatching away, the catching up into the air. This is beautiful. He is coming to receive us unto Himself. We are going to be in His presence.

In I Thessalonians 4:13-18 the apostle is speaking to the people about the coming of our Lord. "I would not have you to be ignorant, brethren, concerning them which are asleep. . . " Then he goes on to speak of the coming of Christ.

Look at this verse: "For the Lord himself shall descend from heaven with a shout, with the voice of the archangel, and with the trump of God: and the dead in Christ shall rise first" (I Thess. 4:16). Then, it goes on to state that the living shall be changed.

What is he doing? Giving the picture of the rapture,

THE WRAP-UP ON THE SECOND COMING

the snatching away. Dr. McGinley, the late Scottish preacher who has been with us quite a few times, said when he was once preaching on the second coming and about the dead in Christ rising first, a lady came up and asked, "Doctor, why do they rise first?" He replied, "I don't know except that they have farther to go."

The dead in Christ will rise first, the living will be changed and caught up into His presence. First the rapture, then the revelation.

There is one second coming. He is coming to receive us unto Himself. That is what we read in John 14:3, "I will come again, and receive you unto myself..."

First is the rapture, then the revelation. The revelation is pictured in many places, but I read one especially in Matthew 25:31,32:

> *When the Son of man shall come in his glory, and all the holy angels with him, then shall he sit upon the throne of his glory:*
> *And before him shall be gathered all nations: and he shall separate them one from another, as a shepherd divideth his sheep from the goats:*

The revelation of Christ: this is when He comes out of the air. When He comes (the first stage) at the rapture, we will be caught up to meet Him in the air. In the second portion, we will come with Him. He will come as King of kings and Lord of lords for the Battle of Armegeddon, the judgment of living nations, and the establishment of His thousand-year-reign upon the earth. All of this is going to take place at the end of the tribulation time.

When we are caught up in the air, two things transpire: first, the judgement seat of Christ; second, the marriage supper of the Lamb. After this (which is a full space of seven years, according to the Book of Revelation), we will come with Him in the revelation, as He comes out of the air, down

THE WRAP-UP ON THE SECOND COMING

upon this earth, and we will reign with our blessed Saviour. This is what is in the Scripture we have been studying tonight: "I come quickly" means that He might come at any moment. At any second of time the Lord Jesus might appear. When He comes, He comes first for us who are saved. We will be caught up in the air to meet Him. We will be with Him in the air. Then, we will come with Him out of the air, down to this atmosphere to reign with our Saviour upon the earth. Behold, He cometh!

II. BEHOLD HE REWARDETH

Look at Revelation 22:12:

And, behold, I come quickly; and my reward is with me, to give every man according as his work shall be."

Behold, He rewardeth! He is coming. "... my reward is with me, to give every man according as his work shall be." I mention three judgments.

<u>First, the judgment seat of Christ</u>. This is given to us in Romans 14:20, I Corinthians 3:12-15, and II Corinthians 5:10. This is all about the judgment seat of Christ.

For other foundation can no man lay than that is laid, which is Jesus Christ.
Now if any man build upon this foundation gold, silver, precious stones, wood, hay, stubble;
Every man's work shall be made manifest: for the day shall declare it, because it shall be revealed by fire; and the fire shall try every man's work of what sort it is.
If any man's work abide which he hath built thereupon, he shall receive a reward.
If any man's work shall be burned, he shall suffer loss: but he himself shall be saved; yet so

THE WRAP-UP ON THE SECOND COMING

as by fire.
                                      — I Cor. 3:11-15

These are some portions to make you think of the judgment seat of Christ.

My dear Christian friends, if you are saved, a child of God, and ready for Heaven and the coming of Jesus Christ, you are still going to stand before the judgment seat of Christ and give an account of yourself. Not of your salvation, but you are there to give an account of your works. Some will be saved and have rewards coming. Some will be saved and have no rewards. "If any man's work shall be burned, he shall suffer loss: but he himself shall be saved, yet so as by fire." Sometimes we say a person is saved, "by the skin of his teeth," but he is saved.

Don't come back to me and say, "Well, Brother Roberson, if I can just get into Heaven, that is all I ask for."

No, it is not. If you are a child of God, you will want to hear Him say, "Well done." If you are a child of God, you will want to receive a reward from His hand. Why? Because you were faithful. This reward is for the man, woman, young person who is found faithful in His service upon this earth. This is the judgment seat of Christ. Behold He rewardeth! He is coming and will reward His own. This is the first of the judgments.

<u>Second, the judgment of living nations.</u> When does this take place? At the end of the tribulation time. This takes place at the revelation of our blessèd Saviour, when He comes out of the air and down to this atmosphere. We'll be gathered before Him after the Battle of Armegeddon. Then all the nations of this world will be judged.

> *And before him shall be gathered all nations: and he shall separate them one from another, as a shepherd divideth his sheep from the goats: And he shall set the sheep on his right hand,*

THE WRAP-UP ON THE SECOND COMING

but the goats on the left.
— Matt. 25:32,33

This is the picture of the judgment of living nations at the coming of our Saviour, at the close of the tribulation period.

When Jesus comes, first will be the rapture when we are caught up to meet Him in the air. Second, the revelation when we will come out of the atmosphere, out of the air, down to this earth. When He comes, we will be caught in the air to meet Him. We will come before the judgment seat of Christ, the marriage supper of the Lamb, which is a blessed truth given to us in Revelation. When we return, we come this time with Him. He comes as the Judge. He comes as the King of kings. He is coming to reign upon the earth. There will be the judgment of living nations. They will be judged at the time of His coming.

The third judgment is the Great White Throne Judgment. This is given in Revelation 20:11-15, a portion that you know quite well.

> *And I saw a great white throne, and him that sat on it, from whose face the earth and the heaven fled away; and there was found no place for them.*
> *And I saw the dead, small and great, stand before God; and the books were opened: and another book was opened which is the book of life: and the dead were judged out of those things which were written in the books, according to their works.*
> *And whosoever was not found written in the book of life was cast into the lake of fire.*

This is the judgment of the lost dead, and it comes at the close of the thousand-year reign of Christ. This is another judgment. ". . . it is appointed unto men once to die, but after this the judgment." Men, death, and judgment is the

THE WRAP-UP ON THE SECOND COMING

truth given here.

You will have to decide where you want to stand. If Jesus comes tonight and receives us unto Himself, every child of God will be caught up and the Christians will stand at the judgment seat of Christ. If you have turned your back upon the Son of God, you are lost and you are here for the tribulation time of seven years. You are here for the other events that I have mentioned. If you die without Christ, you will come before the Great White Throne Judgment, which is a sentencing of those who have rejected the Saviour. This will determine the extent of your punishment in Hell on the basis of that judgment before the King.

There are three judgments I want you to see. He is coming again. The child of God should be careful and earnest in His work. Labor lovingly, labor willingly, labor unselfishly and labor faithfully for God's glory. He is coming again.

III. BEHOLD HE WARNETH

Look back at Revelation 22:7:

Behold, I come quickly: blessed is he that keepeth the sayings of the prophecy of this book.

Behold, He warneth. He is giving us a warning. Listen to this:

Watch therefore: for ye know not what hour your Lord doth come.
— Matt. 24:42

He is warning you to be ready for the coming of the blessed Saviour at any time.

<u>Christian, get ready</u>, for He is coming again. Look at your life. Are you ready to stand before the judgment seat? He said He would come. And He is warning you to get ready for His coming.

THE WRAP-UP ON THE SECOND COMING

We should look at ourselves daily and judge our lives, look at what we're doing, how we're working and know what we're doing.

Thomas Carlisle had a message to people about how to begin their days. He said folk would put on their suit or dress, shoes, and so forth, then look at their clothes and say, "Behold the clothes I'm wearing." That is the attitude many take. He said people did all these things for self. He said what they needed was to stop, look at their soul and say, "Lord, what about my soul? Behold my soul! I want to think now of my soul. Am I saved or lost? Where do I stand?"

Christian, watch therefore. Quit covering your sins, your sins of omission, your sins of commission. Quit alibiing for the wrong things in your life. You're going to stand before the judgment seat and give an account of yourself to God.

If you have no passion for souls, then confess it. If you have no concern for others, confess it. You may be saved, but saved yet so as by fire, saved without a reward coming to you, because your own heart is not stirred for the things of God. O God, help us to be stirred! Lord, help me be my best for Christ.

An outstanding Christian was talking to someone out of China about communism. When he was asked the question, "Why did the Chinese people turn their backs upon Christianity and turn to communism?" the Chinese gave this answer: "They have done so because communism has a philosophy, a program, a passion."

Are you listening? We have a philosophy written down in the Word of God for us. We have a program given to us by the Saviour, "Go ye into all the world, and preach the gospel. . . " We miss it where they have been succeeding, and that is the passion. The communists have a passion for what they are doing. They'll die for that cause. They stand for what they think is right, and would die in their tracks for it.

With Christians it is a rather lackadaisical, half-hearted,

THE WRAP-UP ON THE SECOND COMING

indifference. It doesn't get down to the soul of the individual. The child of God is so easily discouraged, so easily turned away.

The early Christians had a passion. That's why they succeeded in the first century in such a mighty way. Every church that has ever succeeded in history has had a passion for souls, a passion for doing things. Not simply a cold, calculated, methodical way of operation, but a passion that comes from God, a passion that will cause us to launch out in the deep and do the job God wants done.

If God has blessed here, it is because of a passion. Not because I bring in the best preachers, not because of our staff, but because we have taken the Word of God with complete and utter faith, and at the same time, we try to have a passion for the souls of men. We could stop all the missionaries, we could put up the most beautiful building this country has ever seen. We can stop operating all the chapels, or stop spending all the money we're spending, or stop building Sunday school buildings and school buildings, and everything else we are trying to do. But if we did so, we would be dead. The whole thing centers on passion for souls.

Child of God, ask God to give you a passion for the souls of others.

Backslider, get ready. He is coming again. Backslider, you may know Jesus as your Saviour and yet be in a backslidden condition. You're away from God, your heart is cold. If you're in a backslidden condition, it's hard to differentiate between the one we call "Christian" and the backslider. We know that some who are saved are yet far from God.

Somebody calls this the "Holiday Inn Age." Why? Because people are running hither and yon, searching, but finding nothing to satisfy their souls.

Oh, the great need to settle down. If you're a Christian living on the mere fringe of things, ask God to help you. Ask Him to put you where you can serve Him with all your heart, with everything you have.

THE WRAP-UP ON THE SECOND COMING

Backslider, away from God, cold in heart, tonight turn from your sin and claim the promise of I John 1:9. Renounce your indifference. Take your place in the service of Jesus Christ.

If you have been sitting on the fringes, on the edge of things, then ask God to stir your heart and help you to be right with Him. You don't want to be counted a backslider, away from God, cold and sinful in heart.

O God, help us to see ourselves as we are.

Look, friends, don't jump on somebody else. Husband, don't criticize your wife if she is a Christian. Wife, don't say, "My husband says he's a Christian, but look at him!" Don't criticize your neighbor. Look at yourself, then say, "O God, help me to be what you want me to be; help me to be ready for Your coming."

Henry B. Thoreau, a name known to all educators, said, "I have traveled much in Concord." This man wrote many mighty things. He got it all from one place - from a study of the situation in the place where he lived.

Dear friend, look at yourself tonight where you are, then ask God to help you be your best for your Christ. He is coming again. We shall see Him face to face. I want to have done my best for the blessed Saviour when He comes.

<u>Sinner, get ready</u>. Without the Lord Jesus Christ you're lost and undone. There is no hope without the Saviour. To have Him, you must repent of your sin and receive Him as your Saviour as simply as a child.

How are people saved? By simple faith. How are they saved? By repentance and faith. You cannot separate the two: repentance and faith - repentance toward God, and faith in our Lord Jesus Christ. Tonight you can be saved by His faith.

Tonight, I'm appealing to the theme of the second coming of Jesus Christ. This might be controversial to some. You might try to argue about the second coming and what it is. But, I want you to see that Christ is coming and that you

THE WRAP-UP ON THE SECOND COMING

need Jesus as Saviour. You need to be ready for His coming. You need to know that He is your Lord and Master so that you can stand before Him unashamed at His coming.

The second coming of Jesus calls for four things.

<u>First, it calls for awareness</u>. It calls for awareness of the conditions around us: the hardness of men's hearts, the increase of sin, the weakness of our churches.

<u>Second, it calls for alertness</u>. It calls for the child of God to be wide awake and alert in the things of Christ, ready to serve God with all your heart. The Bible says,

> *The night is far spent, the day is at hand: let us therefore cast off the works of darkness, and let us put on the armour of light.*
>
> *Let us walk honestly, as in the day: not in rioting and drunkenness, not in chambering and wantoness, not in strife and envying.*
>
> *But put ye on the Lord Jesus Christ, and make not provision for the flesh, to fulfill the lusts thereof.*
>
> — Rom. 13:12-14

Yes, God is calling us to be alert. It is so very, very important that we be alert and ready, that we be conscious of the world around us. We must be alert to the needs of this hour, seeking to get out the Gospel to as many as we possibly can.

A man had visited one of the beautiful art galleries where many lovely things were placed. He saw something strange. One fellow brought his lunch and sat in one corner and ate. He seemed to have no interest at all in art. Another couple came in and found a little nook in the art gallery where they could sit and talk. Others came inside, because it was raining outside. Few, it seemed, had any interest at all in art.

I'm afraid that is the picture of Christians today. No concern, no awareness, no alertness to the things of God. They all pass it by. It doesn't matter at all to them. They

THE WRAP-UP ON THE SECOND COMING

are unconcerned, untroubled about it.

Third, there must be readiness. Prepare for His coming. Be ready to meet Him when He comes. There should be one great thought in our minds, and that is that we be ready when Jesus appears, that we might stand before our blessed Saviour unashamed.

It is my business to live victoriously. It is my business to grow in grace, and to keep on growing as long as I live. There is no plateau, no stopping, no going back. Some Christians grow for a while, then stop. Some of them turn back and fall away. That is not for the child of God. We are to go forward, on and on, up and up, as long as we live, serving and growing in grace, and getting ready for His coming.

Fourth, it calls for unselfishness.

"Others Lord, yes others,
let this my motto be.
Help me to live for others,
that I might live like thee."

This is my message on the second coming of the Lord Jesus Christ and of being unselfish with what you have to share with others. Let people know that you're saved. Let them know that you love God. Let them know that you love Jesus. Let them know you are looking for His return. Let them know you want to serve Him and want to share what you have with them.

When I go back to Louisville, Kentucky to visit, I think of my early days. I went to the University of Louisville, but before that to Louisville High School. I took a two-year business course, including typing, bookkeeping, and other courses. I finished and got my diploma when I was fourteen. I went back to high school for four more years.

But, I thought: *What if somehow, something had gotten hold of my life and caused me to turn away from the thing God had called me to do?*

Dear friends, what an awful waste! God called me for a special task. If I had been selfish, looking for money and

THE WRAP-UP ON THE SECOND COMING

gain for myself, I would have lost all the joy and blessings God has given me through this work here.

God has something for you. Is your desire to be unselfish? Unselfishly, I want to share what I have with others, that others might hear and know of Jesus, the blessed Saviour.

Yes, Revelation says, "Surely I come quickly." Back in John 1:29 we read, "Behold the Lamb of God, which taketh away the sin of the world."

Chapter 13
Life Is A Lollipop

And he spake a parable unto them, saying, The ground of a certain rich man brought forth plentifully:
And he thought within himself, saying, What shall I do, because I have no room where to bestow my fruits?
And he said, This will I do: I will pull down my barns, and build greater; and there will I bestow all my fruits and my goods.
And I will say to my soul, Soul thou hast much goods laid up for many years; take thine ease, eat drink, and be merry.
But God said unto him, Thou fool, this night thy soul shall be required of thee: then whose shall those things be, which thou hast provided?
So is he that layeth up treasure for himself, and is not rich toward God.
— Luke 12:16-21

But this I say, brethren, the time is short: it remaineth, that both they that have wives be as though they had none;
And they that weep, as though they wept not; and they that rejoice, as though they rejoiced not; and they that buy, as though they possessed not;
And they that use this world, as not abusing it: for the fashion of this world passeth away.
— I Cor. 7:29-31

LIFE IS A LOLLIPOP

About twelve months ago, on January 13, I sat on a cold bench on a chilly Sunday morning near the empty tomb of the Lord Jesus in Jerusalem listening to a speaker for the early morning service. He was not a Baptist, but of some other denomination. He said this: "Life is a lollipop - eighty or ninety years - then you are no more."

The exact quotation did not have a very fitting symbol, it seemed to me, with the tomb so nearby and the fact of the resurrected Saviour. But I did remember what he had said so that I could use it as a theme for my thinking in a service such as this.

Just before me and a few feet away, was the hill called Calvary. I could see it from where I was seated, right near the tomb.

Before me, also, was Joseph's tomb, where the body of Jesus was placed after His crucifixion. It was in that tomb that He remained until a glorious Sunday morning when He arose from the dead. The angel of the Lord rolled back the stone from the door and sat upon it. The angel said to the women who came to the tomb, "Fear not ye: for I know that ye seek Jesus, which was crucified. He is not here: for he is risen" (Matt. 28:5,6).

In light of the speaker's statement, in light of our Lord Jesus who conquered death and the grave and rose again, I want you to look at life tonight and think about it for awhile.

I. THE SWEETNESS OF LIFE

Life is made sweet by three very simple things.

<u>First, by knowing Christ</u>. Knowing Christ changes everything. Knowing Christ changes everybody. When a man gets saved, everything around him changes. For example, when a man gets saved, he sees people in one of two ways - saved or lost. Before, he sees them differently, but after he gets converted, he sees them another way.

Christ's coming into the heart makes man a new creature (II Cor. 5:17). Knowing Christ brings the Holy Spirit into

LIFE IS A LOLLIPOP

your life. He abides with you. Knowing Christ brings you into the family of God. Knowing Christ opens the Book to you. Knowing Christ gives usefulness to life. Knowing Christ makes one ready for the coming of Christ. Knowing Christ guarantees Heaven for us. Knowing Christ gives us eternal life. Knowing Christ gives us the privilege of prayer.

What else could we say? Many, many things would follow in this matter of simply knowing Christ. Life is made sweet by knowing Him.

<u>Second, knowing His will</u>. God has a will for every single person and He wants you to know His will. If we know His will, good. If we have turned away from His will, or refuse to know His will, then we suffer. Life is unsteady until His will is known. Life will be uncertain until you can say, "This I know is the will of God for my life."

Life is made sweet by knowing His will. God has a will for your life and He knows what it is. It is your business to find it. God is not playing hide-and-seek. He is not trying to keep anything from you. He wants you to know His will and will help you to know it. He is trying to help you. But, somehow, you have so enshrouded yourself with the things of this world that you are not seeing, not understanding. Yes, God has a will for you and He wants you to know His will.

<u>Third, by doing His will</u>. Some people know His will but do not do it.

I'll always recall, always be repeating the story of my call to the ministry. As I stood by the crowd of young men at the church in Cedar Creek, in Louisville, a Mr. W. A. Lucky came by, shook my hand, and said, "I'm glad that you've been called to preach." Then he bent over and whispered in my ear: "Young man, when I was your age, God called me to preach, but I turned away. I refused. I went into business and made money. I got married and had a family. I'm now up in years. I've never preached a single sermon, though God called me. Every time I pray, I'm reminded that I'm out of

LIFE IS A LOLLIPOP

the will of God."

How pitiful that is! Yet, many folk are like that. They know His will, they know what God wants, yet refuse to do it.

In Greensboro, North Carolina, a man said to me, "I know I've been called to preach. I retire from my business when I'm 65, which I am now approaching. I've been called to preach, but I've never yet preached a single sermon. I've written out a lot of them, but never preached one. Perhaps someday, a little later, when I retire, I'll get to it."

I doubt that he ever will. He is a miserable, unhappy man. Life is made sweet by doing the will of God.

How blessed to know Him! How blessed to know His will! How blessed to do His will!

Yes, Christ loves us. God loves us. Christ died for us on Calvary, and we are saved by simple faith in Him. The first thing is the sweetness of life. I could not begin any other place than to talk about the sweetness of life found in Jesus Christ, the blessed Saviour.

I heard about a colonel from the Air Force who was giving a speech to a business meeting of men. He said something like this: "Major So and So was lost in flight. We began calling for help. After awhile hundreds of planes were searching for the colonel. We put out 10,000 lights in different places." (I don't understand their techniques nor language, but that's the way he said it.) He kept on talking. "We found the Major, but it cost almost ten million dollars to do it. Planes by the hundred were flashing through the sky searching for him."

Now that is a whole lot of money; but it cost God His life to save my soul. Jesus died upon the cross for me and for you. Then when I think of my salvation, I think that I'm saved by the great sacrifice of the Son of God and by my acceptance of Him to cleanse my soul and to make me God's child.

LIFE IS A LOLLIPOP

II. THE BITTERNESS OF LIFE

All days are not fair. We must face it as we think about life. The minister at the tomb said, "Life is a lollipop - eighty or ninety years - then that's all." We have to face the fact of the bitterness of life.

All associations are not pleasant. All work is not successful. We must face the many things that come to us as children of God.

First, the sweetness of life; second, the bitterness of life.

What do we face? Persecution is one thing. "Yea, and all that will live godly in Christ Jesus shall suffer persecution" (II Tim. 3:12).

Discouragement is another. We get worried with our discouragements - discouragement because of failure, discouragement because of adversity, people against us in the work we do. But discouragement is a part of life.

Again, sorrow will come to all of us - the passing of a loved one.

I mentioned twenty-eight deceased bodies in one single funeral home in this city. I'm sure others are also full. This is a tragic hour when many are going out from us by death. But death for the child of God is just the knock that opens the door of life. When one knows Jesus Christ as Saviour, he enters at once into the presence of God. Sorrow will come to us all.

Affliction comes, too, affliction of body. A man is in the hospital now, one who helped me in the baptismal work for some twenty-five years. For more than twenty-five years Brother Huber would climb the steps and help me change clothes every Sunday morning, every Sunday night, and every Wednesday night, missing only a few services in these many years. I thought this man would just help me on and on. Now, today, he lies helpless in St. Barnabas Hospital, a rest home. He cannot speak, talk, nor move.

Oh, affliction can come to each one of us. We must face the bitterness of life. Some will come because of the sorrows

LIFE IS A LOLLIPOP

and afflictions of life.

I was reading again this week of George Matheson, the fine preacher of Scotland. He was just a young man when he went to the doctor for an eye examination. The doctor said, "Mr. Matheson, in just a few month's time you will be blind."

George Matheson was engaged to a young lady. He loved her very dearly. The date had been set for the marriage. He went to tell her: "I've been to the doctor. After he examined my eyes, he said that I'll be blind in a short time. Now I want to release you from your promise to me. Surely you wouldn't want to marry a blind man and have to lead him around throughout life. So we'll break the engagement."

To his surprise, she accepted his offer. "All right, we'll terminate the engagement now. You go your way, and I'll go mine."

George Matheson came away with a broken heart. Oh, but this man with a poetic mind became a mighty preacher. A short time after the broken engagement he put into words the song,

> O love that wilt not let me go,
> I rest my weary soul in Thee;
> I give Thee back the life I owe,
> That in Thine ocean depths its flow
> May richer, fuller be.

Back in 1928, in my first year of college at Russellville, Kentucky, that song had been voted the most popular gospel song (or hymn) in the world by one certain denomination. They read it, they sang it, they talked about it.

George Matheson had an affliction. He had a problem. Here came bitterness of life, the loss of a dear one. Friend, this can happen to any of us.

How do we bear these experiences? How should we bear them? Certainly God can make them sweet if we bear them in the right way. "And we know that all things work together for good to them that love God, to them who are the called according to his purpose."

LIFE IS A LOLLIPOP

I want you to see the bitterness of life. Hold to that thought.

III. THE BREVITY OF LIFE

For what is your life? It is even a vapour, that appeareth for a little time, and then vanisheth away.
— James 4:14

The days of our years are threescore years and ten; and if by reason of strength they be fourscore years, yet is their strength labour and sorrow; for it is soon cut off, and we fly away.
— Ps. 90:10

"Life is a lollipop. It's soon gone - eighty, ninety years."

The Bible says, "threescore years and ten," and if life is longer, there will still be more labor and sorrow.

Sweet, brief and troubled is the lesson life is trying to give us. The brevity of life.

Some are reckless with life. Are you listening? Some do not appreciate the gift of life. They are reckless in the use of life. They are throwing away their days. Oh, let God speak to you. Be not reckless with your life.

Nations are reckless with life. Through the centuries, history books tell us how thousands and thousands have been killed. Lives are lost. Some are reckless.

Some are foolishly cautious about life, so cautious that they do nothing. They just stand still. Yet God says to launch out into the deep, to go and do what He wants done, to go and obey. But many refuse. They stand back and refuse to move out by faith.

Some are forgetful of the power of a single life. Your life has power for good or for evil. This you must face. God says, "For none of us liveth to himself, and no man dieth to himself." Oh, the power of one life for Christ or for

LIFE IS A LOLLIPOP

Satan! Yes, somehow, we forget the brevity of life, the uncertainty of these days.

How should we consider our lives? Certainly, we ought to consider them as God-given. Some of you are not doing that, and you know it. I'm speaking to you now. Some of you are not considering your life as God-given. You are not doing what He wants you to do. You are not using your life to please God. Listen to Job 12:10: "In whose hand is the soul of every living thing, and the breath of all mankind." Your life is God-given.

These lives of ours are targets for the Devil's tricks. No one is exempt. The Devil is always fighting. He goes about "as a roaring lion, seeking whom he may devour." The Devil never, never stops. You are never out of his range. You are always where the Devil can tempt you and where he can work. My dear friend, are you by your faith in God and by your stickability to the Word of God, able to resist the Devil? Turn from him? Cast him aside? Get rid of his temptations? Remember, he is out for your downfall.

How do we view life? As capable of bringing much blessing to others, to bless others around us? I am conscious, as I give the message tonight, that this is the last Sunday in this year. This year is about over. In a few hours we will be celebrating the coming in of the new year. Have you used this past year in the right way? Have you given your life to God? Have you tried to bring blessings to others? Or, are you a stumblingblock, causing sorrow and tears? What are you doing? Think about how you used your life in the past twelve months. Can you improve it? A new year is about on us. If God spares us, we shall see it, too, through in twelve months. But what are you doing <u>now</u>? Are you using your life now to bring blessings to others? You have the power and capability to bless those around you. Yes, everyone can do that. The timid little mother can. The quiet working father, who has nothing to say publicly, can. The man in the school administration can. The man in the business world can.

LIFE IS A LOLLIPOP

No matter who you are, you can be a blessing. There is something each of us can do. So help others in the brevity of these days, in the use of your time. Use your life to glorify God.

What a beautiful story is given about the great singer, Jenny Lind. This incident came to me this past week.

She sang in Washington, D.C., almost one hundred years ago. Later, she dropped out of public view and took a different line for life. But back in Washington she gave a final concert in the big city auditorium. Great crowds came, packing every portion of the building. The President of the United States was there. So were the cabinet members. The senators and representatives were present. Officials from the army and navy were there. Diplomats were there to hear her. It was an august body who had gathered to listen to Jenny Lind sing on that night.

As Jenny Lind sang, the people applauded. How blessed they were by this wonderful singer whose life had been given over to God. Christ had meant so much to her. She had a tremendous testimony for the Saviour.

She came to her farewell number. As she was about to sing, she looked up in the balcony, and saw a man whom she recognized. The man was John Howard Payne. She changed the song and began to sing his song, "Home, Sweet Home."

>   Be it ever so humble,
> there's no place like home.
> Home! home! sweet home,
> There's no place like home,
> There's no place like home!

As Jenny Lind sang, she looked up toward the lonely, humble man in the balcony. His heart had been broken by a number of incidents, and this song came out of the many heartbreaks of his own life.

Soon tears were flowing. The President, cabinet members, senators and others were weeping.

People finally stood to their feet to applaud this great

LIFE IS A LOLLIPOP

singer and the song. Soon it was whispered, "John Howard Payne is here . . . John Howard Payne is here." Jenny Lind had recognized the great man and wanted to bring a little joy to his heart. She was singing his song because she wanted to bring a bit of joy to another. She did just that - and to many other hearts that evening.

Oh, the brevity of life! Use it wisely !

IV. THE JOY OF LIFE IN HIM

We could easily spend much time discussing the emptiness of life. I've seen the empty faces of the lost all over this country. I've seen them in Japan. I've seen them in Israel. I've seen them in the islands of the sea where I have visited. I watch people, and my heart goes out to those who are lost.

Oh, how long we could talk tonight about the emptiness of life! How empty is the heart and life of those without Jesus Christ! But now I speak about the joy of life in Him.

<u>There is the joy of living for Him</u>. People say it is too hard these days to live for God. There are too many temptations, too much sin, too many things to distract us. So many complain that it is impossible. Shame on you! You can live for God no matter what the circumstances are.

Stand for your faith! Stand for your God! Stand for your convictions! Rest upon Him! Live for Him daily. There is a joy in living for Him, a joy in letting others know that you are on the Lord's side.

<u>There is the joy of working for Him</u>. That is a joy. Work, for the night is coming. Now is the hour given us when we can work. Next to salvation, the greatest thing we can do is enjoy what God gives us to do.

A few hours ago I was speaking to our evangelists in one of our special meetings. I told them a story that I had just read, the story of Stanley Stine. He was blind. He was helpless. And he had leprosy. He was put in the leprosy hospital in Carville, Louisiana. His body had wasted away until he was helpless. Then he got to thinking: *What can I do with what*

LIFE IS A LOLLIPOP

I have left? He still had his mind. He could still think. He still had his brain. *There is something I can do. I'll write a book.*

So Stanley Stine went to the library found a book, then started back across the grounds to his room. A doctor met him and asked, "Stanley, where have you been?"

"I've been to the library."

"What have you got?"

"I've got a book right here in my hand."

"Well, what are you doing with a book? You can't read. You're blind."

"I know. But I'll get somebody to read it to me."

"What kind of book is it?"

"It's a book that tells me how to be a writer. I'm going to use my mind, my brain, to write something to help other people, if I can."

The doctor said, "You can't do that, Stanley. You're helpless, you're blind. You can't be a writer."

"You watch me," Stanley replied.

He found someone to read it to him. He began learning what he could from what he heard. Then he began dictating a book.

After awhile the book was finished. It was entitled, *Not Alone Anymore* - a testimony of his own heart. It became very popular in sales.

They say now one can go to Carville, Louisiana and find a man at certain hours walking around the campus with a transistor radio and dictaphone over his arm. He will dictate, and he will ask others to talk to him. He records what they say and listens back to it again and again. Writing all of the time, using the life he has.

What can I do with the life God has given me? What can I do with the time I have left? What can you do with yours? Do something! It may be the choir. It may be the orchestra. It may be to be an usher. Or to teach in the Sunday school. Or to work with young people. Whatever it may be, give yourself to God. Oh, the joy of working for Him, doing

LIFE IS A LOLLIPOP

something for Him in this hour!

How many people waste their time! They know not what to do, so they refuse to do anything. Volunteer your life to God and say, "O God, here it is. Take and use it for Thy glory. I give it unto Thee." There is a joy in working for Jesus Christ.

If you enjoy just sitting on the sidelines and doing nothing, just folding your hands, you have nothing inside, neither in your heart nor in your brain. The child of God with anything moving will want God to use him, will want to be used in the service of Christ.

There is the joy of working. I pray tonight that you will determine that this coming year you will find a place of opportunity, that you will enter into soul winning and witnessing, into the work of the Sunday school and the Baptist training union. In some way, serve God. Use your life in the best way.

There is the joy of waiting for Him, the joy of looking for His return. We don't know when Jesus is coming. I'm not trying to set dates. But He instructed us: "Watch therefore: for ye know not what hour your Lord doth come." I don't know when His coming will be, but I'm looking for His return.

The Apostle Paul never tired of looking for the return of Jesus Christ. He was always searching, looking. He was ready for the moment when the Son of God would come and receive him unto Himself. So should we be.

It may be this year, next year, ten years from now, or fifty - I know not when, but I know there is a joy in waiting! I know there is a joy in believing this Book. It says I'm going to see Him face to face. It says I'm going to be in His presence. And I believe this Book. That one day we shall see Him is our joy.

Joy! Life! Call it what you will, but this is a blessed life that God has given us. There may be bitterness. There may be disappointments. But in all of that, there is still a sweetness

LIFE IS A LOLLIPOP

about life. There is the joy in living for Jesus Christ because we belong to Him. We who have been saved by the grace of God and are in the family of God have a place of service and something to do for Him.

Tonight, think of it: the sweetness of life, the bitterness of life. Yet, the bitterness can be turned to sweetness. The brevity of life. How short are these days that we have! Just a little while and we're gone. Just a brief time and it is all over.

Will you say, "O God, take my life and use it for Thy glory for the days to come. I want to be fully surrendered to Thee"?

A great story is told about Dr. Ray Petty, successor to Dr. Conwell at the famous Baptist Temple in Philadelphia. Dr. Petty was a very fine, fundamental preacher. He suffered with heart trouble. He was in the hospital often. It came a time when he was seriously ill. He was placed in the hospital. His wife stood by. The doctor was there and the nurses. Friends were nearby.

Dr. Ray Petty turned to the doctor and said, "Doctor, tell me, am I going to go?"

The doctor tried to control his voice as he said, "Yes, Ray, it's your time to go."

Dr. Petty reached over, took the hand of his wife, then reached over and got the hand of his doctor, then he began to pray like this: "O God, bless them. O God, help them now to look to Thee, to have faith in Thee; help them dry their tears away."

He kept on praying fervently for a long time. When he finished, he dropped their hands, then raised his two in the air and said something like this: "The records are all in. I'll soon be Home with Mother, my brother, and with my Lord. When I go through, I'm going to walk straight up to the gates and salute My Lord and Master and tell Him I'm ready for the next task He has for me to do."

I like that! Heaven is going to be a place where we are kept busy. Heaven! Let us busy ourselves serving God here, living for Him now, for one day we shall step into His presence.

LIFE IS A LOLLIPOP

What joy there is in working and in waiting for Him!

Chapter 14
This Bus Stops At Calvary

And when they were come unto a place called Golgotha, that is to say, a place of a skull,

They gave him vinegar to drink mingled with gall: and when he had tasted thereof, he would not drink.

And they crucified him, and parted his garments, casting lots: that it might be fulfilled which was spoken by the prophet, They parted my garments among them, and upon my vesture did they cast lots.

And sitting down they watched them there;

And set up over his head his accusation written, THIS IS JESUS THE KING OF THE JEWS.

Then were there two thieves crucified with him, one on the right hand, and another on the left.
— Matt. 27:33-38

The most famous bus stop in the world is at Calvary, or Golgotha, "a place of a Skull." Standing a few feet away, it resembles a skull, with the indentations of the eyes and mouth.

This is the place where Jesus died for the sins of the world.

This is where Christ shed His blood that others might be saved.

This is the place where Jesus fulfilled the Old Testament prophesies regarding His death.

As you stand in the garden where the tomb is located, just

THIS BUS STOPS AT CALVARY

a few feet away is the hill called Calvary, not a high hill, just a rocky knoll, actually, as we think in this country. On the top of this today is a cemetery, placed there in recent years. Today one cannot go to the top, except by some special dispensation.

At the foot of the hill of Calvary is a bus stop. The buses come and go rapidly, pulling in and pulling out. The average bus they use on the streets and for tours in Palestine today are $85,000 Mercedes Benz, located at the very foot of Calvary.

The hill called Calvary or Golgotha, and the bus station right at the foot. You see people busily getting on and getting off. The drivers and the riders seem oblivious to the fact that they are in the proximity of the most famous spot in the world - the place where Jesus died, the place where He rose from the dead.

When I looked upon that scene - the hill called Calvary or Golgotha, and the bus stop down below - these thoughts kept pressing upon my mind:

I. THE WORLD TRIES TO IGNORE CALVARY

Man tries to ignore Calvary. Some denominations call Calvary "a bloody religion," and take the songs about the blood out of the hymnbooks.

Governments try to ignore Calvary. This is true of Russia and her atheism, of America and her secularism.

Education tries to ignore Calvary. Bible reading and prayer have been taken out of our schools. There is a laughing attitude toward the message of the cross. It is denounced on every hand. The world tries to ignore Calvary.

II. THE WORLD MUST STOP AT CALVARY

Christ cannot be ignored. "Oh," you say, "but they do ignore Him." No. He can't be ignored. Jesus said, "He that hath the Son hath life; and he that hath not the Son of God hath not life." There is no way to ignore Jesus Christ. If you

THIS BUS STOPS AT CALVARY

turn your back on Him you have not ignored Him but rejected Him and you are lost. If you refuse Him, if you laugh at Him, if you turn away, you have not ignored Him but doomed your own soul.

According to the Bible, man is lost or saved, depending upon what he does with Jesus Christ. It matters not what he thinks; it matters not how he has been reared; it matters not about his church; it matters not about his nationality: all that counts is whether or not he knows Jesus Christ. I say, the world must stop at Calvary.

People try to ignore it. The buses come in; the buses go out; people walk; people go. But they can't change the fact that "He that believeth on him is not condemned: but he that believeth not is condemned already" (John 3:18), and "He that hath the Son hath life; and he that hath not the Son of God hath not life" (I John 5:12). There is no escape. One must face Calvary. There are no exceptions. No matter who you are, you have to face it.

You say, "I don't want to." You don't have to want to, but you have to anyway. You are either for Him or against Him, said our Lord Jesus Christ Himself. Accept the sacrifice of Calvary and you are saved. Reject the sacrifice of Calvary and you are lost. The world must stop at Calvary.

III. THE WORLD MUST BOW AT CALVARY

And being found in fashion as a man, he humbled himself, and became obedient unto death, even the death of the cross.

Wherefore God also hath highly exalted him, and given him a name which is above every name:

That at the name of Jesus every knee should bow, of things in heaven, and things in earth, and things under the earth;

And that every tongue should confess that Jesus Christ is Lord, to the glory of God the Father.
— Phil. 2:8-11

THIS BUS STOPS AT CALVARY

Every knee must bow - the saved and the lost. The lost will reject Him and turn away, but they will bow nevertheless one day before the Son of God. At the judgment, there will be a bowing. All saved will be with Him, but all the lost must bow before Him at this time.

The world must bow at Calvary. They can reject Him, ignore Him, turn away from Him, but they must one day bow. They can laugh at Him, deride the second coming, ridicule the Word of God; they can ignore salvation by grace through faith in Jesus Christ, but that doesn't change the fact that the world must bow - saved or lost - at Calvary.

IV. THE WORLD NEEDS CALVARY

The world is lost. ". . . the soul that sinneth, it shall die" (Ezek. 18:4). We have all sinned and come short of the glory of God. Man is "dead in trespasses and sins" (Eph. 2:1). Man is dead, he is helpless, he is hopeless.

Christ, the one Mediator, is man's only hope. "For there is one God, and one mediator between God and men, the man Christ Jesus" (I Tim. 2:5). You see, that changes the picture. One will say, "Well, I believe this way;" others, "I believe this way." It doesn't matter: you have to come before the Lord Jesus Christ and see Him. He is the One you need. The world needs Calvary. Multitudes may drive by, they may rush by, they may say, "I'm too busy for Him," but that doesn't change it. They can say, "I was brought up a different way," but that doesn't change it either. It has to be based on Jesus Christ. A man is saved or lost by what he does with the blessed Saviour.

Someone said, "We have the glare of the world so much in our eyes today." We see the world around us; all the processes of this present day and time - educational, governmental, social - everything is rushing in upon us. But we need to get the glare of the world out so we can see Jesus with clarity. We need to see His power to save.

Somebody tells about the picture of Holman's Head of

THIS BUS STOPS AT CALVARY

Christ being painted and placed in London. People were allowed to come and see it. They were taken through an almost completely dark hallway. There was a little bit of gray light shining inside the hallway.

They stepped from the hall into a room that was totally dark, so dark you couldn't see your hand before you. They were told, "You must stand here until the glare of the world is gone, then, you can step in to see Holman's Head of Christ."

They stood there in total darkness, and finally were led into another room to see this magnificent picture. Now they could see the face of Jesus in all its beauty as painted by the artist.

The world needs Calvary. We have to get aside from this world to see Jesus. Oh, the world needs Him.

The bus stops at Calvary. People stop, but do they stop to think? Do they stop to recognize the Lord Jesus and His power to save? Have they received Him? Or, have they turned away from Him? Have they rejected the blessed Son of God? What have they done with the Holy One, the Lord Jesus Christ?

My friend, what have you done with Him? Have you accepted Him? Do you honor Him in your life? Are you living for Him? Are you testifying for Him? Are you showing forth Jesus in your life day by day? Or, do you reject Him and turn away from His side? What have you done with the blessed Son of God?

May the world stop and receive Him and say, "Yes, this is Christ. This is the Holy One of God. And I have come to receive Him as my blessed Saviour."

Chapter 15
Cure for Excusitis

Then said he unto him, A certain man made a great supper, and bade many:

And sent his servant at supper time to say to them that were bidden, Come; for all things are now ready.

And they all with one consent began to make excuse. The first said unto him, I have bought a piece of ground, and I must needs go and see it: I pray thee have me excused.

And another said, I have bought five yoke of oxen, and I go to prove them: I pray thee have me excused.

And another said, I have married a wife, and therefore I cannot come.

So that servant came, and shewed his lord these things. Then the master of the house being angry said to his servant, Go out quickly into the streets and lanes of the city, and bring in hither the poor, and the maimed, and the halt, and the blind.

And the servant said, LORD, it is done as thou hast commanded, and yet there is room.

And the lord said unto the servant, Go out into the highways and hedges, and compel them to come in, that my house may be filled.

For I say unto you, That none of those men which were bidden shall taste of my supper.
— Luke 14:16-24

Most of you surely recognize this as the story that is used by so many people. This passage has been used in the last

CURE FOR EXCUSITIS

year in our church by three men. I have their names here in my Bible. (I keep note of these things.) Dr. Don Jennings preached on this portion; Evangelist Darrell Dunn preached on it in one of our chapel hours; and Dr. E. J. Daniels used the same scripture.

But I want to turn tonight to this matter of excuse-making and show the "Cure for Excusitis" and give a few thoughts that might help us.

One person said, "I have bought a piece of ground and I must needs go and see it."

Another said, "I have bought five yoke of oxen, and I go to prove them."

The third said, "I have married a wife, and therefore I cannot come."

The master of the house, troubled by all these excuses, sent his servant out into the streets and lanes, saying, "Bring in the poor, the maimed, the halt, and the blind." And they did as told.

You know the general story in Luke 14. Excuses are common things. We hear them everywhere. Think of your individual Christian life and let God speak to you about this matter. When you have an opportunity for service, when you should do something that God wants you to do, what is your answer?

Some years ago I invited a man to teach a Sunday school class. He was in the church and a very faithful, good man. When I asked him if he would take a class, he made this answer: "Sir, I am sorry, but I am too busy. I promise you I will teach later, but not until I get out of my present crisis in business. I work at it night and day. I cannot teach now because I am too rushed."

There came a time when he was free from the rush and the pressure of his job, but then he died quite suddenly. He was sincere when he said, "I plan some day to help you, but I can't now."

A lot of people are like that. They make excuses and say they cannot do so and so. A man goes into sin and excuses

CURE FOR EXCUSITIS

himself by saying, "The pressures of life were so upon me that I couldn't help what I did."

A man neglects his family, then excuses himself for it. When he doesn't take proper care of them, doesn't administer the affairs of the home, doesn't meet with them for a family altar, he excuses himself. One may neglect the worship of God and offer excuses for not coming to church on Sunday morning, Sunday night, or Wednesday night.

That is the simple thing to do. Folk do it all the time. A husband and wife neglect the family altar and excuse themselves by saying, "We don't have time." Or, "The schedule is so broken. My husband works certain hours, I work certain hours, so we have no time when we can get together for a family altar."

Making excuses and trying to get around certain things that may come to us is common - just as common as the dirt around us.

A popular psychologist of this day said, "There are four common forms for excusitis in the business world, especially. One fellow says, "My health isn't good. I am not well, so I cannot do certain things." So, if he fails, he blames it on his health. Strange - that is used in churches also. People say about coming to church, "Well, I am not well. I can't go Sunday night. I quit going Wednesday night years ago because of my health." Not being well doesn't stop them from doing anything else. They still go to work on Monday, they still take a vacation, they still do a lot of other things. But they make excuses. How feeble is this! The part they fail to see is that most of work is being done by sick people. Isn't that strange? Check it out. Most of the work of the world is being done by those who have some infirmity. Yet, still some say, "My health isn't good."

Another excuse is: "You have to have brains to succeed. I don't know enough to do it." I have folk tell me that they couldn't teach Sunday school because they don't know enough about the Bible, or they don't have brains enough to

CURE FOR EXCUSITIS

know what to say to people, so they turn away from teaching. They fail in Christian service. God can use any of us, if we will apply ourselves and give ourselves to Him, not offer some excuse such as, "Well, I just can't do it."

Some say, "I am too old," or "I am too young." I saw a man yesterday, a graduate of Tennessee Temple, twenty-nine years of age, who pastors one of the outstanding churches of the northland. This graduate is a great preacher. He could have said, "Well, I am too young. I can't do it, so I will turn away." But he said, "If God wants me here, I will do the best I can." And he is doing a big job. The church is growing and souls are being saved.

Some men say, "Well, I am too old. I can't do it." Some of the world's greatest works have been done by those in advanced ages.

Some men say, "My case is different. I attract bad luck. In spite of it all, I just seem to have bad luck in everything I do. I just can't get ahead."

People fail in life and fail in serving Christ. Sometimes it is because of selfishness that they turn away. "For all seek their own, not the things which are Jesus Christ's," said the apostle. Some are selfish.

Some are lazy and so refuse. Somebody asked R. G. Le Tourneau years ago, "Mr. LeTourneau, when should a child start working?"

He replied, "At three years of age."

"Mr. LeTourneau, what do you mean at three years of age? That is like child labor."

"No! No!" he said, "A child should start working just as soon as he is old enough to get around. Some duties ought to be given him. The trouble with the American home today is because we have not given our young people something to do." And Mr. LeTourneau went on to discuss what he meant by giving young people something to do in life. He was thinking about his own young life when he had little tasks to do. He said, "This is important. It is pure laziness today."

CURE FOR EXCUSITIS

Some people fail because of greed. They desire certain things for themselves, thus they fail in life because of that greed.

Some people fail because of low standards, standards not as high as God would want them, so they fail.

Most people fail because they are not willing to take a job and do it. They simply make excuses. Sometimes they are gracious and nice about it when they excuse themselves.

A lady in this church several years ago reached the age of retirement, retiring from her job with the city of Chattanooga. She came to me one day and said, "Brother Roberson, I have retired from my job."

I said, "God bless you! You can have more time for the church now."

She replied, "No, I am quitting the church, too."

You won't believe this, but she did quit. I mean she quit-quit! I never saw her again back in church.

You say, "You mean a woman of intelligence enough to teach school would say a thing like that?" Yes, she did. She is still living today in our city but never goes to church.

I am trying to make you see something. Watch yourself! The flesh is subtle. The world and the flesh join together to deceive you, turn you aside, get you to say foolish things, and do foolish things even as she did. I told the lady that when she mentioned her retirement. I have been to see her. She has suffered physically, and perhaps much of it because of being out of the will of God.

The flesh seeks to escape responsibility, seeks to satisfy its own desires; therefore, the flesh is quick to make excuses.

Is there some cure for excusitis? A cure for this excuse-making? The Bible says, ". . .they all with one consent began to make excuse." What can we say? Let me suggest a few things whereby you can avoid excuse-making and make your life count.

CURE FOR EXCUSITIS

I. THERE SHOULD BE A VITAL VISION

Get the vision. Keep it before you continually! Get a vision of what you think God wants you to do. If God changes that vision, then enlarge it and move on out. If God says, "This is as far as I want you to go." then take it that far and stop. But do what God says.

That has been the secret of what we have done here through the years. I have to pray much about this. I have to pray much about this church, about Tennessee Temple University, about Camp Joy and everything we are doing. I do not like to move unless I feel so led of the Lord. If God says, "Move out and do more," then I want to do that. But we have to have a vision.

First of all, a vision of a lost world. Jesus looked upon the multitudes and had compassion upon them (Matt. 9:26-38). The Apostle Paul had this and was so concerned (Acts 13). He went out as a missionary. He expressed his great burden for souls in Romans 9:1-3.

A vision of the lost world takes away indifference. When you are concerned about others, it makes a big change.

You see, the selfish person has such battles. Even going to church is a battle! For a selfish man or woman or boy or girl, it is a battle! If the benches in the church are too hard, they don't like it. If the service is too long, they complain. If the ushers are not friendly as they come in, they fuss about that. They are here for self, to gratify self.

But if you are here because of a desire to see the job done and to get the Gospel to the ends of the earth, if you have a vision of a lost world, these mundane things do not concern you.

Second, get a vision of your family. Perhaps many of your family members are lost. Maybe Mother or Father are unsaved, maybe brothers and sisters. Get a vision for your family.

Third, get a vision of the awfulness of Hell as pictured for us in the great message of Jesus in Luke 16 - the story of Lazarus and Dives. Get a vision of the eternal abode of the

CURE FOR EXCUSITIS

damned.

All these things we could enlarge upon. They are familiar to you. I am trying to help you see how to make your life count and how to avoid excuse-making. Get a vision! Do what God says.

II. A RESTING ON FERVENT PRAYER

To make your life count and to escape many things, fervently pray.

A resting upon fervent, honest prayer will settle the excuses of most. You are not praying at all when you offer some feeble excuse that even the Devil himself would offer. You are trying to make it sound nice and real when you say, "That's why I don't do so and so."

No! No! No! You have not prayed at all, for a real fervent prayer life will change that.

<u>Prayer means contact with the Heavenly Father</u> - feeling His presence and His nearness day by day.

I visited the Billy Sunday home one day in Winona Lake, Indiana. Ma Sunday, Billy Sunday's wife, was here some years ago and spoke in the chapel next door. I had been to the home many times before, but on this particular day I thought of Billy and of his prayer life, of how he had prayed.

Billy Sunday prayed walking around. He prayed when he was shaving or riding in a car. He prayed and talked to God with his eyes open. He prayed all the time. He just talked to the Lord.

A lot of things you can say about Billy Sunday's ministry. Some people criticize it. I get that once in a while in certain places. But he preached the Word of God. He preached the message of salvation. He prayed about everything and brought himself before God.

Prayer means contact with God.

<u>Prayer brings a clear vision of yourself and your needs.</u> You see what you are, you see how weak you are, you see how sinful you are, when you seek the face of God. The

CURE FOR EXCUSITIS

self-righteous person hasn't prayed much. The self-righteous are not going to see themselves. They haven't prayed enough to get their eyes open to what they are.

<u>Prayer activates your mind and heart</u>. How sluggish we become unless we pray daily and seek the face of God. I have discovered this in my experience. I have been at this thing a good long while and I have had a lot of ups and downs. Many things have happened.

I can always get answers from God when I pray. If my mind and heart are slowing down and I am not excited about the work of the Saviour, I simply pray and ask God to help me. He always does. He rejuvenates my heart. He stirs me up and makes me want to do more.

Have you been praying? For yourself? For your family? For your loved ones? I am not talking about reciting words but really praying.

I think some of you sitting here tonight have been fooling, kidding yourself. You have been lying to yourself and to God. Had you been praying, God would have given you an answer. Some of you have confessed to me that you don't get answers; yet you say that you know the Saviour.

Prayer will activate the mind and heart and will send you out to do things for God. Prayer keeps us in tune with God and keeps away from us the things that will hurt and hinder our lives.

III. UNDERSTAND THE MATTER OF INFLUENCE

When you understand this, you will jump to do certain things. You will get out of bed on Sunday and be in Sunday school and church! Why? Because of your influence. Sunday night, you will jump at the opportunity to go to church because of your influence. Neighbors and friends are watching you. You will be to church on Wednesday night because somebody is watching you, because you know not to go will hinder others. "For none of us liveth to himself, and no man dieth to himself," said the apostle.

CURE FOR EXCUSITIS

We all have an influence. Our failures, our indifferences, our excuse-making may influence many.

The pastor who does not reckon with the power of influence will fall. His life, his example touch many. This must not happen.

The deacon who does not reckon with the power of influence will fail. The deacon who is unfaithful in attendance in the church - that does not go unnoticed. People see that! The deacon hurts himself and the cause of Christ. Deacons! Deacons! Deacons! Be faithful to God in your church attendance, in your giving, in your witnessing to lost souls. Deacons should be faithful men.

Also Sunday school teachers reckon with the power of their influence. Some Sunday school teachers leave after Sunday school. God pity their poor little pusillanimous souls! God pity any man, any woman, any teacher who would dare teach a class, then go home after you teach. Nothing is as dispicable as that. Yet, some do that. Pastors with broken hearts over such things, talk to me about it.

I was in a big church up North. I met with the Sunday school teachers and officers at 7:00 one Monday night. The superintendent of the Sunday school wasn't there. The next night I returned to the church. I had the crowd in front of me for the Sunday school meeting. A man was sitting in the back of the room, dressed in some dirty clothes, leaning up against the wall. I said, "Is the superintendent here?"

He raised his hand, "I am the superintendent."

I said, "I missed you last night."

"Yes, I moved my trailer last night."

Wait a minute! That was not a dead church. This was one of the so-called good churches up North, with a beautiful building, air-conditioned, moneyed people - all of it.

I said, "Well, I am glad you are here tonight. I want to talk to you about the Sunday school. I went back and spoke to him at the end of the Sunday school meeting. I said, "Now, let's go on to the church service. I have a few more

CURE FOR EXCUSITIS

things to say in there."

"I'm not going to church."

I finished preaching that night and the pastor drove me to the airport. As we drove along I said, "Pastor, you have a problem, haven't you?"

He replied, "I sure have. I have been here seven years. For five years this man has been superintendent of our Sunday school and he hasn't been to church once in five years."

"Why don't you fire him?"

"If I fire him, then I fire over half the church," he answered.

"I think I would fire him anyway."

"It would kill my church."

"It is already dead," I said. "All you have to do is stick a lily in its hand and go ahead."

"You are right about it, Brother Roberson." By now he was crying. This fellow was running the Sunday school and never came to church. He never came Sunday morning, Sunday night, or Wednesday night. He came to Sunday school, then left.

Sunday school teachers, watch your life! Watch your influence.

A preacher and his three boys found a dog. They liked him, like the way he looked. So they decided to adopt him, to bring him in the home and keep him as their dog.

They saw an announcement in the paper that a man lost a dog. The announcement said: "He has just a few white hairs on his tail." The preacher and the boys looked at the dog. Sure enough, the dog had a few white hairs on his tail. So the preacher said, "We will fix that. We'll just pull them out!" So they pulled out the white hairs in the dog's tail.

Somehow the owner of the dog found out who had the dog and came to the home. The dog recognized him right away. The pastor and his three sons were there. (The pastor himself had pulled the hairs out of the dog's tail.) The man looked and said, "Why, this is my dog!"

The pastor said, "Does it have any white hairs on the tail?"

182

CURE FOR EXCUSITIS

The fellow looked and said, "No, it doesn't."

"It is not your dog then."

The pastor said, "I kept the dog but lost my three boys. They saw what I was - a liar and a cheat. My influence was hurt with my boys. I never got over it."

They never got over it, either. They saw their daddy, a pastor, a preacher, lie to another, and this ruined his influence with his own sons.

What am I saying? Get an understanding of the power of influence.

IV. HAVE A CULTIVATED DETERMINATION

Christ illustrates this by saying, "I set my face like a flint" toward Jerusalem (Isa. 50:7b). The Apostle Paul illustrated this when he said, "This one thing I do. . . "

Determine to make your life count for Christ. Work at it. That eliminates indecision. It takes away indifference, excuse-making. Just follow a straight course and don't turn right nor left. Just go right on down the line serving God.

You don't take a vacation from God. You don't take a vacation from church. You don't take a vacation from spiritual activities. Remember that, and it will direct you in all ways. It will help in Bible study, in prayer, and help you grow in grace and touch others.

It is almost impossible to stop a determined Christian. Get a young man determined to serve God and you can't stop him. He just puts his head down and says, "This is it. God has called me; I am determined to follow Him." He fires on and does the job.

Watch yourself. A lot of people take the easy way and they fail. They side-step the responsibilities God has placed on them.

Yesterday I heard a story, perhaps I should not repeat it but I guess it will be in the newspapers eventually, so you will read it then. A pastor that I have helped in meetings (not a Baptist, but he invited me to come and speak to his

CURE FOR EXCUSITIS

Sunday School Convention), took a bankrupt law for his church and the institutions around his church, for 25 million dollars. You know what that has done? It has made all the enemies of our Lord stand and laugh with glee and say, "Ah, look at him! Look at him! Look what he did!" If I would call his name, most of the preachers here would know him. He took the bankrupt law last Monday morning for 25 million dollars. He said he couldn't pay the bills. He kept buying and buying and selling bonds and doing more, until the thing got deeper and deeper. He tried the easy way out, but couldn't find an easy way out. Now he says the bankrupt law is the way.

You have a cultivated determination to be honest and upright with God in all your dealings!

IV. THERE MUST BE A COMPELLING COMPASSION FOR OTHERS

That will help you to be steady. That will help you to grow in grace. Learn compassion.

Learn compassion by studying about Jesus, a Man of compassion, One who looked upon the multitudes with compassion. Study others. See their needs and see how you can help them.

Learn compassion by looking into your own heart. Look with honesty. Do you care for others? Are you concerned about those around you? Do you have compassion?

To have compassion, we must feel as others feel. We must endeavor to stand where they are standing. We must see from their eyes.

One learns a lot from visiting a sick room in a hospital, or in a home. One learns a lot about people from visiting a rescue mission. You see their hearts. I don't put blame on some of the bums who come to our mission! I love them. I blame them for going on that way after they hear the Gospel, but some are just doing what Mother and Dad did before, just following after Mother and Dad. They ignored

CURE FOR EXCUSITIS

them. They ignored their spiritual interest. They didn't take them to Sunday school and church. They didn't give them the Bible at home. I have talked to these men. I know.

We also learn a lot from visiting a jail or a penitentiary. There is a lot to be learned of compassion.

We lack compassion because we are so selfish. We live in tight compartments of self. Our Saviour knew men, their pain, their heartaches, their discouragements, and He cared. That is the way we should be.

Oh, my dear friend, making excuses is an old business that failed a long time ago. Let God stir your heart tonight. Be determined to be your best for the Saviour. Let others see Jesus in you. Don't make excuses, but serve God in the best way you can, and with determination. If neighbors laugh at you, you still be determined. If family laughs, still be determined. Whatever it may be, still be determined to let God have the first place in your life.

Chapter 16
America — Where Are Thy Gods That Thou Hast Made?

As the thief is ashamed when he is found, so is the house of Israel ashamed; they, their kings, their princes, and their priests, and their prophets,
Saying to a stock, Thou art my father; and to a stone, Thou has brought me forth: for they have turned their back unto me, and not their face: but in the time of their trouble they will say, Arise, and save us.
But where are thy gods that thou hast made thee? let them arise, if they can save thee in the time of thy trouble: for according to the number of thy cities are thy gods, O Judah.
Wherefore will ye plead with me? ye all have transgressed against me, saith the LORD.
In vain have I smitten your children; they received no correction: your own sword hath devoured your prophets, like a destroying lion.
— Jer. 2:26-30

America is without question the richest nation on earth. She has the strongest and largest churches in the world. America has more ordained ministers than any other country in the world. She has more Christian colleges, more Christian universities, more Bible schools than any other country.

Yet, in spite of all these things, sin is in our midst. The Devil is making an appeal and an attack upon this nation that we cannot fail to see. He would like to destroy everything

AMERICA — WHERE ARE THY GODS?

worthwhile. He would like to destroy every soul-winning church, every evangelistic school like ours. He would like to destroy every radio broadcast, every summer camp like Camp Joy. There are movements on right now to put out of business every Christian camp in America.

The same is true regarding schools. In certain states it seems Christian schools may be closed because of rules and regulations the government has brought up. All this is because we've turned away from the simple faith that God has given us. Multitudes have turned to modernism.

Only a small percentage - twelve or fifteen percent - attend church on Sunday morning in America, maybe not that many at times. Sunday evenings, even a smaller percentage. Almost none at all for our Wednesday night prayer meetings.

Our text comes from the book of Jeremiah "the weeping prophet." Jeremiah looked upon the people of Israel with amazement and tears. He was amazed that they had turned away from the eternal God. He was in tears as he pled for their return to God. He gives the message of God to Israel: "Return, thou backsliding Israel . . . . I will heal your backslidings."

Three separate thoughts I will try to join together in this brief message.

I. THE DUMB GODS OF MAN

The people of Israel turned away from the living God to the dumb gods of man. They had turned to mountains and hills for salvation. It says in verse 28, ". . . the number of thy cities are thy gods, O Judah." They turned away to false gods, to idols.

Our mind goes back to the story of Elijah on Mount Carmel and prophets of Baal standing and prophesying. Elijah said, "Build your altar. Set it afire with your prayers. I'll build an altar and set the fire with my prayers."

The prophets built the altar. They prayed. Nothing happened. Dumb gods! Dumb gods! But God answered the

AMERICA — WHERE ARE THY GODS?

prayer of Elijah.

Man Is a Worshiper

He has to worship something or someone, no matter who. And he often worships himself, his own ingenuity, his own inventiveness. He thinks he can do all things. He worships himself.

How often I've watched a puny little man stretch himself and say, "You Baptists have certain ways. You think certain ways. I have my own way!"

My dear friend, the only way is the Bible way. I'm not bragging about being a Baptist. I'm bragging about being a Christian, one who believes the Word of God. This is the Bible, God's holy Word. We stand for this. But many have turned away and refused to receive it.

Man worships objects, money, houses and lands. Jesus gave the parable, in Luke 12:16-21, about the rich fool, saying of this one, "Thou fool, this night thy soul shall be required of thee."

And, again, we have the story in Luke 16:19-31. "There was a certain rich man, which was clothed in purple and fine linen, and fared sumptuously every day." Man - worshiping objects, worshiping things.

Man worships his own inventiveness. He feels that he can work it out. In his shrewdness, he says, "Look what I've done! Look what I built!" Man's way of doing it.

Now, my friend, you can worship a helpless god, as did the worshipers of Baal. You can worship a god who can't hear you. You can worship a god who can never help you in your time of need. That god is a failure, and your life is also a failure. What a waste it is when people fall for the false worship of this world!

I want you to see this, this morning. Hold to this if you will. Think of your life. Are you worshiping God? Or do you worship the things of this world? Are you falling for some of the sinful escapades of the world and its sinful pursuits? Are you falling for the money, for the riches, for the power,

AMERICA — WHERE ARE THY GODS?

the things of this world, the dumb gods that cannot answer prayer nor do one thing for you?

I saw a pitiful story the other day that came out in the newspaper. It told about a woman thirty-seven years of age named Carol Sabalski who died as a result of the bite of a four-feet-long rattlesnake. She was a divorcee, despondent, and had just quit her job. In her job she handled a rattlesnake out on the platform, a water moccasin, and other poisonous reptiles.

She got despondent, quit her job and went home. The police statement was, she committed suicide by allowing the rattlesnake to bite her.

The emptiness of life. When one comes to the end of his way, then there's no way out, nothing else to do. She had no hope. Our hope is not in things of this world! It is not in attracting people by physical beauty or physical aims, or by our abilities. She felt a complete failure.

But, she is not alone. There are other folk who are failing in the same way by following dumb gods.

II. THE DANGER ZONE OF MAN

Today we fear certain things. For example, we fear price inflation. There is a lot of talk about that. What is happening today? Prices are going up, eating up our comfortable salaries, eating up what we've saved and making it difficult to live comfortably. We fear the curtailment of commodities, as we have to do in certain areas of life and as we've been asked to do in certain circumstances.

Then, we fear the inconvenience of a depression - the loss of salary, the loss of mortgaged property, the loss of position. All these things we fear.

But the danger zone is that we do not fear what we ought to fear. For example, we do not fear sins. We've grown so used to sin that we flippantly look over it, saying, "What difference does it make?" We take sin like a policeman who is used to seeing crime every day. We take sin like the lawyer

AMERICA — WHERE ARE THY GODS?

in the courtroom, who is used to the trials and the sentencing. We take sin like the doctor takes sickness. He's used to seeing it. We get accustomed to it! This is the tragedy. We do not fear sin. This is the danger zone. So alert yourself!

This world is filled with sinful people, wicked people, beer drinkers, those who are immoral, immodest in every way. They are used to the sin of this world.

We need to fear sin.

We do not fear indifference toward holy matters. People are indifferent. "So what?" They care little about the church, about the Bible, about prayer, about giving, about missions - about anything. Indifferent to it all. Nobody is troubled!

Jeremiah pointed this out, saying to the people, "This is one of your problems, You are indifferent toward the things of God. You've turned away. But where now are thy gods that thou hast made? What can you do? What can you say?" They had nothing at all. They were empty. This is what Jeremiah, "the weeping prophet," is trying to point out to them.

We do not fear indifference. But, my friend, do fear it with all your heart!

We do not fear wasting of a life. "Just one life, 'twill soon be past; only what's done for Christ will last." We do not fear the wasting of a life.

I have only one life. Maybe I'm not doing what I ought to do. But, oh, I pray every day, "O God, let me use this one day in the best way." I've got eternity! I've got Heaven awaiting me! But, I've got just this one life in which to serve Him.

Back in the old days, I enjoyed hearing Jack Benny on the radio, and later, on television. Jack Benny was a comedian. He died recently. The Rabbi had his service. Bob Hope was there. George Burns was there. Many unbelievers, many profane people were there.

I have no objection to a man being a comedian, if that comedian knows what it is to know Jesus Christ as Saviour. But without knowing the Son of God, no one has anything.

AMERICA — WHERE ARE THY GODS?

You can have all the people attend and mourn. The multimillionaires can stand by the casket. You can have present all the Rabbis. But none of these will help. Without Jesus Christ, there is nothing. We do not fear the wasting of a life. One's life is wasted, if he lives it outside the knowledge of Jesus Christ. Know Him today. Serve Him today. Live for Him today. Love Him today with all your heart.

There are three conditions facing us in this hour. <u>First, the nonchalance of youth</u>. I know young people. I love young people. They know I love them. There's not a problem they have that I do not understand. If I can talk to them, pray with them, I can understand it. I'm older than they, much, much older. I know them. But young people are nonchalant, careless.

God bless the young folk here in this church. God bless you and keep you faithful, keep you true, keep you caring.

"What does it matter if I steal? What are they going to do to me if I do, if I rob, if I get into some other meanness?" And you go on your way. The nonchalance of youth. O God, help us to influence and stir young people to think, to be excited about life, to live as God wants them to live.

<u>Second, the occupation of adulthood</u>. Adults are so busy, working, building, planning until they have left God out altogether. That's surely true of America. People say, "I don't have time to go to church." Or, "I don't have time to read the Bible and pray!" Or, "I don't have time for family altar! I'm a busy man!" I have a lot of men tell me that. That's a lie! "Ah, preacher, I'm busy. I wish I could do like you do - go to church all the time - but I'm just too busy."

It's a funny thing. The same ones can take two, three and four weeks off for vacation and think nothing about it. They take off. I don't blame them. It's all right, but they shouldn't lie about being too busy for God's work.

Sometimes doctors tell me, "I rush, rush all the time!" But they can take off for a vacation. Lawyers are the same way and other professional people, and other working

AMERICA — WHERE ARE THY GODS?

people - all the same. The occupation of adulthood: watch it! Keep God in first place!

<u>Third, the blindness and deafness of age</u>. Tears are gone! Concern is gone! Old age has taken it's toll. Now you think only of yourself! Watch it, old people! Watch it! There are some advantages of growing old. I can talk on your level now. And I'm going to. When I was younger, I could talk to the young people. I'm still going to talk to them. But I can talk to you older folks now.

Both young and old come to the place where you do not care, where there's a deafness, a blindness to everything except yourselves! That's all you think about! You can talk about nothing except your aches and pains, what you have and what you don't have. Now it's only self.

Lots of times adults and those older lose your convictions about right and wrong. You give them up, cast them aside. Oh, alert yourself to the danger zone of this day!

I used to give a message on "The Danger of Getting Used To Things." We should ever be sensitive to the cross of Christ, sensitive to what it means. Sad, sad when our hearts are not moved at the cross.

We must be sensitive to the cry of the lost world.

We must be sensitive to the conversion of sinners, people coming to Jesus Christ.

These things should alert us. The danger zone is the danger of indifference. I care not about your blase' statements, about how you don't care about this, that, and the other. Wake up, my friend! Be alert to the things of God, alert to the tragedies of this hour, alert to what's happening in America, alert to your home life, your business life. Keep Jesus in the very center.

III. THE DELIVERANCE OF MAN

First of all, the dumb gods of men. Second, the danger zone of man. And third, the deliverance of man. There's a way out for the individual. There's a way out for the nation.

AMERICA — WHERE ARE THY GODS?

It's God's way.

First, we have the goodness of God. God longs to help us. And God is ready to help us. I'm continually amazed at the goodness of God. I don't understand it.

A man walked up to me yesterday at the close of a wedding ceremony and handed me a $100 bill. "Just want you to have it. You recall when I gave you one before."

I said, "No sir, I don't."

"Well, I gave it to you years ago at a certain place " (I think out in Tulsa, Oklahoma).

I said, "Praise God! I'm glad to have it. Thank you, sir."

God keeps on supplying. I had no sooner gotten out of the auditorium from the wedding ceremony, when I handed $50 of it to a couple who just sent a boy down to Roloff in Corpus Christi, Texas. They had to have this amount to get him there and to get one of the fellows back.

God is supplying every need. The goodness of God!

Second, we have the promises of God. The promises of God to a nation: "If my people, which are called by my name, shall humble themselves, and pray, and seek my face, and turn from their wicked ways; then will I hear from heaven, and will forgive their sin, and will heal their land " (II Chron 7:14).

We have the promise to the Christian away from God. "If we confess our sins, he is faithful and just to forgive us our sins, and to cleanse us from all unrighteousness " (I John 1:9). That's for you, child of God.

There is a promise to the church. "Behold, I stand at the door, and knock: if any man hear my voice, and open the door, I will come in to him, and will sup with him, and he with me " (Rev. 3:20).

Then there is a promise to the sinner: "I tell you, Nay: but, except ye repent, ye shall all likewise perish " (Luke 13:3). "He that believeth on the Son hath everlasting life: and he that believeth not the Son shall not see life . . . " (John 3:36).

Third, we have the power of choice: God's goodness,

AMERICA — WHERE ARE THY GODS?

God's promises, and to us has been given the power of choice. You can choose to walk with the world, or you can choose to walk with God. You have a choice.

Enoch made a choice. He chose to walk with God. This is what you should choose this morning.

I bring this message to bring peace to troubled hearts. I know I am praying and you're praying about our nation. Things are tragic now; they may get worse. I'm not a prophet. I do not know what's going to happen. No one else seems to know what the next thing will be. But, my friends, we can have peace of heart by resting upon the promises of God.

I bring this message to strengthen our faltering hearts. "Draw nigh to God, and he will draw nigh to you..." That promise God has given us.

What is your need this morning? Let God supply it. He can do so. "My God shall supply all your need according to his riches in glory by Christ Jesus."

Suppose your business had failed completely. A millionaire comes along and says, "I want to pay your bills and get you going again." Would you take him up on that offer? Sure you would.

Well, there is One who is worth more than a million, ten million, ten trillion. When I have needs, I can come to my God and say, "Lord, God, I have need of help." And He has promised to help me. He has the power to help. He has the resource to help. He has the compassion to help. He wants to help. We can have His help by simple faith in Him.

Oh, the dumb gods that cannot do one thing for us; the danger zone of life, and the deliverance that God wants to give to each one through faith in His name.

On this last Sunday of this year, won't you say, "O God, let me so live that this coming year shall be a year of victory. If I live the whole year, or if I live just a part of it, I want to be victorious down to the end. I want to direct my family in the right way. I want my life and influence to count for you. I want others to see Jesus in me. I surrender my all to Thee."

AMERICA — WHERE ARE THY GODS?

My friend, if you've never been saved, if you've never accepted Jesus as your Saviour, there couldn't be a better time than right now. You may be trusting in things. You may be trusting in church membership. You may be trusting in baptism. You may be trusting in good works. You may be trusting in your acts of philanthropy, giving to others. But I hope you will come forward to say, "I put my faith and my trust in Jesus Christ, the Son of God."

Dr. Fuller was pastor of the First Baptist Church in Atlanta, Georgia, and later president of the Southern Baptist Seminary in Louisville, Kentucky. I was with him on the platform in a number of meetings where both of us spoke. Dr. Fuller was an outstanding Gospel preacher, a unique preacher in some ways.

He was conducting a meeting in a big tent seating some five thousand or six thousand. God was blessing. Souls were being saved.

One afternoon a young fellow came to him and said, "Dr. Fuller. I want you to go with me to see a man. It'll take just a little while."

"Where is this man?"

"He lives thirteen miles out of town."

"Son, I can't go. I've got a sermon to get ready. Young man, excuse me. I can't make it."

The boy wouldn't take no. "Sir, you've got to go. You've got to go."

Dr. Fuller said, "If that's the way it is, I'll go."

They got in the car and drove to a beautiful farm home.

"There's a sick man here I want you to see. His name is Mr. Penson."

They led him through the house to the side porch. It was the hot summer-time, with no air-conditioning in that day. The man was lying on a cot on the side porch. He was introduced to Dr. Fuller.

Dr. Fuller said, "Sir, I just want to ask you something. I don't have much time here, but are you saved? Are you a Christian?"

AMERICA — WHERE ARE THY GODS?

He answered, "Dr Fuller, I'm glad you're here. I've always been a good citizen. I've always paid my bills. I've got a high reputation. I provide for my wife and daughter. They have the very best. I'm a leader of my community. On every civic matter, I take the lead. Just a moment. Let me call my wife and daughter."

He called and they came out on the porch. "I want you to tell Dr. Fuller what you think about me and my life."

The wife spoke with tears, "Why, you're one of the best husbands in the world. You've done everything for us that anyone could ever do."

The daughter in tears also said, "Why, daddy you've done everything. Your life is exemplary. There's nothing else that could be desired."

When they got through, Dr. Ellis Fuller, in his quiet but positive way, said, "Sir, I'm sorry. You're going to die. What you are trusting in now will send you straight to Hell."

The man, in shock, said, "Why, sir what do you mean? I've done my best."

"I know, but that's not enough. That won't save your soul."

"What do you mean?"

"There is only one way to be saved, and that is by faith in Jesus Christ."

Dr. Fuller took his Bible, read to the man the Word of God, read where Jesus said, "I am the way, the truth, and the life, no man cometh unto the Father, but by me." He read, "He that believeth in me hath everlasting life." He said, "Jesus Christ is the only Saviour, the Way to Heaven. Now we'll pray."

They prayed. He asked the man to put his trust in Jesus, and asked him to pray the sinner's prayer, "Lord be merciful to me and save me for Jesus' sake." The man prayed.

When Dr. Fuller finished, the man opened his eyes, looked around and said, "I've never felt like this before. This is wonderful! This is what I've been wanting all the time! Salvation through faith in Jesus Christ. This is peace! This is what I need for my heart and life."

AMERICA — WHERE ARE THY GODS?

Dr. Fuller prayed and thanked the Lord, then went on his way. In one single week Dr. Fuller was asked to come back for the funeral service for this outstanding farmer. For just one week he had known the Saviour!

My friend, God is speaking to you this morning. This is your hour to be saved. You come today. Maybe you want to come for rededication of life.

Tabernacle
Revival Sermons

by
LEE ROBERSON, D. D.

PREFACE

The sermons contained in this book were preached in the Lord's Day services of the Highland Park Baptist Church of Chattanooga. Some were given in the old saw-dust floor tabernacle and the others in the new concrete and steel tabernacle (completed in 1947).

All of the services of our church are characterized by the revival spirit. Souls are saved and saints are revived in every meeting. Both preaching and singing have one end: Decisions for Christ.

I make no claim for originality. Thoughts ,illustrations, and outlines from other sources now long forgotten—may appear in this book. The goal of my ministry is the winning of the lost—those who are likeminded do not object to seeing their words repeated, if by doing so souls are brought to the Blessed Saviour.

TABLE OF CONTENTS

What Held Jesus to the Cross?............................ 5

Death Bed Repentance.......................................13

My Peace..18

Whosoever Is Fearful and Afraid...................24

The Shoulders of Jesus......................................32

Cross Bearing..39

Does Jesus Live at Your House?......................46

A Death Vision..54

Do We Need a New Gospel?..............................63

Heaven Is Looking On..70

Chapter 1
What Held Jesus to the Cross?

"*If thou be the Son of God, come down from the cross.*" *Matt. 27:40.*

"*And they that passed by reviled him, wagging their heads,*

"*And saying, Thou that destroyest the temple, and buildest it in three days, save thyself. If thou be the Son of God, come down from the cross.*

"*Likewise also the chief priests mocking him, with the scribes and elders, said,*

"*He saved others; himself he cannot save. If he be the King of Israel, let him now come down from the cross, and we will believe him.*

"*He trusted in God; let him deliver him now, if he will have him: for he said, I am the Son of God.*

"*The thieves also, which were crucified with him, cast the same in his teeth.*" *Matthew 27:39-44.*

The Bible definitely tells us what held Jesus to the cross. It was not simply nails, though He was nailed to the cross. The Son of God, with power to raise the dead, heal the sick, make the blind to see, still the storm-tossed sea, surely had power to step down from a cross, even though He was nailed to it.

It was not human weakness which bound Him to the cross, for He said regarding His life, "No man taketh it from me, but I lay it down of myself. I have power to lay it down; I have power to take it again. This commandment have I received of my Father." John 10:18.

It was not because He was friendless that He stayed on the cross. In the garden of Gethsemane, when Peter drew his sword and began to battle in defense of the Master, Jesus said, "Thinkest thou not that I cannot now say to my Father, and He shall presently give me more than twelve legions of angels?" The twelve legions of angels were still available when Jesus was on the cross.

What then is the answer to the question, What held Jesus to the cross? Here is the answer.

I. HIS LOVE FOR US HELD HIM TO THE CROSS.

Jesus said nothing and did nothing when the scoffers passed by reviling Him and wagging their heads. They called to mind a statement that He had made regarding His death and resurrection. He had said that if they destroyed the temple, He would raise it up in three days, He was speaking of Himself, but they thought He spoke of the temple in Jerusalem; therefore, they said, "Thou that destroyest the temple, and buildest it in three days, save thyself. If thou be the Son of God, come down from the cross."

The chief priests, the scribes, and the elders also came by and said, "He saved others; himself he cannot save. If he be the King of Israel, let him now come down from the cross, and we will believe him. He trusted in God; let him deliver him now, if he will have him."

Surely these taunting statements were enough to try the soul, even of the Son of God. He did not come down from the cross, for His love for a lost mankind held Him to the cross.

Many verses declare this great truth unto us. Jesus said, "Greater love hath no man than this, that a man lay down his life for his friends." Paul tells us in Galatians 2:20 that the Son of God loved us, and gave Himself for us. John tells us in I John 3:16, "Hereby perceive we the love of God, because he laid down his life for us, and we ought to lay down our lives for the brethren."

There are three things I would like to say about the love of Christ.

First, His love was unusual. It is an ordinary, everyday thing for us to love those who love us, but Jesus loved those who hated Him. "But God commendeth His love toward us, in that, while we were yet sinners, Christ died for us." Romans 5:8.

Jesus loved His enemies, and even on the cross, He said, "Father, forgive them, for they know not what they do." The love of Christ was unusual, and this is the love that He beseeches us to have for our fellowman.

The story is told of Peter Miller, a plain Baptist preacher of Ephrata, Pennsylvania, in the days of the Revolutionary War. Near his church lived a man who abused the pastor to the last limit. The man became involved in treason, and was arrested and sentenced to be hanged. The old preacher started out on foot, and walked the whole seventy miles to Philadelphia, that he might plead for the man's life. Washington heard his plea, but he said, "No, your plea for your friend cannot be granted."

"My friend!" said the preacher, "He is the worst enemy I have!"

"What!" said Washington. "You have walked nearly seventy miles to save the life of an enemy. That puts the matter in a different light. I will grant the pardon."

That is what makes the love of Christ unusual. He loved His enemies, and this love bound Him to the cross.

Secondly, His love was unending. "Now, before the feast of the Passover, when Jesus knew that His hour was come that he should depart out of this world unto the Father, having loved his own which were in the world, he loved them unto the end."

Sometimes even the love of a mother for her child fails. Occasionally even a father may turn against his own son, but the love of Jesus never fails. It continued to the cross—beyond the cross, and abounds unto us today. His love bound Him to the cruel tree.

Thirdly, His love was unselfish. Man had nothing to give to Jesus that He did not have already. All things belong to Him. The silver and the gold, the cattle upon a thousand hills, and yet, the Saviour died in our behalf. It always seems like a foolish thing to beg people to receive Jesus, when the giving must be all on His side. All we can do is surrender ourselves. There is nothing in a material way that we can give to God that He does not already have. All things are His by act of creation, and yet, the Son of God condescended to die for us, and His unselfish love bound Him to the cross of Calvary. It is a rare and beautiful thing to see people give and love when nothing can be given to them in return.

The Sunday School Times tells the story of a group of dirty, ragged, poor children who were waiting in a mission one afternoon for their teacher and leader to arrive. They were children from the poorest homes. Most of them were hungry. All of them were familiar with hardships. As they sat waiting, a boy appeared leading by the hand two children, a little more forlorn looking than the others. The leader of the group jumped up and said, "Hey, fellows, these kids ain't got nobody to take care of them. They sleeps in a box, and ain't had nothing to eat today. Can't we do something for 'em?"

The crowd stared at the newcomers, and then one boy suggested, "Let's take up a collection," and they did. Grimy hands plunged into the recesses of tattered garments for pennies, and the collection was taken. The result—seven cents. A large committee was appointed to go to the nearest bakery, and invest the funds. Some small cakes were bought, and these were put into the hands of the two poor, hungry children. The rest of the dirty, ragged boys and girls gathered around to watch the two little ones eat their cakes. They were giving unselfishly.

When Jesus died upon the cross, bound by the divine love for poor, lost sinful mankind, His love was unselfish.

II. HIS SUBMISSION TO GOD'S WILL HELD HIM TO THE CROSS.

The bitter, angry mob, especially the religious leaders told Him to come down from the cross if He were the Son of God. One of the malefactors railed on Him, saying, "If thou be Christ, save thyself and us."

In the common parlance of today, they were saying, "If you are not a liar and a hypocrite, come down from the cross. If you are such a big person, if you are what you claim to be, then show us by coming down from the cross." But Jesus could not come down, for His submission to God's will bound Him to the rugged cross.

Let me pause here to make this plea. May our lives be so submissive to the will of God that we will be unable to do anything but say, "Thy will be done." May our submission to His holy will bind us to separated living, to soul-winning, to consecrated service, to liberal giving, to earnest praying. May our submission to the Father's will bind us to do His divine purpose and plan for our lives.

Jesus said, "Lo, I come to do thy will." It was the will of God that He should die for sinful mankind. It was the will of God that He should enter into the holy of holies, and there make one sacrifice for sin forever. It was the Father's will that He should pour out His blood upon Calvary's hill. Jesus was submissive to the will of God.

III. OUR SINS HELD HIM TO THE CROSS.

The trail of sin from the Garden of Eden to the present time is a bloody and tragic one.

Sin separates men from God, just as it drove the first pair from the garden.

Sin brings shame. Adam and Eve sought to hide from God. Sinners are still ashamed, and try to hide their sins; therefore, men love darkness rather than light.

Sin brings sorrow. See it for yourself. The life of sin will end in sorrow. The home of sin will end in sorrow.

Sin brings suffering. All of the world's suffering came about because of sin. Mental anguish, physical suffering, all come from sin.

But the crowning act of sin's dastardly career came in the death of Christ. But let us not stand back and say, "Shame on you, sin, for crucifying the Saviour." For let us remember it was our sins which nailed Him and held Him to the cross."

"But he was wounded for our transgressions, he was bruised for our iniquities: the chastisement of our peace was upon him; and with his stripes we are healed.

"All we like sheep have gone astray; we have turned every one to his own way: and the Lord hath laid on him the iniquity of us all." Isaiah 53:5,6

1. He bore our sins to satisfy the law of God. God's law says, "The soul that sinneth it shall die." "The wages of sin is death." Because of our sins, we deserve the penalty of death and Hell, but Christ came and died in our place. He satisfied the law of God. God accepted His death as payment for our sins.

"Who gave himself for us, that he might redeem us from all iniquity, and purify unto himself a peculiar people, zealous of good works.

Who his own self bore our sins in his own body on the tree that we being dead to sins, should live unto righteousness, by whose stripes ye were healed."

What Held Jesus to the Cross? 11

2. He took our sins that He might bear them away from us. John announced the ministry of Jesus by saying, "Behold the Lamb of God which taketh away the sin of the world." Just as the priest in Leviticus could lay his hands upon the head of a live goat and confess over him all the iniquities of the children of Israel, and all their transgressions, and send him away into the wilderness, so did Jesus bear our sins that He might bear them away from us.

The picture is also given in the Passover scene of the Lamb slain, and the blood put upon the door posts. Jesus is our sacrificial Lamb. His blood covers our sins, and releases us from the penalty of Hell. John writes, "And ye know that he was manifested to take away our sin, and in him is no sin." I John 3:5.

3. He bore our sins in His own body on the tree that He might bring us unto God. The redemptive work of Jesus is to take out of this world a people for His name. The whole world will not be saved, but some will be saved, and with them God is going to abide forever.

Yes, your sins and mine bound Him to the cross. Christ was fully conscious that only His death could satisfy the law of God, bear away our sins, and bring us unto the Heavenly Father. Therefore, though men scoffed at Him and accused Him of lying and hypocrisy, He stayed on the cross, bound by our sins, to the tree.

There is but one way open to the fair minded person who realizes that his sins nailed Jesus to the cross, and that is to receive Jesus as Saviour. He died that you might live. You cannot live without Him.

A big, brawny cultured athlete was once asked why the word "mother" was so sacred to him. In reply, he told how, when he was born, the doctor told his father that either the mother or the child must die. The doctor said, "Decide quickly, so that I can go to work." The young athlete said, "My mother overheard what the doctor said, and putting her arms around my father, said to him, 'I will die. Let my baby live.' My mother passed away. She gave her life for me, but her supreme sacrifice has enobled my whole being, and has endeared all mothers to me. Only Christ, my Saviour, could have done more."

Come to Jesus today and live. Let Him plunge all your sins in the fountain filled with blood. Let Him write your name upon the Lamb's book of life. Let Him keep you in the hollow of His hand. Receive Him as Saviour, and know the blessedness of salvation.

"I'll go to Jesus, though my sin, like mountains round
    me close,
I know His courts, I'll enter in, whatever may oppose;

Prostrate I'll lie before His throne, and there my guilt
    confess,
I'll tell Him I'm a wretch undone, without His sovereign
    grace.

I can but perish if I go—I am resolved to try,
For if I stay away, I know I must forever die."

Chapter 2
Death Bed Repentance

"All that the Father giveth me shall come to me; and him that cometh to me I will in no wise cast out." John 6:37.

"And one of the malefactors which were hanged, railed on him, saying, If thou be Christ, save thyself and us.

"But the other answering rebuked him, saying, Dost not thou fear God, seeing that thou art in the same condemnation?

"And we indeed justly; for we received the due reward of our deeds: but this man hath done nothing amiss.

"And he said unto Jesus, Lord, remember me when thou comest into thy kingdom.

"And Jesus said unto him, Verily I say unto thee, Today shalt thou be with me in paradise." Luke 23:39-43.

Quite a number of times in my ministry people have asked me, "What do you think about death-bed repentance? Will God accept it? What does the Bible say about it?"

By the expression, "Death-bed repentance," we commonly mean the turning to God of some lost sinner in the moments just before death steps in. It is human for us to question whether or not God will accept a person who neglected or ignored God during the days of life and then turned in the hour of death.

The answer to the question is surely given in the passages I have read to you. In John 6:37, we have the promise of Jesus of "Him that cometh unto me, I will in no wise cast out."

In the 23rd chapter of Luke we read of the salvation of the thief on the cross. Yes, God will honor repentance and faith at any time if it is sincere. He will honor the repentance and faith of a young child and of the aged person. The Scriptures indicate from Genesis to Revelation that God will pardon, forgive, and save the sinner when he comes to Him in true repentance and faith.

Of course, we need to emphasize that word "sincere." If the sinner is not sincere in his repentance, it will avail him nothing. It was Spurgeon who said, "I have no confidence in death-bed repentance, because so few live up to it after they get well." We can all catch the humor of Mr. Spurgeon's statement, but he, too, believed in the love of God and the gracious willingness of our Father to forgive sinners whenever they may come.

In the light of all of this, we find ourselves facing two problems. First, to get to men before death comes. In love, we must race to the unsaved with the gospel. We have delayed too long to take the gospel to the people of this earth. There are millions who have never heard the name of Christ. Again, we must take the gospel to our loved ones who are lost. Let us not wait until some great catastrophe comes upon us or them, but let us speak now and win them now.

Our second problem is to get men to accept the Lord Jesus at once. We need to emphasize that little word *now*. Men and women, boys and girls, need Christ now, and they will need Him in eternity.

With Christians praying earnestly, I want to point ont to the unsaved of this audience the folly of delay—of putting off your acceptance of Jesus.

I. IT IS UNFAIR TO CHRIST HIMSELF.

The Lord Jesus died for us on the cross. He deserves to have the best of our lives. It is not fair to give your life to the devil, and then hand to the Lord a few dying moments. It is like the drunk who takes his pay check and spends it in drunkenness and sin, and then brings home to his wife, the mother of his children, a few paltry pennies. It is not fair.

I have a certain respect for the infidel, who, when his loved ones begged him to turn to Christ in the hour of death, said, "I will die as I lived. I have lived for the devil, therefore, I will die and take my place in Hell. I will not run to God as a coward in this dying moment."

The infidel was a fool in life and a fool in death, but I have respect for his sense of fairness.

Lost friend, it isn't fair to Jesus to live for the enemy of God and righteousness and then give the Lord a few weak, pitiful, dying moments. Therefore, I plead with you to accept the Lord now as your Saviour.

II. BY DELAY, YOU ARE LOSING JOY.

The happiest life is the Christian life. Jesus said, "I am come that ye might have life, and that ye might have it more aboundantly." You cannot know what true joy is until you make Christ your Saviour. The world's joy turns to ashes, but the happiness of Christ is a deep settled abiding peace.

Sinner after sinner has told me after conversion, "I did not know there could be anything so wonderful as this."

Come to Christ, rest in Him, and receive the greatest joy this world knows anything about. The Lord can remake your home, transform your life, give you a new incentive for living, and put a perpetual song in your heart. Every day that you stay away from Him, you are losing that much joy.

III. BY REJECTING CHRIST, YOU ARE A DAMNING INFLUENCE TO OTHERS.

Paul said, "For none of us liveth to himself, and no

man dieth to himself." This can apply to the unsaved as well as to the Christian. Without Christ, your life and influence can point in only one direction—away from God and toward the world, the flesh, and the devil.

The school teacher without Christ is a damning influence. If I cared to take the time, I could illustrate over and over again. Here in our city are teachers who have rejected the Saviour and who add insult to injury. They mock Him and His cause. It is impossible at this time to estimate the extent of their damning influence. And notice this, a popular teacher who rejects and reviles the Saviour is worse than an unpopular one, for a charming and persuasive personality can lead multitudes astray.

The big business man, the employer of men, without Christ is a damning influence. In many case employees look up to their employers, and these employers are lost. They wield a damning influence over their men who are lost. We need more out-and-out Christian business men —men who are not afraid, and unashamed to speak of Jesus to others. Incidentally, business men, if you will firmly and courageously take your stand for Christ, others will respect your position. They will not laugh at you. They will look up to you. Don't be afraid to read the Bible and pray in your establishment. Do it quietly, but do it without fear.

Again, mothers and fathers without Christ are a damning influence. Boys and girls often come to the Saviour in spite of their parents, but it is hard for them, and the odds are against them. The hands of many parents will be stained with blood of their children, because they have pointed them toward Hell. Parents, your children need an example. They need to see Christ in your life. They need to know where you stand on this all-important question.

IV. Delay Is Dangerous.

Not only is it unfair to Christ, not only are you losing joy day by day, not only are you a damning influence to others, but putting off Christ is dangerous—it is exceedingly risky.

The common answer given by those who are urged to accept Jesus is, "Not now, some other time." All men intend to be saved some time, but they forget the awful uncertainty of life.

Yes, you mean to repent, but suppose there is no time for repentance. Your good intentions will not save you. You meant to do right about this matter, but there was no time.

I need not remind you of thousands who die daily, who had no opportunity to repent. Death came quickly. I wonder how many of those who go from us by sudden death meant to make things right, but there was no time. Millions will be in Hell who intended to be in Heaven, but life ended suddenly for them, and they were lost.

Often it is said of the penitent thief on the cross that one such case is recorded in Scripture that none may despair of repentance on a death-bed. And only one case is given that none may presume. Do not take the story of the thief on the cross and say that you will be saved at the last hour. It is entirely possible that the thief was hearing the gospel for the first time. Many of you have heard it over and over again. Now is the time to accept.

Take no chance of losing your soul. Flee to the Saviour at once. Life is uncertain, and eternity is long. Therefore, be saved now.

Chapter 3
My Peace

"Peace I leave with you, my peace I give unto you: not as the world giveth, give I unto you. Let not your heart be troubled, neither let it be afraid." John 14:27.

When Christ was about to leave the world, He made His will. His soul He committed to the Father, His body He bequeathed to Joseph to be decently buried. His clothes fell to the soldiers. His mother He left to the care of John, and to His disciples, "My peace I leave with you."

What gracious things are promised to us in the 14th chapter of John. First, we have His promise of a home in Heaven. "In my Father's house are many mansions; if it were not so, I would have told you." Secondly, we have a promise of a way to Heaven through Jesus Christ. "I am the way, the truth, and the life; no man cometh unto the Father but by me." Thirdly, we have the promise of doing greater works than Jesus. "Verily, verily, I say unto you, he that believeth on me, the works that I do shall he do also, and greater works than these shall he do, because I go to my Father."

A fourth promise concerns prayer. "If ye shall ask anything in my name, I will do it." Fifth, He promises to give us the Holy Spirit. "And I will pray the Father and He shall give you another Comforter that He may abide with you forever." Sixth, we are given His peace. "My peace I leave with you."

Let us remember that this bequest of Jesus is for those who have been saved. First, we must make our peace with God before we can receive the peace of God.

There are three distinct marks of a consecrated Christian:

The first is courage. The message of God to His followers is "Fear not," but this is a day of great fear. We fear men. We fear circumstances. We fear the future. We fear sickness. Some fear growing old. Others fear death. The world is in the grip of fear. But to the child of God whose faith is fixed in the eternal, there should be no fear. Therefore, I say it is a mark of consecration when Christians are courageous.

A second distinguishing characteristic of a consecrated Christian is power. The closer we link ourselves to God, the greater our power. The farther we are from the Lord and His will, the less will be our power. Let us not be deceived. We cannot expect to be Christians of power unless our lives are separated and surrendered. When Simon Peter followed afar off, he was powerless, but when he drew nigh to God, and was filled with the Spirit, he had power. When we make a sorry mess of life, the Lord does not tell us to try harder, for this in itself would drive us to despair. But the Heavenly Father says, "Draw close to Me and My strength will be yours." Paul said, "I can do all things through Christ who strengtheneth me." Christ pours power into us when we are near to Him.

A third mark of consecration in the Christian life is peace. Some Christians are as serene and peaceful as our Lord. This is because they have received His peace. They have taken it by faith. They have said goodby to worry and concern. They have learned how to live in the midst of an angry world, but still retain an inner peace.

My friend, is this not the thing we all need so much? Then let us listen to the Saviour who said, "My peace I give unto you."

Underscore the words, *"My peace."* The peace that Jesus had is our peace through His gift. The disciples were often troubled, but Jesus was always peaceful and serene. On the sea of Galilee, when the storm was raging, they were afraid, but Jesus said, "Fear not; peace be still." When the mobs cried, "Crucify! Crucify!" the disciples fled away, but Jesus stood still in perfect peace. Surely this is the peace that we need and we want.

What was the peace of Christ which He gives to us?

I. IT WAS THE PEACE OF ASSURANCE.

Jesus knew that He was God's Son. There was no doubt about this, and, therefore, He had great peace in His heart. John 14:20, He said, "I am in my Father and ye in me, and I in you." Again and again He spoke of His Father. There was complete assurance on the part of Jesus that God was His Father.

The peace of assurance can be ours too. We can know that we are saved. We can know that we are in the family of God, that God is our Father, Christ our Saviour and elder brother. If you have received Jesus as your Saviour, you have the promise of God that you are saved. Any doubts about your salvation cast reflections upon God Himself. Years ago, Dr. J. Wilbur Chapman went to Mr. Moody and said that he was having serious doubts about his salvation. He said, "I do not have the assurance that I am saved." Mr. Moody tried to help him, but could not until he bluntly said, "Mr. Chapman, whom are you doubting?" Dr. Chapman saw that he was doubting God, and from that day he stopped this unintentional sin.

Oh, friend, we may have our good days and our bad days, but God is ever the same. And if our faith is in Him, we can be assured that all is well with our souls.

Assurance of salvation will give us peace as we contemplate death or the second coming of our Lord. Many people fear death. Many do not enjoy sermons on the imminent return of Jesus, for they are conscious of an unreadiness. But when we are ready, we will not be afraid. The story is told that back in 1833 there was a great meteor shower. There lived a boy by the name of Sandy—he was small, not too bright, but filled with faith in God. On the night when it seemed that every star was falling from the heavens, people were alarmed and crying, thinking that the final day of doom had come. Sandy's mother was frightened also, and she aroused him from his sleep, saying, "Sandy, Sandy, get up, will you? The day of judgment has come!" Instantly the boy was alive to the call, and was on his feet shouting, "Glory to God! I am ready!"

Assurance of salvation will also qualify us to help others. If we are doubters, we cannot help those who are lost. We must have a firm hold upon our own salvation before we can help someone else.

There is wonderful peace in knowing that you are saved. Jesus knew that He was God's Son. We, too, can know that we are the children of God by faith in Christ. "To as many as received him, to them gave he power to become the sons of God, even to them that believe on his name."

II. JESUS HAD THE PEACE THAT COMES FROM UNLIMITED RESOURSES.

There was no worry or concern in the Saviour's heart about spiritual or material resources. He knew that the wealth of Heaven belonged to Him. He knew that the power of God was His; therefore, He was serene and untroubled.

Most of us have spent troubled hours thinking about our depleted resources. Sometimes we have recognized that our spiritual resources were small because we were not trusting sufficiently in God. We realized our weakness, spiritually as we faced the duties of life.

Ofttimes we have been troubled about our inadequate material resources. We worry about making ends meet —about getting by. In our worry we further weaken ourselves. We become faithless Christians. We ignore every promise of God's Word.

Jesus knew that He had unlimited resources. From the world's standpoint, He seemed exceedingly poor, but He knew the golden streets of Heaven belonged to Him. The cattle upon a thousand hills were His. The worlds and all that were in them were recorded in His name.

If Christ is your Saviour, then you, too, have unlimited resources. Paul said, "But my God shall supply all your need according to his riches in glory by Christ Jesus."

Have faith in God. He is able to supply every need of life. Jesus said, "My peace I give unto you." Take this peace of Christ about your daily needs.

III. JESUS HAD THE PEACE WHICH COMES FROM UNBROKEN FELLOWSHIP WITH GOD

One thing breaks fellowship with God: SIN. Christ did no sin, therefore, His fellowship was never broken. He was always at one with the Father.

If you would have the peace of God in your hearts, then the line between you and Heaven must be kept intact. When sin enters in, fellowship is broken and peace is gone.

The heart of Jesus was clean. There were no memories of sin to mar His thoughts. He did not have to hear a prophet stand before Him and say, "Thou art the man," as did David. Christ was always able to talk to the Father in unbroken fellowship because of His sinless, pure life.

What terrible things sin does in our lives.

1. It keeps us from prayer. It not alone keeps us from prayer, but makes it impossible for God to answer our prayers when we sin. "If I regard iniquity in my heart, the Lord will not hear me."

2. Sin shuts us off from the Book. The Bible is still in our possession, but we do not read it and love it and meditate upon its pages when fellowship with God is broken through sin.

The Bible is as a mirror, and when the flesh is ruling, we sometimes rebel at seeing ourselves as we are.

3. Sin destroys peace. Sin is as a cancer. It is like a throbbing nerve that does not let us rest. But think of the joy and peace that we have when we have fellowship with God.

Christ is offering His peace to you tonight. Will you accept it? We have mentioned three conditions for having His peace. First, if you are trusting Christ, be assured of your salvation. Secondly, trust in the Lord to supply all of your needs. Third, keep an unbroken fellowship with the Father. If this is not done, there can be no peace.

Chapter 4
Whosoever Is Fearful and Afraid

"Now, therefore go to, proclaim in the ears of the people, saying, Whosoever is fearful and afraid, let him return and depart early from Mount Gilead. And there returned of the people twenty and two thousands; and there remained ten thousands." Judge 7:3

Every portion of God's Word has spiritual significance for all people of all ages. The ancient story of Gideon found in the book of Judges would seem to many people a mere historical account, but to the careful student of the Word of God, there are tremendous spiritual teachings found in this account.

The children of Israel, God's people, were oppressed by the Midianites. In the hour of trouble, it was God's plan back in that day to raise up a leader for the people —someone to deliver them from their enemies. When the Midianites came against Israel, God spoke to Gideon. Let us not forget this, that Israel's difficulties came because of their sin. In the case of the Midianites, God delivered Israel into their hands for a period of seven years because His people did that which was evil.

But, though God allowed His people to be chastened, He also provided a deliverer. Gideon was chosen for this specific task. He tried as Moses did to escape the call of God. He made excuses and would not accept the call until God gave an evident token of His presence. Finally, Gideon began his task. He issued a call for the Israelites to help him. Thirty-two thousand came to his side.

In my imagination, I can hear Gideon saying, "Thirty-two thousand is a mighty small army to fight against the large army of the Midianites. He might have prepared to issue another call for additional warriors, but God put an end to this by saying, "Gideon, you have too many men."

There are three main divisions to my sermon for this morning: God's Purge, God's Plan, and God's Purpose.

I. GOD'S PURGE.

Thirty-two thousand men came to assist Gideon in delivering the nation from the hands of the Midianites. God said, "The people that are with thee are too many for me to give the Midianites into their hands, lest Israel vaunt themselves against me, saying, Mine own hand hath saved me." We see at once why God said there were too many. He knew that if they won the battle with an army of thirty-two thousand, they would have reason to boast, but they had won in their own strenth and without the help of God.

Therefore, a first test was put to the people. It was a very simple thing, but it was effective in reducing the size of Gideon's army. He simply said, "Whosoever is fearful and afraid, let him return and depart." With this simple statement twenty-two thousand departed. They resigned their places in the army.

It is always easy to thin the ranks of Christian volunteers by the simple expedient of saying, "If you are afraid of the task and fearful that the job is too much for you, I would suggest that you quit now." I believe I can take a hundred volunteers in the church, perhaps a hundred teachers and officers of the Sunday School, and say such a thing to them, and perhaps from twenty-five to fifty per cent of them would say, "Well, I believe I will resign now."

In my nineteen years of preaching, I have noticed a very interesting thing about consecration invitations. If I give a general invitation for people to come forward who want to give themselves completely to the Lord and to live closer to Him, the response will be quick and quite numerous. But I have observed that if I will stop in the midst of such an invitation and say, "Please do not come unless you mean it. This invitation is wholly for those who mean business," at once the general movement of the people will cease, and the flood of forward marchers will diminish to a mere trickle.

I do not have time to enlarge upon this portion of the message except to say God is calling for brave, courageous, whole-hearted followers. The fearful and afraid will not stand long in the heat of battle.

When the army was cut to ten thousand, still God said, "You have too many." This time God gave directions for the final sifting. It was a simple, but remarkable test. The remaining ten thousand were ordered to go down to the water's edge and to take a drink. The Lord said, "Divide the men according to the way they drink. If they drop to their knees and put their faces into the water and drink, forgetful of all else, put them in one company." Then He said, "The men who stand on their feet and dip up the water with their hands, put them in another company." When the test was over, nine thousand seven hundred of the men were in the group of those who dropped to their knees and drank to the full. Only three hundred had remained upon their feet, watchful and alert, ready for any emergency. God said, "By these three hundred men that lapped will I save you and deliver the Midianites into thine hands: and let all the other people go every man unto his place."

There is little place in the service of Christ for the self-indulgent. The whole cause of Christ is injured by those who want to do something, but cannot put self out of the way. These three hundred men who stood the test were self-disciplined and self-controlled men, eager for the fight and ready to obey orders at any time.

Here is God's purge: Let the fearful and the afraid go home. Send home the self-indulgent. God's battles can be won by those who have courage and those who know the meaning of self-denial.

II. GOD'S PLAN.

With only three hundred men, God gave to His servant a plan for defeating the hosts of the Midianites. To human eyes, this plan seemed foolish, but it was God's plan. God's way of salvation, through the crucified and risen Son of God, looks foolish to people of the world, but it is God's plan.

The following equipment was given to each man: A trumpet, an empty vessel, a lamp, and, of course, each man had the example of Gideon to follow.

The trumpet represents the gospel message which is to be sounded out. If we fail to sound the gospel trumpet, the blood of others will be upon our hands. Christians are to be watchmen. Here is the word of Ezekiel 33:6 "But if the watchman see the sword come, and blow not the trumpet, and the people be not warned; if the sword come, and take any person from among them, he is taken away in his inquity, but his blood will I require at thine hand."

Secondly, the empty vessel is a picture of the redeemed sinner. If the child of God is to be used, he is to be emptied of all pride, self-esteem, self-sufficiency, and all that would hinder the purpose of God through him. Paul said, "But we have this treasure in earthen vessels, that the excellency of the power may be of God and not of us." II Cor. 4:7. Again the apostle speaks in II Timothy 2:21,

"If a man therefore purge himself from these, he shall be a vessel unto honor, sanctified, and meet for the master's use, and prepared for every good work."

Are you an empty vessel for God to use?

Thirdly, the torch is the Christian's testimony. Jesus said, "Let your light so shine before men, that they may see your good works, and glorify your Father which is in Heaven." Matt. 5:16

The apostle tells us, "That ye may be blameless and harmless, the sons of God, without rebuke, in the midst of a crooked and perverse nation, among whom ye shine as lights in the world." Philippians 2:15

It was said of John the Baptist that he was a burning and shining light. Christians are to be firebrands, burning for Christ, and only as we burn for Him shall we shine for Him.

Fourth, they had an example and a leader. Gideon said to the three hundred, "Look on me and do likewise: and, behold, when I come to the outside of the camp, it shall be that, as I do, so shall ye do."

Christ is our example. He calls us to follow Him and He will make us to become fishers of men. He is our example in love. He said, "A new commandment I give unto you that ye love one another, as I have loved you; that ye also love one another." John 13:34

He is our example in self-denial. "Verily, verily I say unto you, Except a corn of wheat fall into the ground and die, it abideth alone; but if it die, it bringeth forth much fruit." John 12:24

He is our example in service and tells us, "For I have given you an example that ye should do as I have done to you. Verily, verily, I say unto you, The servant is not greater than his lord; neither he that is sent than he that sent him." John 13:15, 16

He is our example in humility. "And being found in fashion as a man, he humbled himself, and became obedient unto death, even the death of the cross." Philippians 2:8

He is our example in the Christian walk. "He that saith he abideth in him ought himself also so to walk, even as he walked." I John 2:6

He is our example in suffering. "For even hereunto were ye called, because Christ also suffered for us, leaving us an example that ye should follow his steps." I Peter 2:21

Gideon's three hundred men had a trumpet, a empty vessel, a torch, and a leader.

Gideon divided his men into three companies. At the appointed time they stood around the camp of the Midianites. When Gideon gave the signal, they blew the trumpets and broke the pitchers which were in their hands and held high the torches in their left hands. They waved the torches, blew the trumpets, and shouted between their blowing, "The sword of the Lord and of Gideon." The enemy was routed, and in their confusion, they began to kill one another. The victory was gained by following God's plan.

Yes, the plan of God may seem simple, unusual, and even foolish to the wordly minded, but it must be followed. Salvation comes through following God's way. Success in the Christian's life can be achieved only by obeying God. Victory can only come through a church as it obeys God and follows His plan.

III. God's Purpose.

It seems to me that the purpose of God in this remarkable occurrence is quite evident.

First, God was revealing His unlimited power. Modernism and faithless Christians have just about made the world believe that God is powerless, but not so. Our God is able to do great and mighty things for His own.

Jesus said, "All power is given unto me in Heaven and in earth. Go ye therefore."

To the disciples on the day of His ascension, He said, "But ye shall receive power, after that the Holy Spirit is come upon you." God has power, and He gives this power to those who will receive it.

You may not be much. Your talents may be few, but God has the power.

Secondly, God's purpose in this account is to show what faith will do. Gideon had to have faith. His three hundred men had to have faith, both in God and their leader. The fearful and the afraid did not have much faith, therefore, they went home. I believe that faith in God will accomplish anything. It will save souls, build churches, transform lives, heal the sick, feed the hungry, comfort the sorrowing. No wonder Jesus said, "Have faith in God.

Thirdly, God's purpose was to bring glory to Himself. Glory belongs to God. If thirty-two thousand men had defeated the Midianites, there would have been nothing but self-boasting. But when three hundred won the battle, it had to be by the hand of God; three hundred men with their trumpets—three hundred men with empty vessels and torches. Incidentally, let us remember that the broken vessels represent the Christian, empty of self and broken and submissive to the will of God. Note also that when the empty vessels were broken, the lights were made to shine forth. But with this small army and small equipment, the victory was won.

Let us beware of glorifying self. Spiritual disaster and destitution await that person who takes glory to himself which belongs to God.

Let it be known far and wide that the work of salvation is God's work and not man's. Let us in humility recognize that the building of the church must be the work of God and not the work of any individual.

In Acts 12 we read of Herod the king, who gave not God the glory, and he was eaten of worms, and gave up the ghost. This verse following this record of Herod's demise tell us, "But the Word of God grew and multiplied."

God has a purpose for you, my friend. Are you willing for God to have His way in your life? If you have never accepted Christ, then do so at once. There comes a call for Christian soldiers, for those who love God and seek His will.

Chapter 5
The Shoulders of Jesus

"For unto us a child is born; unto us a son is given: and the government shall be upon his shoulder: and his name shall be called Wonderful, Counsellor, The mighty God, The everlasting Father, The Prince of Peace." Isaiah 9:6

Sermons have been preached about the eyes of Christ, the hands and feet of Christ, the voice of Jesus, but I do not recall any sermon on the shoulders of Jesus. And yet the Word makes a number of references to His shoulders. These references illustrate the past, present, and future working of Jesus.

Let us seek to exalt Christ again as we turn to the Word of God.

I. THE CROSS ON HIS SHOULDERS.

Here is illustrated *substitution*.

"And he, bearing his cross, went forth into a place called the place of a skull, which is called in the Hebrew, Golgotha." John 19:17

As we see the cross on His shoulders, we are reminded of three things.

First, *His willingness to bear the cross*. Even from before the foundation of the world, Jesus manifested a willingness to bear the cross for us. The answer of Jesus to the challenge of the cross is given in Hebrews 10:9, "Then said he, Lo, I come to do thy will, O God." When Jesus bore the cross and died upon it, there was no coercion. He willingly gave Himself. They did not take His life—He laid down His life. Hear these words:

"Therefore doth my Father love me, because I lay down my life, that I might take it again.

The Shoulders of Jesus

"No man taketh it from me, but I lay it down of myself. I have power to lay it down, and I have power to take it again. This commandment have I received of my Father." John 10:17, 18

With all willingness, the Saviour hastened to do the will of God. He was not drafted—He volunteered. He did not draw back—He pressed forward to the cross.

Secondly, we remember His determination to bear the cross. It is written that He set His face as flint toward Jerusalem and Calvary. Peter tried to reason with the Lord, and deter Him, but He said, "Get thee behind me, Satan." There are not many of us who cannot be persuaded to turn from any hard or trying path. We may be willing to suffer for Jesus if it is absolutely necessary, but if an easy path is offered us, small persuasion will cause us to take it. Jesus was determined. There was no looking to the right, nor to the left, but straight forward to the cursed tree.

Thirdly, the cross on His shoulders reminds us of His purpose. The purpose of Christ was to bring many sons unto glory. Yes, He took the sinner's place. He bore the cross which we should have borne. He carried it for us. Here is the glorious doctrine of substitution. "Who his own self bore our sins in his own body on the tree."

Isaiah 53:6 tells us that He took our place. "All we like sheep have gone astray; we have turned everyone to his own way, and the Lord hath laid on him the iniquity of us all."

Perhaps the best Scriptural illustration of substitution to be found is in the story of Barabbas. Barabbas was condemned to die, but the people said, "Release him and crucify Jesus." It may be on that day when Barabbas was released, he saw the great crowd going toward Mt. Calvary. Perhaps he followed the crowd, and stood in the surging mob around the cross. As he stood there, he must have realized that Jesus was dying in his place. This is the doctrine of substitution—Christ dying for sinners.

> "I see my Saviour with thorn-crowned head,
>   Bearing His cross for me;
> Thorns pierced His brow as by soldiers led,
>   Bearing His cross for me.
> "I see Him pass through the city gates.
>   Bearing His cross for me;
> On midst the taunts and the people's hate,
>   Bearing His cross for me.
> "I see Him burdened with this world's sin,
>   Bearing His cross for me,
> Willing to suffer all hearts to win,
>   Bearing His cross for me.
> "Bearing His cross for me,
>   Bearing His cross for me.
> Wonderful Saviour, what anguish He bore,
>   Bearing His cross for me."

II. THE SHEEP ON HIS SHOULDERS.

Here is *salvation*.

"And when he had found it, he layeth it on his shoulders, rejoicing." Luke 15:5.

One of the notable parables of Jesus concerned the man who had a hundred sheep. Ninety-nine of them were safe in the fold and one sheep was lost. At once the man went searching for the lost sheep, and when he found it, he laid it on his shoulders and brought it home rejoicing.

The sheep on His shoulders illustrates the following:

First, it illustrates His concern for the lost. Here we see the Saviour going after those who are wandering away from God and lost. Lost friend, remember this: No one is so concerned about your condition as Jesus. It was often written of Him that He had compassion when He saw the multitudes. The concern of the Saviour's heart was the winning of the lost. He did not write books. He did not engineer the building of roads, bridges, or buildings. He did not ask for a place of prominence. The Lord was concerned about the lost. He is the seeking Saviour. This same concern should characterize the lives of all Christians. Without concern for the lost, we will be dry, dead, and formal in our religious life. It is anxiety for lost loved ones and friends that changes our lives and makes our hearts warm with concern for others.

A mission paper came to my desk during the past week and caried the headline, "Dry Eyes and Cold Hearts Have Been the Curse of Us." The sub-headline read, "Do We Substitute a Bank Book for Bleeding Hearts?" I have tried to throw away that little mission magazine all week, but have been unable to do so because of that headline. Yes, it is true that dry eyes and cold hearts have been the curse of us. Jesus was concerned. His heart was warm and throbbing for others. He went out seeking the lost, and He goes today seeking the lost.

Secondly, His power is illustrated by the sheep on His shoulders. If the sheep will stop and surrender, the shepherd will lay it on his shoulders and bring it to safety. Think of the wandering lost ones Jesus has found and laid on His shoulders. Simon Peter, a rough, profane fisherman of the Sea of Galilee was found by Jesus. Paul, the persecutor of Christians, a most unlikely man, was found by Jesus and laid upon His shoulders. John Bunyan, a swearing, profane tinker, was found and carried by the Shepherd. Martin Luther, a half-starved monk, seeking to work his way into Heaven, was found by the Shepherd. Oh, the mighty power of Jesus to seek and to save! "He layeth it on his shoulders rejoicing."

Friend, do you feel that your life is meaningless and empty? Do you feel that all joy has gone from you? Then listen, Christ is seeking for you, and He has the power to save and give meaning to life. It is said that one Sunday Dr. F. B. Meyer paused in the middle of his sermon and stooping down to where the orchestra was, he picked up a piece of string that had been thrown away by a player. Holding it up, he said, "There shall never any more music come out of this, but though your heart be broken and your life be broken, God can bring harmony out of them again."

Again, we have illustrated the Saviour's complete and final success, for He tells us that when He found the sheep, He layeth it on His shoulders, and "when he cometh home." The Lord does not save and then toss away. He saves eternally. Every mention of salvation is eternal salvation. Those who are in the Saviour's hands are kept forever, for He tells us, "And I give unto them eternal life, and they shall never perish, neither shall any man pluck them out of my hand. My Father which gave them me is greater than all, and no man is able to pluck them out of my Father's hand."

Every sheep found by the Saviour will be brought safely home without the loss of one.

III. THE GOVERNMENT ON HIS SHOULDERS.

This speaks of *completion*.

"For unto us a child is born; unto us a son is given: and the government shall be upon his shoulder."

Throughout the Old and New Testaments there are prophecies of the coming of Jesus and His personal reign upon the earth. Christ is coming to rule the world. The world is now ruled by Satan, who is the prince of this world. But one day Satan shall be overthrown and Christ will reign supreme.

When you get discouraged and dismayed because of the sin of this world, look to the time when Jesus is coming in power and great glory.

He is coming to resurrect the dead in Christ. When He comes, those who died in the Lord will come forth from the tombs.

He is coming to change the living and to snatch them up into the air, the dead first, and then the living. The Lord is coming according to His promise in John 14 to receive His own.

He is coming to reign as King of kings and Lord of lords. Universal righteousness will cover the earth. Justice, love, and mercy will be known between all men. The Lord is going to reign. The government shall be on His shoulder.

If our blessed Lord is coming to rule the entire world one day, then surely we need to let Him rule our lives now. What a mess we make of things when we seek to run our own lives and ignore Christ.

This week I was called to the hospital to visit a man who had attempted to take his life. He had slashed his throat from side to side. I was taken to the emergency room and found him still lying upon the table. He was almost completely covered with blood. When I introduced myself, he put out a hand that was completely blood-covered. The nurses stepped out of the room and I talked with him. I said, "My friend, your condition has come about because you have tried to run your own life." He said, "That's right." I said, "Man always makes a mess of things when he leaves God out of his plans. What you need is the Lord Jesus as your Saviour and Lord and Master." He replied, "I wish you had told me this yesterday. I'm afraid it's too late now." I said, "No, it is not too late. If even now you will repent of your sins and believe on Jesus, He will save you." After prayer he said, "I will do it," and I shook again the hand which was completely covered with blood.

His words which I cannot forget are the words, "I wish you could have told me this yesterday. Things might be different now."

I am saying to you friends tonight—some of you may have come to the end of yourselves. You need Christ. Let him rule and reign over your life. Let the responsibility of your life be upon the Saviour. He is fully able to bear. Let His will be your will. Let His way be your way. Let Him be your Saviour now.

See Christ with the cross on His shoulders. This speaks of substitution. See Christ with the sheep on His shoulders. This speaks of salvation. See Christ with the government on His shoulders. This speaks of completion. One day He shall reign over the whole earth—but now let Him reign over your life.

Chapter 6
Cross Bearing

"*And as they came out, they found a man of Cyrene, Simon by name: him they compelled to bear his cross.*" Matthew 27:32

And they compel one Simon a Cyrenian, who passed by, coming out of the country, the father of Alexander and Rufus, to bear his cross." Mark 15:21

"*And as they led him away, they laid hold upon one Simon, a Cyrenian, coming out of the country, and on him they laid the cross, that he might bear it after Jesus.*" Luke 23:26

There are many opinions as to why Simon was compelled to carry the cross of Jesus. Almost all of the commentators draw the conclusion that Simon was compelled to bear the Saviour's cross because he was staggering and sinking beneath its weight. There is no word in the Scripture to support such a conjecture. Some commentators reason that the enemies of Jesus were afraid that He might faint and die beneath the load of His cross, and thereby prevent them the pleasure of crucifying Him.

At any rate, this is what we find. After the soldiers had mocked Jesus, they took off the purple robe they had placed upon Him, and put His own clothes on Him, and then led Him out to be crucified. Matthew, Mark, and Luke tell us that a man by the name of Simon, a Cyrenian, who was coming out of the country, or out of the fields, was compelled to bear the Saviour's cross. Mark tell us that Simon was the father of Alexander and Rufus. Many believe that he was a disciple of Christ.

It was a Roman custom that a criminal should bear his own cross to the place of execution. But in this case, another was forced to bear the cross. It is almost certain that Jesus bore the cross for a time until Simon was forced to do it.

From this picture of Jesus, making His way toward Calvary's hill, and Simon following after carrying the cross, we find many lessons.

I. SIMON, BEARING THE CROSS, TELLS ME THAT WE HAVE CROSSES TO BEAR.

When we use the term, *cross*, we use it to stand for suffering and affliction.

Sometimes the cross may come upon us suddenly, even as it came on Simon. In Mark's gospel, it is indicated that Simon was passing by, coming out of the fields, when suddenly the cross was thrust upon him.

There are crosses we must bear, and ofttimes we are surprised when we find them upon our shoulders.

There is the cross of suffering. You may have spent many years in perfect health until one day you found yourself with the cross of suffering. You hardly knew that you had it. You tried to say that it wasn't so, but there it was. Suffering and affliction of body are widespread throughout the world. Those of use who are in good health should ever be sympathetic toward others, patient and eager to help them, and thankful to God for His blessings to us.

There is the cross of disappointment. Very few people go through life without at some time bearing this heavy cross. It may be that you had high hopes for your family. You sought to make your children into honest, respectable citizens, but they refused to accept such a place. Bitter disappointment was yours. Again, life may have disappointed you greatly because of your own failure. In young days a person sets a high goal for himself, and when that day remains a distant star, never to be reached, the disappointment is great. It is a cross to bear.

Again, there is the cross of sorrow and loneliness. Loved ones have been taken from you, and in spite of your submissiveness to the will of God, there is still the cross of sorrow and loneliness. This is not a cross to throw away, but it is one to bear. Our Saviour was a Man of sorrows, and has often been charactertized as the loneliest Man who ever walked upon the earth—lonely, because there was no one to fully understand; sorrowful because of the world's sin and rebellion against God. Yes, our Saviour surely knows how to sympathize with those who bear the cross of sorrow. Because He was lonely, He offers His presence to all who will receive Him, and says to us, "Lo, I am with you alway, even unto the end of the age."

There is also the cross of persecution. Jesus knew the full meaning of this. The apostle Paul bore this cross, "and all who live godly in Christ Jesus" must bear it also. Our lives are not Christ-like when all men speak well of us. When we stand for something, there will surely be persecutors. This is a cross to be borne.

There are three attitudes you can take toward your cross. First, you can refuse to bear it, and take the coward's way out. Between 25,000 and 30,000 choose this way each year in our country. Most of these thought the cross was too heavy. Life was meaningless. They did not have the courage to fight on, therefore, they took the quick way out.

Secondly, you can take your cross, bear it, but complain about its weight. This is the predicament of so many complaining Christians. They take the crosses of suffering, sorrow, persecution, and disappointment, but they continually complain about the hardness of the way. They make themselves miserable and everybody about them.

Thirdly, you can take the cross and bear it in the

spirit of Christ. There was no complaining on the part of our Master when He bore His cross. Simon was later compelled to bear it, but the Word does not record any complaint on His part. No one races to get a cross, but when the cross is placed upon us, we should bear it in the spirit of Jesus.

Yes, we have crosses to bear. How are you bearing yours?

II. Simon, Bearing The Cross, Tells Me That We Can All Have A Place In The Work Of Christ.

It is true that Simon was drafted, but he carried the cross nevertheless.

Bearing the heavy, unwieldly cross was not a pleasant task, but think of the honor bestowed upon Simon of Cyrene. He carried the cross but a few minutes, but his name is written down in the Word of God forever. Wherever this gospel is preached, and this Book read, his name is mentioned, for he bore the Saviour's cross to Calvary's hill.

My friends, any work for Jesus is an honor. Though the task be small, obscure, and thankless, it is an honor to work for Jesus. Even though it be mopping the floors in God's house, we should deem it a great honor. If we could have such an appreciation of the Lord's work, it would be so much easier to get workers.

Simon was compelled to bear the cross, but let us respond joyfully to the call of Christ to work for Him. In whatever field of service He may want us, may we with alacrity hasten to His side. Take any position offered you in the Lord's work, and work joyfully, knowing that it is for Him. If no place is offered you, then do the task which you see needs to be done, and give it the very best you have.

III. SIMON, BEARING THE CROSS, TELLS ME THAT IT TAKES COURAGE TO BEAR HIS CROSS.

Matthew and Mark tell us that they compelled Simon to bear the cross. It is quite evident from these words that no one volunteered to bear it. Apparently there was no one in all that crowd with sufficient compassion and courage to volunteer to carry it for Christ. It was a reproach and none would do it, but by compulsion.

We cannot bear the actual heavy, troublesome cross which Simon bore after Jesus. But we can spiritually bear the cross of Christ. It takes great courage to do so, but thank God, many are doing it.

To those who are fearful of the shame and reproach in bearing his cross, let me say:

First, have the courage to identify yourself with the cross. There are still enemies of the cross of Christ who would seek to turn you aside by making you ashamed of the cross. That is the reason we have modernism today. People are seeking for a religion without the cross. They do not like to hear about the shed blood of Christ. They are ashamed of the simple gospel, salvation by substitution.

The apostle Paul identified himself with the cross. We find it oft mentioned in his writings.

"For Christ sent me not to baptize, but to preach the gospel, not with wisdom of words, lest the cross of Christ should be made of none effect.

"For the preaching of the cross is to them that perish foolishness; but unto us which are saved, it is the power of God..." I Cor. 1:17, 18

"But God forbid that I should glory save in the cross of our Lord Jesus Christ, by whom the world is crucified unto me, and I unto the world." Gal. 6:14

Have the courage to identify yourself with the old-fashioned gospel of the cross.

Secondly, have the courage to feel the weight of the cross. By this I mean do not draw back from the hardships which come along the Christian way. Welcome every suffering and heartache if it be for Jesus' sake. Paul wrote to the Philippians, saying,

"That I may know him, and the power of his resurrection and the fellowship of his sufferings, being made conformable unto his death."

Christ-likeness is not achieved by easy living. We become more like the Master as we suffer for Him. Note carefully, you are not to make yourself suffer, but suffering will come if you live a true, consecrated life.

Thirdly, have the courage to testify to the meaning of the cross. What is the meaning of the cross? I think it is all summed up in these five words of I Cor. 15:3—

"Christ died for our sins."

This must be our constant theme. All others are secondary. Men must be pointed to the Lamb of God who taketh away the sin of the world. Unless people come to the cross, and see Jesus dying for them, all else is in vain. All knowledge and achievement are nothing unless there is salvation. This salvation comes from Christ who died upon Calvary's hill and rose for our justification, and comes again to receive us unto Himself.

The story is told of a man and woman who were leaving a mission in London, where the song had just been sung:

"Down in the valley, or upon the mountain steep,
 Close beside my Saviour would my soul ever keep;
 He will lead me safely, in the paths that He has trod,
 Up to where they gather on the hills of God."

"What are the hills of God?" asked the woman.

The man slowly replied, "I don't know, but I should think one of them would be Calvary."

Yes, friends, one of God's hills is Calvary, and this must be climbed before we can see Him.

May we ever have the courage to testify to the meaning of the cross. Let us not be ashamed of it. Let us not be led aside by any socialistic gospel, or any modernistic philosophies. Let our theme ever be, "Christ and Him crucified."

A little boy, cold and hungry, was found by a city missionary in London. He was invited to go to the mission for food and shelter. He was told to ring the bell and when they asked him who he was, to say three words: "In His name." The little fellow went to the mission. He ventured up the steps and true to the promise of the worker, he received a royal welcome, a good supper, and a warm bed. A few days afterward, he was hurt in a London thoroughfare by a passing car. The card of the rescue home was found in his pocket, and after he was taken to the hospital, word was sent to the mission. During the last few days of his life, he was tenderly cared for by loving Christians. They told him of Jesus, the only Saviour. They pointed him to Heaven, and said, "There is just one way in, and that is in His name." It was said that often during the last hours of the little fellow's life, he would repeat the words, "In His name, in His name, that's what gets you in."

Yes, it is by the name of Christ that we receive admittance to Heaven. It is in His name that we can live victoriously here below. It is in His name that we are empowered to do His work. It is in His name that we can bear the cross which life gives to us.

Look unto Jesus today. Believe on Him, and in His name, Heaven's door will open wide to receive you.

Chapter 7
Does Jesus Live at Your House?

"Now it came to pass, as they went, that he entered into a certain village: and a certain woman named Martha received him into her house.

"And she had a sister called Mary, which also sat at Jesus' feet, and heard the word;

"But Martha was cumbered about much serving, and came to him, and said, Lord, dost thou not care that my sister hath left me to serve alone? bid her therefore that she help me.

"And Jesus answered and said unto her, Martha, Martha, thou art careful and troubled about many things:

"But one thing is needful: and Mary hath chosen that good part, which shall not be taken away from her." Luke 10:38-42

Perhaps no better time could be selected for a message on the home than this Christmas season. This is a time when people think about home. It is a time when people living in distant places plan to be home for Christmas.

As far as I am concerned, there is nothing beautiful about a home that does not have Jesus in the center of it. Through the years it has been my privilege to observe hundreds of homes. I have found that a home without Christ is a desolate, dreary, miserable spot. All of the fine furnishings, all of the social gatherings, cannot change a Christless home into a beautiful, happy spot.

For a home to be its best, the presence of Christ must hallow each room.

A simple poem came to my desk a few days ago. The title is, "Does Jesus Live at Your House?" Let me read it to you:

Does Jesus Live at Your House?

"Does Jesus live at your house?"
    I heard a child once ask:
Her little brow was furrowed
    As she struggled with a task,
I saw her eyes were shadowed,
    Her face marked with a tear;
The voice a wee bit wistful
    For the answer she might hear.

"He used to live at our house,
    With Mamma—Daddy, too,
But now He's gone away somewhere
    I don't know what to do,
For Daddy's not the same today,
    And Mamma laughs no more,
They never bother much with me,
    They say I'm just a bore.

It didn't use to be this way
    With Jesus in our home,
For every night my Daddy came
    When all my curls were combed,
To help me say my bedtime prayer,
    (And Mamma helped me too.)
And they'd smile and tuck me in,
    But now—they never do.

"Could you tell me where Jesus is?
    For everything seems black:
We want Him in our house again
    We want Him to come back.
And when He comes we'll keep Him
    For we truly need Him so—
If Jesus lives at your house,
    Oh! don't ever let Him go!"

> "The child then turned and left me
> While I pursued my way
> And thought of many home-fires
> That could be bright today.
> Does Jesus live at your house?
> How much these words portend
> Yea! On this question's answer,
> Our hopes—our all—depends."

Yes, there are some homes that were once Christian, but they are no more. Certain things took place, and now the presence of Jesus is no longer felt in the home. In some cases, the making of money became paramount, and allegiance to Christ was forgotten. In other cases the pursuit of pleasure began to take first place, and the home disintegrated. Yes, many homes were once beautiful and happy through the presence of Christ, but not today.

Again, there are some homes that have never known what it means to be Christian. They have never honored Christ—they have never received Him.

The first great essential in the building of a Christian home is to receive Jesus. He must be admitted into the heart of the members of the home. This is not a polite acceptance of the fact that Christ is the Son of God, but it must be the experience of receiving Him as Saviour, which results in the New Birth. We must not at any time deceive ourselves into thinking that a home can be made Christian simply by uniting with the church. The homes of many church members are as hellish and miserable as the homes of out and out sinners.

Therefore, the first prerequisite to a Christian home is to receive Christ as Saviour.

After acceptance of Christ, there are still some things to do in order to make your home a Christian home.

May I suggest some of them.

I. HONOR THE CHURCH.

The Bible gives many good reasons why we should honor the church. First, we should honor it because it was purchased by the blood of Christ.

"Take heed, therefore, unto yourselves, and to all the flock, over the which the Holy Ghost hath made you overseers, to feed the church of God, which he hath purchased with his own blood." Acts 20:28

And again, in Ephesians 5:25 we read, "Even as Christ also loved the church, and gave himself for it."

We should also honor the church because Christ is the head of it. Ephesians 1:22, "And hath put all things under his feet, and gave him to be the head over all things to the church."

And in Ephesians 5:23 "For the husband is the head of the wife, even as Christ is the head of the church; and he is the Saviour of the body."

The church is God's evangelizing agency in this age. We cannot ignore the commission of our Saviour. He has given us His command to go into all the world and preach the gospel.

Therefore, we should honor the church by attending the services. The first step to a backslidden Christian life is to absent onself from the house of God. I'm sure that one reason for the sinking condition of so many homes is the failure to attend the house of God. When I say that we ought to attend the services of the church, I speak of all of our specified meetings. All of the Sunday services should be attended and the Wednesday prayer service. Too many people have a Sunday morning type of religion. You can't build a Christian home on anything as shallow as that. You cannot tie your home to the church of God by a single service on Sunday morning. There are 168 hours in the week; at least six of these should be given to the Lord, and as many more as we can.

Mothers and fathers need not lament the wayward, drifting condition of their children if they persist in staying away from God's house. I can name a number of homes in our church today where mother and father used to attend regularly, and their children came with them. Today, the parents come only occasionally, and the children come not at all. Some parents have told me that they do not know what to do with their children, for no amount of persuasion will bring them to church. Parents, you are reaping what you sowed.

Again, we should honor the church by giving our money. I make no apology for saying that every child of God should be a tither, and I say without any fear or contradiction that every home would be blessed materially and spiritually if the tithing plan were adopted and followed. God has had a plan in everything He has done, and He has a financial plan. We cannot prosper if we ignore God's financial program. I am still ready to give $500.00 to anyone who can produce a consistent tither who is a beggar, or is forced to depend upon welfare agencies for his subsistence.

Thirdly, honor the church by giving your talents to the Lord's work. There is such a desperate need for work, even in a church such as ours where scores have enlisted in service, we still have great need. Some phases of our work suffer at all times because of the lack of faithful servants.

If your home is to be a Christian home, then you must honor the church of Jesus Christ.

II. HONOR THE WORD OF GOD.

You cannot hope to build a Christian home without

daily consultation with God's guide book. Almost every home in America has a Bible, but the Bible is read in few homes.

Here is a rule for your home: The Bible should be read aloud in your home, in the presence of your family, at least once each day. Find the time best suited to the family, and establish the rule that the Bible will be read each day at that time. It may be at the breakfast hour, or it may be at the evening meal, or it might be before retiring at night. But if you are willing to pay the price, to put first things first, there is a time when your home can be blessed by the reading of the Word of God.

A dusty Bible will never bring blessings to your home. Someone has said,
"These hath God married, and no man shall part;
Dust on the Bible, and drouth in the heart."

A clean, unmarked Bible is not a good testimony. The Bible is to be read, yea, to be worn out with much handling. When one copy is torn up, another can be purchased. But let your home be blessed by the reading of God's Holy Word.

III. To Build A Christian Home,
 Give Due Place To Prayer.

After the reading of the Word should come prayer time. You will find that serious, earnest prayer will put your home in direct contact with Christ. Prayer will drive out bitterness, harshness, yea, and even infidelity.

Prayer is the key to every needed thing.

Prayer is the way to victory. Prayer is the cord which binds us together. The more we pray, the more blessed and happy will be the home.

Children should be taught the meaning of prayer. Prayerless young people come out of prayerless homes. In my daily visitation, I am astonished to find many homes where people do not know what to do with themselves when I say, "Let us pray." Ofttimes large children will stand in the middle of the floor in amazement when I drop to my knees and begin to pray. They have never seen anything like it, and they do not know what to make of it . On one or two occasions, small children have been frightened into tears when I asked the folks to bow with me in prayer. They could not understand what it was all about. I do not blame the children, but I blame the parents for failing in their responsibility to teach their children the meaning of prayer and the need of prayer. The little ones need an example on the part of the parents so that to them prayer might be as natural as breathing.

Let there be no lightness, nor levity about spiritual matters. It is never good to joke about the Bible, or to joke about prayer. Any such action will lessen the reverence of young and old for sacred things.

A critical attitude on the part of adults toward the church, the ministry, and the services of the church shall reveal itself in the children in later days. They will begin to question the importance of church attendance, Bible reading and prayer, if we criticize or make light of these vital things. Again, skepticism expressed by adults will reveal itself in the lives of young people. I spoke to a young Intermediate lad about being a Christian, and he replied, "I don't believe the Bible. There are too many mistakes in it." I asked him where he got such an idea, and he said, "Oh, I just thought of it myself." I knew at once that this was not true. I learned later that the boy's father is a snarling, bitter skeptic, who delights in ridiculing the Bible and making fun of Christians. That father will doubtless be priviledged to have the company of his son in Hell for eternity because of his attitude.

Your home needs the family altar. In real earnestness, you need to set aside a time each day for the reading of God's Word and prayer. Your home must honor the church and if Christ lives at your house, He will be directing your steps to the place of worship.

I believe you can tell the home where Jesus lives. There is a blessed peace, a happiness, a gentleness, and a love not found in the home of the world.

The storms may beat upon the Christian's home, but it stands firm and fast. Sorrows, like sea billows, may roll against its walls, but it stands. The sun may refuse to shine for weeks and months and years, but still the Christian home has comfort and cheer. Like Martha of old, receive Jesus into your home. Sit at His feet as did Mary, and listen to His words.

America needs Christian homes. As go our homes, so goes the nation. A wise teacher of ancient days said, "Give me a single domestic grace, and I will turn it into a hundred public virtues." The Christian home contributes to peaceful living, curbs juvenile delinquency, lowers the divorce rate, kills atheism, and builds a wall of security about our nation which no enemy can tear down.

Answer the question today, "Does Jesus live at your house?" If He has never entered, then let Him in today. If He was once there, then open wide the door again, and bid Him enter. Does Jesus live in your heart? If not, receive Him now.

Chapter 8
A Death Vision

"Behold, I see the heavens opened, and the Son of man standing on the right hand of God." Acts 7:56

The world has had but few men as great as Stephen, one of the leaders in the first church of Jerusalem. His life was as a meteor, burning brightly for a time, and then suddenly ending in a martyr's death. But the light of Stephen's life and testimony has never gone out. His life and labors were brief, but his influence and testimony reach into eternity. We need more men of such caliber today. It is such men that move the world for God.

In two chapters of The Acts, we learn much about this man. He was one of seven deacons chosen by the early church.

He was a man of good and honest life. Only men of honest report were considered for the work of deacon.

He was full of the Holy Ghost. This was also a qualification. The fruit of his life verifies that he was full of the Spirit.

He was a man full of faith, for so we read in Acts 6:5. By this we judge that he was not the type of individual who limits God, but believed in God with all his heart, and believed in a God able to perform the hardest task.

He was full of power (Acts 6:8). When one is full of the Holy Spirit, power will be the natural result. Power came because he was separated unto God, and filled with the Spirit. This is the need of all Christian workers today. We need to be endued with power from on high.

A Death Vision

He was full of good works, for he did "great wonders and miracles among the people." You cannot imagine Stephen leading a sedentary life. He was active through every day, serving his Lord.

He was full of wisdom. "And they were not able to resist the wisdom and the spirit by which he spake." (Acts 6:10). We do not know of his educational background, but we surely know that God gave unto him great wisdom for the work he was doing.

Stephen was successful in his Christian work. Souls were saved, and the people were stirred. This deacon did not restrict himself to serving tables, but went out testifying for Christ.

When success came, trouble came. The courageous work of Stephen brought opposition. The official religionists of the day didn't like him. He was a trouble maker. They accused him of trying to change the customs which Moses delivered unto them.

Let me pause to say that the pathway to spiritual success is not smooth. Public opinion often praises a preacher who gets along without opposition and condemns the man who has trouble. But because a man has smooth sailing does not indicate that he is a spiritual success. The successful followers of God mentioned in the Old and New Testaments traveled on rough roads. It was so with Abraham, Isaac, Jacob, Joseph, Moses, Joshua, Jeremiah, Ezekiel, and Daniel. The way was even more stormy for the New Testament followers of Christ. Opposition was everywhere. There were scorners and scoffers galore. Hatred for Christ's followers was a common thing. And let us not forget the Son of God also traveled a stormy and rugged path. He came to do God's will, and did it perfectly, but in so doing, He excited the hatred and opposition of the people. This brought Him to the cross of Calvary, and a shameful, painful death in our behalf.

And let not forget that this opposition to Stephen came from the religious leaders of the day. They feared Stephen because they said he was seeking to change their customs. Ecclesiastical forms and ceremonies have always had their raging defenders. There have always been men who have made more of the outward organization than of the indwelling Spirit, more of ecclesiastical than of divine ordination. Dr. W. B. Riley gives this quotation from another minister: "The Lord Jesus would never have been crucified, neither would Stephen have been martyred, nor Paul imprisoned, but for words and acts deemed derogatory to the tabernacle. And in these days a man may with impunity deny all the vital truths of Christianity, and reject our divine Lord's teachings about the Scriptures which He came to fulfill, and remain in good standing in the church. But let him say a word in disparagement of any human element of the Christian religion, and he is at once cast out of the synagogue." A further comment is as follows: "In the judgment of many it is more essential to remain loyal to the convention than it is to Christ; loyal to leadership of man, than to the leadership of the Spirit; loyal to the drive and plans of ambitious program makers than it is to a divine program and the preaching of the gospel itself."

Early in his work Stephen ran into trouble. False witnesses said that he blasphemed against God, therefore, they caught him and brought him to the council. In chapter 7 of the Acts we have his notable addresses before the council. In this remarkable sermon he gave the history of God's dealing with Israel and of their unbelief and hardness of heart. He told how they rejected Joseph, Moses, and the prophets, and how they had crowned their rebellion by rejecting Jesus Christ, the

Son of God.

These words were delivered in love, but they aroused the fury of the elders, scribes, and church leaders.

"When they heard these things, they were cut to the heart, and they gnashed on him with their teeth."

With these words, we have the beginning of a death scene, the account of the home-going of the first Christian martyr. Death is usually depressing, but the story of Stephen's death is remarkably encouraging.

I. HIS DYING VISION OF CHRIST.

"But he, being full of the Holy Ghost, looked up stedfastly into heaven, and saw the glory of God, and Jesus standing on the right hand of God,

"And said, Behold I see the heavens opened, and the Son of man standing on the right hand of God." Acts 7:55, 56

Here is a priceless passage from the inspired and holy Word of God. While angry men tore him with their teeth, Stephen looked up and saw the glory of God. We cannot know exactly what is meant by seeing the glory of God, but we do know the meaning of these words, "and Jesus standing on the right hand of God."

Only a short time before the Son of God had carried His disciples to the Mount of Olives and ascended out of their sight into the sky. Perhaps Stephen was in the assembly of those who saw Him depart. Now, in this hour of great need, the Heavens are opened, and Stephen is accorded a vision of Christ in glory.

The Word usually tells us that Jesus is seated at the right hand of God, but Stephen saw Him standing on the right hand of the Father; standing, let us say, to welcome home this dying Stephen, who had so faithfully presented the gospel.

Stephen was not by any means the last one to receive a vision of Christ. Many years later the apostle John, on the Isle of Patmos, received a vision of Christ which is given to us in the book of the Revelation.

Jesus has never sought to hide Himself from the eyes of men. As a matter of fact, He came that men might see Him and believe on His name, and desire fellowship with Him and the Father. During His earthly ministry when people came seeking an audience, Jesus was always accessible. The disciples tried to turn away the curious, but the Lord was ready to receive them all.

Think not that Christ is trying to hide Himself from you today. He is ready to reveal Himself through the Word of God; therefore, we must turn to the Scriptures to know Him aright. He is ready to reveal Himself in saving power to all who will repent and believe. He is ready to make known Himself to every Christian who desires His guiding hand.

Stephen saw Christ by looking up. We, too, can see Him by looking up. Read the Bible, pray, witness, live for Christ, and you will both see Him and manifest Him unto others.

II. HIS DYING COMMITTAL.

When Stephen said that he saw the Son of God, they cried out with a loud voice, stopped their ears, and ran upon him with one accord, and cast him out of the city and stoned him. As they were stoning him, Stephen called upon God, saying,

"Lord Jesus, receive my spirit."

These words are much like the words of Jesus, who cried out, saying, "Father, into thy hands I commend my spirit."

It is entirely natural that Stephen should have used these words of the Lord. Christ-like language is natural for those who live in His presence.

A Death Vision

I would have you notice Stephen's committal of himself unto God. By so doing he was manifesting the spirit of Christ, who trusted all to the Heavenly Father. In quietness and serenity Stephen laid himself into the arms of an all-powerful God. The figure is of an infant going to rest in its mother's arms.

What contrast we find in this scene. See the angry mob, foaming at the mouth, casting stones, angry, and demon-possessed, filled with hatred and intent on murder. Upon the ground is Stephen, quiet and peaceful, resting on God.

Stephen had learned the secret of peace. This is a lesson and example for all of us. We fret and worry about the smallest things. We trouble ourselves needlessly about things which may never happen. Let us take this lesson to heart and commit our all to God. The apostle Peter says, "Wherefore, let them that suffer according to the will of God, commit the keeping of their souls to Him in well doing as unto a faithful Creator." I Peter 4:19.

Trust God for salvation and for security. Trust Him for daily needs. Trust Him to supply grace, even to the dying moment.

Paul said, "For the which cause I also suffer these things, nevertheless, I am not ashamed, for I know whom I have believed, and am persuaded that he is able to keep that which I have committed unto Him against that day." II Timothy 1:12

The Psalmist David said, "Commit thy way unto the Lord; trust also in Him, and he shall bring it to pass." Psalm 37:5

III. HIS DYING PRAYER.

"And he kneeled down, and cried with a loud voice, Lord, lay not this sin to their charge."

Again we find Stephen following both the teaching

and example of Christ. In Matthew 5:44 the Lord Jesus says, "But I say unto you, Love your enemies, bless them that curse you, do good to them that hate you, and pray for them which despitefully use you, and persecute you."

When Christ was nailed to the cross, He prayed, "Father, forgive them, for they know not what they do."

You can never make a mistake in following the word and example of Christ. In life and in death we should seek to do what He said and emulate His example.

If you have been wrongly treated and malice fills your heart, go to the Lord in prayer and stay there until you can say, "Lord, forgive them," and, "Lord, bless them." Life is too short between the budding and the falling of the leaf for hatred and malice. Let us always have the forgiving spirit and let us hasten to beg forgiveness if we have wronged others. Only the Spirit of God could have helped Stephen pray such a prayer in the agony of death.

A skeptic and critic one time asked Dr. Joseph Parker of the City Temple, London, "What did Providence do for the martyr Stephen when he was being stoned to death?" Dr. Parker said that he prayed for help that he might give the right answer to this skeptic, and then he replied, "God enabled Stephen to say, 'Lord, lay not this sin to their charge.' This was a greater miracle than deliverance by legions of angels."

We can well understand that this reply was enough to electrify all who heard it, and to put to shame the skeptic who sought to embarrass the minister of God.

IV. HIS DYING VICTORY.

"And when he had said this, he fell asleep."

I do not believe this account could end in a more beautiful way. I have always liked that word 'asleep' as it refers to death. Of course, the soul does not sleep.

It is never unconscious, but the body sleeps to await the resurrection morning. Death is a harsh and cruel word, but sleep is an expression of rest and repose.

Jesus used the word 'asleep" in speaking of those who were dead, yet should live again. In Luke 8, when He came to the ruler of the synagogue's house, He found the daughter dead, but Jesus said, "Weep not; she is not dead, but sleepeth." When the scoffers were put out of the room, He told the girl to arise, and she was raised from the dead.

He used the word 'sleep' also when He spoke of Lazarus. Lazarus was dead, but Christ knew that He would raise him from the dead, therefore, He said, "I go that I may awake him out of sleep."

The expression 'asleep in Jesus' is given to us in the words of the apostle in I Thessalonians 4, "But I would not have you to be ignorant, brethern, concerning them which are asleep, that ye sorrow not even as others which have no hope. For if we believe that Jesus died and rose again, even so them also which sleep in Jesus will God bring with him."

Yes, when Christ comes, the dead in Christ, whose bodies are in the grave, will be raised from the grave. Let us remember that sleep only refers to the body, not to the soul.

What a victory was given to Stephen! He did not fear death, for Christ had taken away the sting of death. Death came as a release and an opportunity to go home to be with God.

There should be no fear of death in the Christian's heart. There should be only a sense of victory, for in Jesus, it is far better to depart this life and be with Him.

When John Huss, who has been described as one of the greatest souls this world has ever known, was dying at the stake, he left behind him a song as sweet as the world has ever heard. His song remained long after the singer had vanished from sight. While dying he said,

"Glory be to God on high, and on earth, peace, good will toward men. We praise Thee, we bless Thee, we glorify Thee, we give thanks to Thee, for Thy great glory."

With Paul we can say, "For I am persuaded that neither death, nor life, nor angels, nor principalities, nor powers, nor things present, nor things to come,

"Nor height, nor depth, nor any other creature shall be able to separate us from the love of God which is in Christ Jesus our Lord." Romans 8:38,39.

L O O K UNTO JESUS TODAY — THERE IS VICTORY IN HIM.

Chapter 9
Do We Need a New Gospel?

"Paul, a servant of Jesus Christ, called to be an apostle, separated unto the gospel of God." Romans 1:1.

There are some people who seem to believe that the world needs a new gospel. The gospel of the Lord Jesus does not satisfy their intellectual minds. They boast that they are searchers for truth, but foolishly they set aside the truth of God as they seek for some new things.

Such people are like the Athenians of the day of Paul. When Paul began preaching about Jesus in Athens, the philosophers listened to him because they were forever searching for some new thing. "For all the Athenians and strangers which were there spent their time in nothing else but either to tell or to hear some new thing." Acts 17:21. The Apostle soon made them see that he was not preaching a new doctrine, or introducing a new saviour, but he was preaching the gospel of the eternal God.

This is the day of itching ears. The Apostle Paul prophesied: "For the time will come they will not endure sound doctrine; but after their own lusts shall they heap to themselves teachers, having itching ears. And they shall turn away their ears from the truth and shall be turned unto fables." II Timothy 4:3,4. The liberals and the modernists of today are trying to satisfy the itching ears of the people; therefore, they preach a social gospel, and laugh at the shed blood of Jesus, and declare that they will have nothing to do with a slaughter-house religion.

Many Bible teachers and evangelists, who proclaim themselves as fundamentalists, are also catering to the itching ears of this modern age. They advertise certain subjects and declare that they will give the people something new, something never heard of before. For example, a preacher in a certain city, put a large paid ad in the newspaper with this heading: "A NEW REVELATION." He then went on to say that on Sunday night he would make a revelation of divine truth which had never been given before.

Yes, I suppose he had a house full on Sunday night. All of the people of itching ears were there. They wanted to hear this new revelation. They were, of course, doomed to disappointment, for there is no new revelation. God's complete and full revelation is given in this Bible. There is nothing more that man can add to it.

Here is an interesting thing. Even sinners, lost sinners, prompted by the devil, are seeking a new gospel. How often I have talked to unsaved ones, and after giving them the plan of salvation, they reply, "Oh, I know all of that, but I still want something else." Apparently, repentance and faith, sound too simple for their minds, and they want something new added to the old gospel.

We do not need a new gospel. God's gospel is sufficient for every hour and every person. It is as unchangeable as God Himself. We simply need more preaching of the old gospel.

In the first verse of Romans, Paul said that he was separated unto the gospel of God. He at once digressed from speaking about himself and began talking about the gospel of Christ. In verses 1 through 18 he says many wonderful things about this glorious gospel. I call your attention to a few of them.

I. THE PROPHESIED GOSPEL.

"Which he had promised afore by his prophets in

the holy scriptures." Verse 2.

Paul declared at once that he was not a setter-forth of a new gospel, but of one which had been prophesied for many hundreds of years. All prophecy of the Old Testament pointed to the coming of Jesus, and His atoning death upon the cross. The scarlet thread is tied in the opening chapters of Genesis and stretches through the thirty-nine books of the Old Testament.

God's gospel is an ancient gospel. It is no new doctrine, but of ancient standing in the promises and prophecies of olden days.

II. THE PERSON OF THE GOSPEL.

"Concerning his Son Jesus Christ our Lord, which was made of the seed of David according to the flesh; And declared to be the Son of God with power, according to the spirit of holiness, by the resurrection from the dead." Verses 3 and 4.

When Paul mentioned Christ, it seems that he could not say enough about him. He endeavored to use all the names and titles he could. He calls Him "His Son Jesus Christ our Lord." He speaks of His human nature, "seed of David." That is, He was born of the virgin Mary, who was of the house of David. He speaks of His divine nature, "declared to be the Son of God." Christ was of the seed of David, according to the flesh, but He was the Son of God, according to the spirit of holiness.

As proof of the deity of Jesus, Paul mentions the resurrection from the dead. The Person of the gospel is Christ, crucified, buried, and risen from the dead. Those who are not convinced by the resurrection would be convinced by nothing.

The Person of the gospel of God is Christ, the Son of God. Leave out Jesus, or deny His deity, and you have no gospel. The gospel is not Christ, plus someone else, but it is Christ, the only Saviour of lost men. The gospel is not Christ, plus law, but Christ alone. The good news of salvation is not Christ, plus the efforts of man, but Christ, the only Saviour. May this truth ring forever in your ears. If you are right about this, you will be right about every truth in the Word of God. If you are wrong about Christ and His place in the gospel of God, you will be wrong about everything else.

III. THE PURPOSE OF THE GOSPEL.

"For I am not ashamed of the gospel of Christ: for it is the power of God unto salvation to every one that believeth; to the Jew first, and also to the Greek." Verse 16.

The purpose of the gospel is to save souls.

Paul said, "I am not ashamed of this saving gospel." He was not ashamed that his gospel was built upon One who was hanged on a tree. He was not ashamed that the doctrine of it was plain with little adornment. He was not ashamed of the gospel which appealed more to the lowly and despised than to the high and mighty. He was not ashamed of this gospel which people spoke against everywhere. He was proud of the gospel because its purpose is the saving of men.

The primary purpose of the gospel is to save. It is not simply to beautify people or to make them good citizens. These are but the by-products of salvation. The gospel's purpose is to redeem men from Hell, and to give them an eternal home with God.

How could we be ashamed of this gospel which has the power to redeem men from Hell, and to bring them safely into the presence of God?

IV. THE POWER OF THE GOSPEL.

"It is the power of God unto salvation to every one that believeth."

It is very difficult to keep separated these tremendous thoughts because they are bound together so closely. But I do want you to see the power of the gospel.

Perhaps no person was better fitted to speak of Christ's power to save than the apostle Paul himself. If ever a man had touched the depths of pure meaness, it was Saul of Tarsus. He so despised Christ that he sought in every way to stamp out the followers of Jesus. He consented to the death of Stephen. He put in prison men and women because of their faith.

He was wicked and mean, but God's power was sufficient to save him.

I wish I knew some way to help you to see God's power to save unto the uttermost. Perhaps it can be best illustrated in this fashion. In the recent Winecoff hotel disaster in Atlanta, the paper said that the firemen's ladders would reach only about six or seven stories into the air. The hotel was about twice that height; therefore, the ladders could not reach the screaming people on five or six floors of the burning building. They were good ladders, substantial, but too short. They failed to reach the people. They could not offer salvation to everyone. Here is the power of the gospel—it is able to save everyone who believes.

In our zeal to preach God's grace and power, we must not overlook man's part in salvation. What is it? To be saved you must believe. The medicine prepared will not cure the patient if it is not taken. The gospel's great purpose and infinite power cannot help either Jew or Gentile unless it is believed.

In that word "believe" we again see the marvelous

love of our God and Saviour. The ladder of salvation is placed within the reach of every man, woman, and child. Salvation does not hinge on behaviour, good works, or wealth. It is to all who believe. Education is not a prerequisite to salvation, for the most illiterate can believe and be saved. Age and experience are not necessary, but simple faith in Christ is sufficient. "Believe on the Lord Jesus Christ and thou shalt be saved."

V. THE PUNISHMENT FOR REJECTORS OF THE GOSPEL.

"For the wrath of God is revealed from heaven against all ungodliness and unrighteousness of men, who hold the truth in unrighteousness." Verse 18.

Here is the interpretation of this verse: The wrath of God is revealed from Heaven against all who hear the gospel, reject it, and continue on in unrighteousness.

We are sad as we contemplate the fact that many people hear, but refuse to heed. They took the truth, but would not permit it to influence them, therefore, the wrath of God will come upon their souls.

This is the part of God's truth that I find it difficult to preach. I do not enjoy telling men that they are going to Hell I would much rather preach of God's love and of Heaven. But one day I shall give an account of myself and of my ministry to God. In that day I do not want my hands to be stained with the blood of others, therefore I must faithfully proclaim the truth of God's wrath upon all who reject the Saviour.

Some modern day theologians have attempted to tear from the Word the teaching of eternal punishment. This is the kind of doctrine all sinners would like to hear. Some denominations have added many names to their roll books because they teach there is no Hell. In that great day when the wrath of God shall be poured out, it will be terrible for the deceivers and the deceived.

We have no new gospel to give unto you, but the old, old story of Jesus and His love. We are not trying to salve your conscience, and ease the agony of your sin-burdened soul by preaching falsehoods. We are endeavoring to proclaim the truth of God that all who believe in Jesus are saved through His shed blood, and all who reject Him shall feel the eternal wrath of a righteous and a holy God. Come to Christ now. Find refuge in Him. Trust yourself and your eternal destiny into the hands of Him who cannot lie and will not change.

Chapter 10
Heaven Is Looking On

"Wherefore seeing we also are compassed about with so great a cloud of witnesses, let us lay aside every weight, and the sin which doth so easily beset us, and let us run with patience the race that is set before us,
"Looking unto Jesus the author and finisher of our faith; who for the joy that was set before him endured the cross, despising the shame, and is set down at the right hand of the throne of God." Hebrews 12:1, 2.

As we read these verses, our imaginations paint for us a mighty picture. It is a picture of the ancient Roman amphitheatre. Rows and rows of seats in ascending stairs surround the arena. In that day when gladiators fought the wild beasts, the cheering thousands would fill every seat surrounding the field. Into the arena would come men selected for their bravery. At a given signal, doors under the stand were opened, and out would dash hungry and ferocious beasts. It was then the business of the gladiator to kill or to be killed. The crowds would cheer the brave and hiss the coward.

Now, Paul tells us that the Christian fights in such an arena. He is surrounded by a great throng of witnesses. Against the Christian come the tigers and lions of sin. Every Christian is drawn into the battle. But he does not fight alone, for a great crowd of witnesses look down to encourage, inspire, and spur him on.

Let us consider our text. Let us gather from this study the elements of faith and courage to help us to victorious living.

I. THE WATCHED.
"Wherefore seing we also are compassed about."

That word "we" refers to all living children of God. *We* are being watched.

We—poor sinners, saved by grace. Even though we have nothing whereof we can boast, we must recognize that we are being watched. By birth we became the recipients of Adam's nature. We were sinners, dead in trespasses and sin. By the new birth we become recipients of Christ's nature. We are now the children of the living God. Still we are only sinners saved by grace.

"Naught have I gotten, but what I received,
Grace hath bestowed it since I have believed;
Boasting excluded, pride I abase,
I'm only a sinner, saved by grace.

"Once I was foolish, and sin ruled my heart,
Causing my footsteps from God to depart;
Jesus hath found me, happy my case,
I now am a sinner, saved by grace."

We are beset by Satan on every hand. Think not for a moment that salvation makes one immune from the tempter. Being saved often causes Satan to redouble his efforts against you. Peter tells us, "Be sober, be vigilant; because your adversary, the devil, as a roaring lion, walketh about, seeking whom he may devour: Whom resist stedfast in the faith, knowing that the same afflictions are accomplished in your brethren that are in the world." I Peter 5:8,9.

The devil is sending all his forces against you, Christian friend. You cannot pray unless you battle Satan. You will not be able to read your Bible unless you war against the evil one. You will not engage in soul-winning unless you confront and overcome the obstacles of Satan. You cannot even go to church without being beset by this roaring lion. The devil is on every hand. He fights viciously and ferociously. He abides by no rules. He is trying to kill your influence and destroy your effectiveness as a Christian.

We—the watched ones—are encircled by an unfriendly world. A few times in my life the devil has deceived me into believing that this world is my friend. When I received such an idea, I was willing to compromise with the world, and worldly interests. Let us not forget for a single moment that this world is against the Christian. It despises God and the Christian way of life. Do not be ensnared by the world's tricks. Cut yourself loose from it. Avoid all doubtful things as you would avoid a room full of rattlesnakes.

Poor sinners, saved by grace, beset by Satan, and encircled by an unfriendly world, are being watched. Paul said, "We are made a spectacle unto the world, and to angels and to men."

II. THE WATCHERS.

"Wherefore seeing we also are compassed about with so great a cloud of witnesses." We can easily see that this Scripture refers back to Hebrews 11. In this chapter we have a list of the heroes of faith. By faith they were saved; by faith they conquered their enemies; by faith they obtained the victory. They are now watching us as we battle sin and Satan.

The Christian is in the arena. The battle is on. The stands are fulll of witnesses.

In one portion of the stands we find an assembly of angels. They are striving to give their friendly encouragement to us as we battle the wild beasts of sin. As we look, we can recognize many of the angels mentioned in the Bible. There is the one whom God placed at the entrance to the Garden of Eden after Adam and Eve lost the Garden through sin. There is the angel who prepared a meal for Elijah when he got under the juniper tree. Twice the angel of the Lord touched him and said, "Arise, and eat." We can see now the angel who appeared unto Joseph in a dream and told him about the Child Mary was to bear. The angel even gave Joseph the name for the Holy Child. "And thou shalt call his name Jesus, for he shall save his people from their sins." There is also the angel who came to Mary and announced to her the great thing which was to happen. We also see the angel of the Lord who announced to the shepherds the birth of Jesus. Still again, in this assembly of angels we see the one who appeared unto Jesus from Heaven when He was agonizing in the garden. We see, too, the angels who announced the resurrection of Jesus to the women on the first day of the week. They are clad in their shining garments, even as on the day they frightened the sorrowing women. We see too the angels who said at the ascension of Jesus, "Ye men of Galilee, why stand ye gazing into Heaven? This same Jesus which is taken up from you into Heaven shall so come in like manner as ye have seen him go into Heaven." Look again into the stands, and you will see the angel of the Lord who delivered Peter when he was cast into prison by Herod.

Yes, the Bible is full of the account of ministering angels. In the great crowd of wittnesses are these holy ones.

Secondly, we find in the stands a glorious assembly of prophets and apostles. We see Elijah and Elisha, Ezra and Nehemiah, Isaiah and Jeremiah. There are Daniel and Jonah.

We must not forget the patriarchs and great men. We can name only a few: Noah, Abraham, Isaac, Jacob, Joseph, Moses, and King David.

Near the patriarchs and prophets we find the apostles. Here James and John are still together. Matthew, the tax collector, who left all to follow Jesus, is present. There is Thomas who had his doubts settled when he viewed the body of the resurrected Christ. Along with the apostles is Paul who met Jesus on the Damascus road. Paul is shouting to us, "Thanks be unto God which giveth us the victory through our Lord Jesus Christ."

Let your eyes move around to another portion of the gallery and there you will find the great host of Christian martyrs. We see the faces of men and women who were hunted down by the forces of evil and burned at the stake. Here are ones who were cast into Roman arenas and torn to bits by ferocious wild beasts. Here are Christians who were soaked in oil by Nero and ignited so that the king's garden might be illumined. Yes, we see the men of the Pleban Legion, that legion which died to a man rather than deny the Lord Jesus. There is John Huss who was burned at the stake because of his bold preaching of the gospel.

The gallery also has its crowd of great witnesses of more recent years—Martin Luther and John Knox; John and Charles Wesley; George Whitfield and Charles Finney; D. L. Moody and Charles Haddon Spurgeon; David Livingston and David Brainerd; Adoniram Judson and William Carey. All these men send their strong encouraging shouts unto us. They are watching us today.

Listen a moment. From another part of the stands we hear sweet singing. Yes, here we have assembled those singers and composers of sacred songs of the ages. David, the sweet singer of Israel, has moved over to this crowd to lend his voice and his talent for praising God.

Heaven Is Looking On 75

Charles Wesley, the brother of John, begins a song of his own composition,

> "Oh, for a thousand tongues to sing,
>   My great Redeemer's praise;
> The glories of my God and King,
>   The triumphs of His grace

> "He breaks the power of cancelled sin
>   He sets the prisoner free,
> His blood can make the foulest clean,
>   His blood availed for me."

Hear now the voice of John Newton who sang,

> "How sweet the name of Jesus sounds
>   In a believer's ear.
> It soothes his sorrows, heals his wounds,
>   And drives away his fear."

We must not forget that Isaac Watts is in this assembly of singers. It was Isaac Watts who wrote,

> "When I survey the wondrous cross,
>   On which the Prince of Glory died;
> My richest gain I count but loss,
>   And pour contempt on all my pride."

He also gave us:

> "Alas, and did my Saviour bleed,
>   And did my sovereign die;
> Would He devote that sacred head,
>   For such a worm as I."

Perhaps the most fitting of all songs written by Isaac Watts for this day is:

> "Am I a soldier of the cross,
>   A follower of the Lamb,

> And shall I fear to own His cause,
> Or blush to speak His name?

> "Must I be carried to the skies,
> On flowery beds of ease;
> While others fought to win the prize,
> And sailed through bloody seas?

> "Sure I must fight if I would reign,
> Increase my courage, Lord;
> I'll bear the toil, endure the pain,
> Supported by Thy Word."

And then we find also the more recent writers of gospel songs who now abide in Heaven's glory. There is Fannie Crosby who gave to the world such noble songs as "Jesus, Keep Me Near the Cross," "Blessed Assurance, Jesus is Mine," "Safe in the Arms of Jesus," and thousands of others.

We have not yet finished. The gallery is still full of witnesses we have not yet named. There are the loved ones who fought to the end and finished the course. They now cheer us from the stands of glory. Your mother and your father who died in Christ are watching you. Mothers and dads, your children who have gone on are now observing your battle down here below.

Yes, there are many watchers. We are encircled by so great a cloud of witnesses.

III. OUR THREE-FOLD RESPONSE TO THEIR WATCHING EYES.

Why do the faithful ones mentioned in Hebrews 11 watch us? Is it to criticize? No, certainly not. They have but one reason, and that is to encourage us and to cheer us on to victory.

And now, notice our text which tells us what to do

in order to run a successful race and wage a successful battle.

1. Let us lay aside every weight and every sin. Nine out of ten Christian people who fail to be victorious because of the weights and sin of the world They are carrying sinful weights and worldly burdens. They have formed entangling alliances with the enemy. They belong to organizations which are a constant hindrance to their best spiritual interests. They need to take the sharp knife of separation and cut themselves loose from all of the devil's entanglements. The watchers in the gallery of Heaven will never see a victorious life on your part if you do not lay aside every weight and sin. Face the issue squarely. What is it that is so hindering you? Be honest with God, and have the courage to drop out of every organization or situation.

2. Let us run with patience the race that is set before us. The Christian life is not resting—it is racing. We are not campers—we are journeying on. We are not simply to sing, "Oh, land of rest, for thee I sigh," but we are to complete the song which says, "We'll work 'till Jesus Comes." All Christians are participants in this race, but how poorly do many of them run!

Begin now to seek a place of service. Commit yourself to a life of activity for Christ. This is surely the will of God and the way to happiness.

3. Let us look unto Jesus. "Looking unto Jesus, the author and finisher of our faith." Every eye in Heaven is fixed on the precious Lamb of God. The watchers in the gallery are ever looking to Him. They encourage us to do likewise.

Christ is our strength. In vain do we look to the things of this world to help us in the race of life. Instead of friends we find enemies of righteousness. The arena of life is full of destructive foes, but there is One who can help us, even Christ. When we are weak, He is strong. If we will but look unto Him, we can be overcomers. He pours His power into us.

Christ is our inspiration. There are times when discouragement lays hold upon us. Some men have fought temptations until they are weary of fighting. They become discouraged and almost succumb to the tempter. But if they will look to Jesus, He will inspire them to keep on fighting and never lose heart. Look unto Jesus now, dear friend. He knows your need and will surely come to your aid. He does not force Himself upon anyone. Your coming to Him must be voluntary. His strength and inspiring presence will not be forced upon you, but the very minute that you recognize your need and look unto Him, He will help you. Impetuous Simon Peter desired to walk upon the water. As long as he looked unto Jesus, he stayed on top, but when he saw the winds and the waves dashing high, he began to sink. Then he cried, "Lord, save me." Christ might well have turned His back upon Peter. He could have said, "Simon Peter, it was your own request to walk upon the water. If you refuse to look unto me, then I will let you sink." But our Christ is ever ready to hear the cry of needy ones. When in sincerity we look to Him and cry for help, He is ready to give it.

Yes, Christ is our inspiration in sorrow, in heartache, in failure, in times of discouragement. If we but look unto Him, He will help us.

There is never any disappointments in looking to Jesus. People and things may disappoint us, but Christ is sufficient for every need. He satisfies every hungering heart.

Not alone is He a giver of strength and inspiration, but He is our intercessor. Our text tells us to look unto Jesus, who endured the cross, despised the shame, and is set down at the right hand of the throne of God. Christ is interceding for you and me right now. Furthermore, His intercession is always successful. Quite often a lawyer intercedes for a person on this earth before the courts, but fails to release him. This is not true of our Christ. He is a successful intercessor. Our souls are safe and secure in His keeping, for He successfully makes intercession for us.

God help us to lay aside the sin and weights of life.
God help us to run the race with patience.
God help us to look unto Jesus.

Let this be our three-fold response to the watchful eyes of God and Christ, and to the cloud of witnesses surrounding the arena of life. What is the shout of every onlooker in Heaven? "Be thou faithful unto death." God is saying it. Christ is saying it. The patriarchs and prophets plead for it. The kings and great men who died in Christ call for it. The martyrs beseech you. The great world of Christians implore you. Your mother and father and loved ones and friends who are now in God's presence beg you to be faithful unto death.